Lee Konitz

W. Royal Stokes
January 9, 2008
Elkins

Lee Konitz

Conversations on the Improviser's Art

Andy Hamilton

THE UNIVERSITY OF MICHIGAN PRESS   Ann Arbor

Copyright © by the University of Michigan 2007
All rights reserved
Published in the United States of America by
The University of Michigan Press
Manufactured in the United States of America
⊚ Printed on acid-free paper

2010   2009   2008   2007   4   3   2   1

A CIP catalog record for this book is available from the British Library.

Library of Congress Cataloging-in-Publication Data

Hamilton, Andy, 1957–
    Lee Konitz : conversations on the improviser's art / Andy
Hamilton.
        p.   cm. — (Jazz perspectives)
    Includes bibliographical references and index.
    ISBN-13: 978-0-472-11587-7 (cloth : alk. paper)
    ISBN-10: 0-472-11587-1 (cloth : alk. paper)
    ISBN-13: 978-0-472-03217-4 (pbk. : alk. paper)
    ISBN-10: 0-472-03217-8 (pbk. : alk. paper)   1. Konitz, Lee—
Interviews.   2. Saxophonists—United States—Interviews.   3. Jazz
musicians—United States—Interviews.   4. Musicians—Interviews.
5. Jazz—History and criticism.   I. Konitz, Lee.   II. Title.

ML419.K66H36   2007
788.7'3165092—dc22
[B]   2006032064

[Frontispiece] "Listen" picture, London, 1987 (Courtesy of Caroline
Forbes.)

To the memory of Lennie Tristano (1919–1978)

That's my way of preparation—to not be prepared.
And that takes a lot of preparation!

—Lee Konitz

Contents

Author's Introduction

The interview form is common in jazz journalism, but a whole book of interviews with a single musician is rare.[1] Lee Konitz is one of the few jazz players who could sustain the reader's interest over so many pages. In conversation Konitz is thoughtful, combative, reflective, and opinionated—a true thinker with gravitas. Unlike many jazz musicians, he is eager to debate the principles of his art, and isn't afraid to pass frank comments on other musicians, including those he has played with. His total honesty and integrity goes with high critical standards, and he is not interested in a mollifying niceness. He has strong opinions on such issues as intuitive improvisation versus "prepared playing," the demands of the group situation, the need for accurate pitch, his inspiration from bebop and Charlie Parker's "compositional" approach. But he also reveals a characteristic ambivalence on many of the deepest questions—such as his Jewish identity, the place of the blues in jazz, and jazz's status as an African-American art form—and also concerning such leading figures in the music as Charlie Parker, John Coltrane, Ornette Coleman, and Wayne Shorter.

Lee Konitz should be heard in his own words, and in contrast to Quincy Troupe's co-written autobiography of Miles Davis and similar efforts, these really are the artist's own words, not an artistic reconstruction. They appear with little editing, though the material has been considerably rearranged to avoid repetition and to produce a more coherent narrative. The interviews were conducted over several years at Konitz's apartment in Cologne, at festivals and gigs in Hull, Coventry, London, Tuscany, and Paris, and by telephone. Extracts have appeared previously in *The Wire* and *Jazz Review*. The project began when Tony Herrington and Rob Young of *The Wire* suggested I subject Lee to an Invisible Jukebox—a kind of "blindfold test" where the artist responds to recordings before they are identified—before his set at the Hull Jazz Festival in 1999. At that first meeting he provided excellent copy, conforming to the stereotypes of grumpy old man and difficult artist. The first disc I played was Anthony Braxton's "April," from a tribute to Konitz's teacher Lennie Tristano, and the diatribe that followed—beginning, "It's the worst solo I've ever heard in my life, I think"—took me completely aback. This was a man with opinions—only later did I appreciate that he is also a

warm, gentle, and artistically vulnerable soul. After that experience, I persuaded Richard Cook, my original journalistic mentor who got me into jazz
writing when he was editor of *The Wire,* to run two very long Konitz interviews in *Jazz Review.* By this time I was getting to know Lee better, and
when I turned up to interview him at his apartment in Cologne, he apolo-
gized for not having any coffee but did offer me a whole orange. Eventually
he became more relaxed, and we got to bantering conversation.

It's fair to say that Lee has found collaborating on this book challenging
and indeed stressful. It exposes him as an artist, and somehow he couldn't—
and I think still can't—believe my assurances that readers would be interested in his opinions and reminiscences at book length. A book, with its
promise of permanence, was more threatening to him than the magazine
interviews that he's mostly been happy to do, and it took a long time to win
him over to the idea. My initial plan was for a co-written autobiography, but
on reading the first results, Lee vetoed the project, complaining that it was
inauthentic. He was onto something important about that overpopular
genre; with interviewer's questions removed, it's hard to see what motivates
the subject's remarks. Honesty and candor are lost when the conversation is
obscured in this way. The Miles Davis case—it turns out that without comment Troupe added material that was not from his interviews—emphasized
how problematic the traditional autobiography is. Even the best-inten-
tioned author has to add material where the interviewer's questions have
been cut, and usually does much more—it is a literary form where a persona
is constructed. As an alternative, Lee and I settled on the question-and-
answer format, with interpolations—though Lee continued to have grave
doubts of the kind I've just described.

These conversations discuss Konitz's life chronologically, broken up by
thematic chapters on improvisation, the instrument, and the material. They
inevitably bring out Konitz's ideas from the interviewer's perspective, and in
particular reflect my long-standing interest in the process of improvisation,
and the perennial question of how genuinely spontaneous it can be—which
is really the question, "What exactly *is* improvisation?" It's evident that the
very same question has long preoccupied Lee Konitz.

Some musicians will have a hidden agenda—in the case of Miles Davis,
Konitz's sometime colleague, almost always. From the 1960s onwards Davis
incorporated the ideas of many musicians that he publicly condemned, in
his own way of course, but not wishing to acknowledge the fact. In Konitz's
case I do not believe that there is any hidden agenda—these conversations
are frank, and any "agenda" is explicit. Konitz rightly believes that the Tristano school, and especially its originator, has not got its due with the jazz

public, even if it might have from historians of the music, and that it has been much misunderstood. He wants to correct that situation—as also will a new book on Tristano by Eunmi Shim in the present series. Konitz also believes that what he calls "prepared" playing, and a focus on harmonic as opposed to melodic considerations, dominate jazz improvisation, and he would like to see that imbalance corrected. Do I—the interviewer—have an agenda? Not that I'm aware of. It's possible that Lee has picked up some of my ideas, but the influence has mostly been the other way round.

Lee has been a close collaborator, reading successive drafts of the manuscript and making corrections and additions. I have mostly incorporated the corrections, but on some occasions, where he has had second thoughts about his criticisms of other musicians, I have persuaded him to retain them for the sake of candor. Occasionally the "censoring" has worked the other way round. This issue of criticism is a difficult one. Lee is known for his uncompromising artistic vision and exacting critical standards, both for himself and others. His outspoken comments on Anthony Braxton in the *Wire* interview, which he amplifies here, received particular attention at the time. (I approached Braxton, via an intermediary, to ask whether he would like to talk about Konitz, but, understandably perhaps, he declined.) The interviews with other musicians were an afterthought that burgeoned, and almost all were conducted as the book was nearing completion. In these interviews, the musicians showed a lot of warmth toward Lee, and their praise helped to give him confidence in the project. Many readers have made suggestions about the organization of the material, and pointed out errors and infelicities in the text, but final editing decisions have been between myself and Lee. The original tapes and minidiscs exist—somewhere—if any archive is interested.

To return to the question of editing. It is difficult to transfer the feel of speech to the written page, and I have rearranged phrases within sentences and sometimes changed individual words to improve the flow. For example, Konitz said: "I'm not sure if this was the same tour or not, but George Shearing, Al Hibbler, and Lennie were standing by the bus before we got on to leave . . ." I changed this to: "I don't remember if this was the same tour or not, but George Shearing, Al Hibbler and Lennie were standing by the bus one time, before we got on to leave . . ." And Konitz says, on playing blue notes: "I can't get away from it. But I'm not exaggerating that feeling, I hope. So I do play [blue notes] occasionally, and hope that they fit into a musical phrase, and make some sense." I have changed this to: "I can't get away from it. But I'm not exaggerating that feeling, I hope. I hope that they [blue notes] fit into a musical phrase, and make some sense." A number of my brief, factual questions have been transformed into Konitz's speech, so that "You joined Kenton in 1952" becomes "I joined Kenton in 1952." On Lee's insistence, "Yeah" mostly becomes "Yes"; on my insistence, "etc., etc." mostly becomes "and so on." Obviously there is much material that I have not included, especially when it repeats other remarks, or where Lee was struggling to express some difficult idea. His memory after all these years is not infallible, and I have done my best to check his reminiscences. Often he would tell me an anecdote, and then some variation on the following conversation would occur: "Can you tell me when that was?" "You know I hate that kind of question!" "Was it the fifties or the sixties?" "I'd say, probably the sixties." Sometimes I could check, but often I could not get a precise date.

I should state my background qualifications for writing this book. Lee Konitz has been one of my musical heroes almost from when, as a student, I first fell in love with jazz. *Lee Konitz with Warne Marsh,* the Atlantic recording from 1955, was one of the first jazz LPs I bought—probably at the record store in St Andrews in Fife, which later closed while I was on student vacation, unable to help sustain its meager cash-flow. It was a surprise to hear Lee, in these conversations, being so self-critical about that almost perfect small-group classic. Later I loved *Jazz à Juan, The New York Album,* and *Ideal Scene.* I heard him live with Harold Danko in the 1980s, and enjoyed their hilarious Keith Jarrett impersonation. I have for many years been a writer on jazz, improvised music, and modern composition, initially for *The Wire* and subsequently for *Classic CD, Jazz Review,* and other publications. I'm a jazz pianist of modest achievements, and it took a lesson with Lee Konitz, reinforced by comments from my friend David Udolf, to make me realize the importance of melody over harmony. This is also the message of Conrad Cork's *Harmony With LEGO Bricks,* an improvisation manual indebted to Konitz's approach, if only I'd had the ears to absorb it. It impressed me that independently these authorities said similar things about my playing—now that I've finished the book, I hope I can put their thinking into practice!

I am grateful to Peter Jones at Edinburgh University for suggesting I combine my day job as philosophy lecturer and my moonlighting as jazz writer into work on the aesthetics of jazz. That's how I got involved in the area of philosophy known as aesthetics or philosophy of art, which I now teach. Teasing out the nature of improvisation is a philosophical matter, so parts of these conversations make up a philosophical dialogue in some sense. At times, Lee commented that he was hoping for some more "philosophy," but

I think we achieve the kind of cautious but significant resolutions that one hopes for in philosophical debate.

Jazz, at the time Konitz was working with Lennie Tristano, was an art music played in nightclubs. For Konitz, it still is, to some extent, and unlike the superstars, he still plays in clubs. Jazz's artistic claims arise in large part from its status as an improvised music, I believe, and intuitive improvisation, of the kind that Konitz practices, is the highest form of improvisation. His career is one of the most consistent examples of commitment to that demanding art.

Acknowledgments

I have had outstanding support from the University of Michigan Press. Series editor Lewis Porter deserves a special panegyric for his assistance from the outset on practical as well as scholarly matters. He has helped to make this a much more accurate book, freer of critical clichés; it would have been far inferior without his frequent input and guidance, and invaluable comments and corrections on the penultimate draft. Chris Hebert was a patient and efficient editor who helped to keep the process of production as painless as possible. My thanks also go to the many others who have read the manuscript or offered comments or helped in other ways: Conrad Cork, whose introduction to jazz improvisation *Harmony With LEGO Bricks* first introduced me to Konitz's method; composer and writer Philip Clark; Safford Chamberlain, whose biography of Warne Marsh, *An Unsung Cat,* is inspirational; James Clarke for his translation of Frank Wunsch's words from German; Connie Crothers, for information about Tristano; Richard Cook, for his support as editor of *Jazz Review* and prudent advice on jazz publishing; Jason Gaiger, for his knowledge of the publishing world; Jack Goodwin, a tireless scholar of the Cool School who has answered many detailed questions; Tony Herrington and Rob Young of *The Wire* for suggesting and running my first interview with Lee; writers Bill Kirchner, Marcello Piras, and Brian Priestley for their lengthy scholarly comments on the manuscript under pressure of time; Mark Levinson, for his photo of Konitz with Tristano; writer Brian Marley, for his stylistic advice and very bad title suggestions; Dan Morgenstern and Tad Hershorn of the Rutgers Institute of Jazz Studies, for photographs and information; Evan Parker, for his comments and encouragement; Enrico Pieranunzi, for insisting that I organize the material more clearly; Ros Rigby of the Sage Gateshead, and Paul Bream, for helping to arrange a rare interview with Ornette Coleman; Alan Ross for his comments; Eunmi Shim for her knowledge of Tristano; Alyn Shipton for his initial help in getting the project off the ground; Nick Southgate for sage advice on style and presentation; James Tartaglia, especially for his knowledge of the saxophone as an instrument; David Udolf for his insight into improvisation; Emma Webb, who read through a late draft and saved me from many errors; Carl Woideck, author of *Charlie Parker: His Music and Life,* for comments on Parker and cool jazz; and Bill Trythall from Discovery Records, Neil Scaplehorn from Ace and Chris Allen of Basho Music. Michael Conklin and Mike Baggetta worked tirelessly on the online discography, and on the online minibiographies and transcriptions respectively; Sergio Bandeira Karam came up with late additions to the discography, which Conrad Cork helped to input. Martin Allison of Durham University Music Department provided technical assistance. Thanks to Oskar Neubauer and Caroline Forbes for their great pictures for the cover and frontispiece, respectively. Ohad Talmor provided at short notice many music examples, including compositions by Lee—as musical director of many recent projects, he is an important archivist of Lee's work. Francesco Martinelli, of Siena Jazz Archive, Siena, Italy, helped with research, and engaged in very helpful discussions on the history of free jazz and free improvisation. I am indebted also to Barga Jazz, Lucca, Italy, for inviting me to the Barga Jazz Festival where Konitz was performing in 2003. I have benefited greatly from reading Eunmi Shim's prodigiously researched dissertation, "Lennie Tristano (1919–1978): His Life, Music, and Teaching" (1999), and from her *Lennie Tristano: His Life in Music* (University of Michigan Press, 2007), in which some of the citations from *Down Beat* and other jazz magazines appear.

Finally, I am greatly indebted for discussions about Konitz's music with musicians who have worked with him, and above all, to Joe Lovano for his foreword. I apologize to those musicians who have worked with Konitz but whom I was unable to contact for a contribution—either because I did not know how to get in touch, or due to pressure of time and space. I could have assembled a further cast as articulate and informative as the one assembled here. In particular, I am sorry that I could not conduct or—for space reasons—include interviews with Geri Allen, Derek Bailey, Chick Corea, Connie Crothers, Don Ferrara, Charlie Haden, Bengt Hallberg, Jim Hall, Peter Ind, Charles Lloyd, Jackie McLean, Brad Mehldau, Bob Mover, Billy Taylor, Clark Terry, and Mark Turner. Last but not least, of course, I must thank Lee Konitz for his patient responses to my incessant questioning, his interest and commitment in pursuing philosophical questions about his art, his hard work in checking the various drafts of the manuscript, and of course his musical inspiration. I am grateful to the editors of *The Wire* and *Jazz Review* for their permission to quote extensively from material that has appeared in their publications. While every attempt has been made to contact relevant copyright-holders, any omissions are regretted and anyone affected is invited to contact the University of Michigan Press.

—Andy Hamilton

Foreword

Andy Hamilton and Lee Konitz have put together an extraordinary retrospective with interviews and commentary on the life of one of jazz music's most beloved and individual voices. Lee Konitz has contributed to the development of this music's life cycles from his emergence onto the scene in the 1940s to the explorations of today. Lee has always tried to be the most creative and spontaneous of improvisers, and has influenced all of us in the most positive way with his passionate and free-flowing approach to standard songs as well as more exploratory forms. In this collection of conversations, Lee gives insightful accounts and critiques of mentors and colleagues. He discusses his early family life growing up in Chicago, meeting, studying, and playing with Lennie Tristano, moving to New York, working with Miles Davis and contributing to the influential recording *Birth of the Cool* with Gil Evans, John Lewis, and Gerry Mulligan, joining Stan Kenton, as well as his associations with Lester Young, Charlie Parker, Warne Marsh, Charles Mingus, and other major musicians.

We come to discover why he plays the way he does, and what has driven him through the years in the world of music. Lee has led a full life as an innovative improviser in the international spotlight, and he is well-respected and revered around the world by musicians and fans. He has taught generations of musicians he's worked with through the years, just being himself and giving all he can with generosity and love. As an alto saxophonist he's developed his own sound and approach, different from Charlie Parker's. I am truly honored to know him and feel blessed to have him as a teacher, mentor, and friend. After my early listening to his records, I've had the great fortune to experience at first hand—or should I say first ear—his sound, feeling, and ideas on many occasions since the mid-1970s, when I moved to New York City. To be in a room with his sound is an inspiration, but to follow his lines on the tune he's exploring taught me so much about how to try and put it all together for myself. Your playing develops from everything you embrace, and Lee's clarity and subtleties, which come through on every phrase, gave me some beautiful things to reach for.

In 1991, Lee joined Charlie Haden, Bill Frisell, Paul Motian, and myself for a quintet session entitled *Paul Motian on Broadway, Volume III* (JMT

Records). This was the first time Lee and I actually played together, sharing melodies and improvising collectively throughout the recording. It is one of the most creative sessions of standard songs I've been a part of, and I am very proud of its success. Some years later, in the mid-1990s, the group did a three-week European festival tour with Marc Johnson on bass instead of Charlie. It was great to travel and play with Paul and Lee on this tour, given their long crazy history together that went back to the Lennie Tristano days in the 1950s—I think it was the first time they toured together. It was fun and challenging to play with these different personalities night after night, at such a high level of musicianship. The magic in jazz is all about communication and sharing ideas spontaneously within an ensemble—when it's happening, there's nothing like it in music! We had some incredible moments during that tour, and I learned a lot about who I am and what I'm trying to do in music and on my horn. Lee's love and dedication have driven his career, and given all of us who know him the confidence to create our own space in this amazing world of music we live in.

Enjoy meeting Lee Konitz in this book on a personal level, as honest and alive as his music.

Sounds and feelings,
Joe Lovano

Prologue

I'm writing this after a trip to Vienna, and while I was there I had the opportunity to hear an Austrian tenor player, fifteen years old, who really played the instrument very well, and wowed the audience with his expertise. And a few days ago I heard an Italian alto player of the same age who was really unbelievably accomplished, instrumentally and musically—and he really got the audience shouting approval. When I was fifteen years old I was playing, but no one had really inspired me like these two guys have obviously been inspired. These two talented people were not aware, as yet, of a true musical statement, without the sensationalism—something they will learn, we hope.

I got my inspiration from Lennie Tristano, and also Lester Young and Charlie Parker. Tristano demonstrated for me a way to play that went deeper than virtuoso musicality—as John Updike wrote, "Virtuosity can seem a distraction—as when you find that you are thinking about how great the musician is instead of listening to the music." I never wowed an audience in my whole life like those two young players did, so I can't help but feel I missed something. But in a more modest way I've been able to continue playing, in private and in public, with occasional comments from people after a concert telling me they like the way I played through the years. So I am grateful to find a place in the improvising neighborhood, and can only wish those two virtuosi a good and real musical life.

Mike Zwerin, who writes a column for the *Herald Tribune* every couple of weeks, just wrote a great piece headlined "Murdering the silence with bad music"—a quote from Joseph Conrad. While in Vienna, I went to the cemetery and saw Beethoven's tomb, next to Schubert's, next to Brahms's, in a small area. They replaced the silence with beautiful music. Jazz is often too concerned with exhibitionism and emoting nonstop, but there have been many beautiful players. Coleman Hawkins's "Body and Soul"; Lester Young's "Lady Be Good" with Basie; Charlie Parker's "Don't Blame Me"; Warne Marsh with Paul Chambers and Paul Motian, four beautiful trio tunes on Atlantic Records; Wayne Shorter at the Plugged Nickel with Miles—and many others . . . Keith Jarrett, Brad Mehldau, Chick Corea, Bill

Evans, Lennie Tristano, and so on. That's the tradition and the intention that hopefully will get to these young players.

I would like to say how much I appreciate working on this project with Andy Hamilton. Left to my own efforts, I would not have written it down, or up! Andy, with great interest and patience, was willing to meet with me a number of times with lists of questions. For instance, we spent a few days together as adjudicators at a big band contest for arrangers in Barga in Italy, and had a few opportunities for discussion.

I also want to thank all my musical colleagues for their great words, in the short interviews Andy did.

Gradually over many months and years, Andy organized the material. I read it, and changed many things, and added much. The last step, after reading, and deleting, and adding; and rereading, and redeleting and re-adding (a few more times) is to get the book published and released. I welcome the opportunity to go public with this musical part of my life, for the people who like my playing. I hope they appreciate the music a little more after getting a look behind the scene—we hope that there are a few insightful moments ahead!

With appreciation for your support,
Lee Konitz

Brief Biography of Lee Konitz

Lee Konitz is one of the most original and distinctive alto saxophonists in the history of jazz. With Sonny Rollins, Max Roach, and a few others, he is one of the surviving master improvisers of the bebop generation. But his apprenticeship to bebop was indirect, and he has carved out an uncompromising solo career guided by a singular artistic vision. He seeks out challenging situations and strives for perfection in the momentary art of improvisation. He is unerringly self-critical and always stretches himself to do the best work possible. Though Konitz is a highly reflective musician, what he plays is intuitive, the product of an intensely emotional sensibility. It's striking how ingenious Konitz has been in creating novel contexts for the traditional approach of "theme and variations" that he follows. In albums such as *Peacemeal* or *Duets* from the 1960s, the solo album *Lone-Lee* from the 1970s, right up to the recent duo album with drummer Matt Wilson, *Gong With Wind,* the saxophonist has been concerned to develop new formats for improvisation.

Konitz was born on October 13, 1927, in Chicago, of Austrian/Russian Jewish parents. At the age of eleven he picked up his first instrument, the clarinet, on which he received classical lessons before switching to tenor and then alto saxophone. In 1943 he met the decisive personal and musical influence of his life, the blind teacher and pianist Lennie Tristano. He joined Claude Thornhill's orchestra (1947–48) and made his first recordings with them. The band, which employed Gil Evans as arranger, was an important precursor of Miles Davis's Nonet, later known as the Birth of the Cool band (1948–50), which Konitz went on to join. It is the latter association for which he remains best known, and he is generally regarded, with Tristano and Miles Davis, as one of the architects of the "cool" style in modern jazz.

Konitz's greatest influence was his still-neglected teacher Lennie Tristano, but he also thoroughly assimilated the heritage of saxophonists Charlie Parker and Lester Young. Konitz's partnerships with Tristano, and with his fellow pupil, the totally individual tenor saxophonist Warne Marsh, were the defining ones of his career. But although Lennie Tristano was a formative influence on Konitz, one shouldn't assume that he was working on a tabula rasa. Although immature by his later standards, Konitz's earliest commercially recorded solos, with the Thornhill Orchestra in 1947, illustrate that he was already developing a unique jazz style, characterized by a highly original tone with a purity unusual in jazz.

An excellent example of Konitz's early style is the solo on the 1949 recording of "Subconscious-Lee" with Tristano—an original Konitz line on the chord changes to "What Is This Thing Called Love?" Tristano often had his students write original lines over standards, but the education also included experiments in free jazz. As leader, Konitz recorded with Warne Marsh (1949), and he worked with the Lennie Tristano quartet (1954–55), recording at the Sing Song Room of the Confucius Restaurant in New York. A period in Stan Kenton's band, 1952–53, extended his experience and range of playing contexts, and periodically he has returned to larger ensembles. But his most original and challenging work has been in smaller groups where improvisational freedom can be given full rein. Konitz is the spontaneous improviser par excellence, constantly finding inspiration in the Tin Pan Alley songs, later known as "standards," that since the 1920s have continued to attract jazz musicians. Throughout his career Konitz has composed, often but not always on the chords of standards.

Konitz's career was at its lowest ebb commercially—though not artistically—in the early 1960s, when he lived in California. In 1961, however, he recorded *Motion*, with John Coltrane's drummer Elvin Jones—one of his finest albums. After his spell in California he returned to New York in 1964 to appear at the Half Note with Tristano. At a memorial concert to Charlie Parker in Carnegie Hall in 1965 he performed a remarkable solo tribute, "Blues For Bird." In 1967 he recorded his *Duets* album, a series of duos with Joe Henderson, Richie Kamuca, Jim Hall, Ray Nance, Elvin Jones, and others, a format that later became a speciality. Later duos were with Sal Mosca (1971), Red Mitchell, Hal Galper (1974–75), Jimmy Giuffre, Martial Solal (1978, 1980), Karl Berger (1979), Michel Petrucciani (1982), and Harold Danko (1984). In the 1970s Konitz was sometimes reunited with Warne Marsh, and in 1975 he returned to the nonet format, which was compared, somewhat inaccurately, with the Birth of the Cool band.

For much of the time since the mid-1960s, Konitz has lived and worked in Europe; he also became popular in Japan. He recorded in Germany with Attila Zoller and Albert Mangelsdorff (1968), and in Italy with Martial Solal (1968) and Enrico Rava (1968). He can be heard on *Mingus at Town Hall* (1972). He recorded with Dave Brubeck and Anthony Braxton, with Andrew Hill, and with Warne Marsh and Bill Evans (1977). He devoted an album to the tenor (1977), played with Paul Bley, and appeared in Europe with Shelly Manne. He rejoined Charles Mingus, with whom he had worked

in the 1950s, in 1978, and played in a duo with Gil Evans in 1980, eventually releasing two albums, *Heroes* and *Anti-Heroes*. In recent years he has
again played more in the United States, and achieved further recognition
there. Konitz keeps an apartment in New York, but in 1997 he married a
native of Cologne, and since then he has lived there most of the time, in a
flat near the city center. As he moves into his later seventies, Konitz is working with much younger players such as Matt Wilson, Joey Baron, and Greg
Cohen, as well as many European players. In his artistic Indian summer,
Konitz's achievement is becoming more widely recognized.

1 ✌ Early Life and Career

We begin with Lee's reminiscences of his upbringing in Chicago in the 1930s, and the influence of his Jewish family background. This material comes from my first extended interview with him, at his apartment in Cologne in 2000. He was a little reticent at first in talking about his parents, but there was a lot of feeling not far from the surface. He is grateful to them for encouraging his love of music, but they did not really understand jazz, and his love for it reinforced his alienation from traditional, observant Jewish culture. The effect of assimilation and the "melting pot" on the first generation in a new country meant that Konitz's attitude to traditional Jewish culture remained ambivalent—as it did with other Jewish jazz musicians and the great songwriters he most loves. John Zorn's short interview, in this chapter, gives a hint of the minefield of identity politics.[1]

I have a few biographical questions and then some musical ones. It's a bit boring, but we'll start at the beginning.
Well, I hate to think of my life as being boring!
I mean starting at the beginning—and it might be boring for you to have to answer questions you've answered before.
Hopefully, with a little bit of different insight, each time is a little different. I don't have a lurid personal story to tell. My niece in Chicago just gave me a review of a recent book on Chet Baker, by James Gavin.[2] And they [Gavin] tear him apart. I don't have any of that dramatic stuff. My pot-smoking would take up a couple of pages at best![3]

My father was Austrian, my mother was from Russia.[4] They came to the United States in the first decade of the last century. They landed eventually on the North Side of Chicago, and the family moved into a few different places in that area. For some reason I can't tell you too much about that—we never talked about it. I guess they emigrated to get a better life. My grandfather—my mother's father—was here in Chicago already, I believe. I don't know why my father came to Chicago—I don't know that he had any family here. My parents met each other, and married, in Chicago. They always lived there.

You have an unusual surname.

I got a tax statement for a *Konits* with an s one time in New York—he's a bass player that lives in Long Island somewhere. Then there's the poet Stanley Kunitz. And someone contacted me whose name was *Kounitz.*

I told my two sons, who are not married, that they would be the end of the Konitz name, and they were visibly unmoved by that, as I was. I never liked the name too much. Both of my brothers changed their name to "Kaye"—they were both businessmen, and felt they could negotiate things better that way, without having to spell their name every time.

A lot of Jewish jazz musicians changed their names—Shorty Rogers, Steve Lacy, and so on.

But you never thought of doing that.

I was named "Leon," and it became "Lee" over the years. And when I was with the Stan Kenton band, a radio announcer introduced me as "Lee Coates"—and from then on, in the band, I was "Coates." I kinda liked it. But when I left the band, it didn't stick.

Did you have a happy childhood?

Well, my two brothers were six and nine years older than me, and they were interested in many things that I wasn't able to join in—I couldn't play baseball with them. They were kind of stuck with me, having to take care of me while my parents worked, so I became like a ball and chain to them, and that was not a happy situation. I paid my dues for being the youngest one. But otherwise the family got along pretty well.

Was it a struggle for your parents to make ends meet?

Yeah, they had to work hard all the time. My father had a laundry and cleaning establishment, and we were living in the back. I remember the "Care" packages for poor families we got at Christmastime, sweaters and things. But otherwise there wasn't a feeling of being without so much, and I appreciated that.

My parents encouraged me to pursue my instrumental interests. They didn't encourage me to finish all of my schooling, which was unfortunate, I felt. I was able to work as a musician at an early age, and somehow that got me out of school. In my sophomore year—the second year—of high school I went on the road with some friends, and then for some reason which I really can't remember my parents didn't encourage me to go back—I was sixteen. When I was eighteen or nineteen I spent a short time at Roosevelt College, as a special student. I hadn't graduated formally from high school, and I took what they call college preparatory courses, like political science, sociology, and so on.

What music did your parents like?

Classical music and opera, but they didn't really listen to it much, except the Saturday afternoon opera programs on the radio. There weren't a lot of records in the house, except the ones that I collected. My parents had a natural instinct to sing, but there was no musical cultivation, so to speak, in the family—that all came from outside. My older brothers were not really interested in jazz, they just liked the popular music of the day. My oldest brother was an amateur comedian, and he liked to burst into spontaneous song, but there was nothing more to it than that.

So what in your upbringing brought you to jazz?

At eleven I got a clarinet, because I was listening to Benny Goodman on the radio, and various other dance bands such as Glenn Miller and Count Basie. Benny Goodman was especially impressive to me. He was my first influence. So I guess I was listening before I was eleven. I heard the music on the radio, and also friends turned me on to it. It was very exciting to me, listening to the radio under the covers late at night.

So you didn't play an instrument till you were eleven.

No—I was just a whistler! I've never been able to figure this one out in retrospect—my parents very graciously got me a clarinet at the Boston department store in Chicago, and included with the clarinet I got a substantial coupon book with free lessons. (Incidentally, I've often wondered if there's a Chicago department store in Boston!) So, a Buffet clarinet, a name clarinet, and many weeks of lessons with a very fine teacher who Johnny Griffin and Eddie Harris also studied with, Lou Honig was his name—a very lucky situation for me.

I kept handing the coupons to this nice man each week for a while, and then I paid a small fee for succeeding lessons. These lasted, I think, a couple of years. I studied classical clarinet and formed a clarinet embouchure, a very rigid kind of muscle formation. Lou Honig was just teaching me the technique of the instrument; it had nothing to do with jazz as such. We did exercises and little pieces from one of the basic clarinet books. He was a dance band player, a club-date musician—he played trumpet and saxophone, and was technically able to adjust to these different instruments. He was quite a well-schooled guy.

The following year—when I was twelve—I got a tenor saxophone and studied it with him. At some point after that I studied with a man named Santy Runyon, who got a little more into the music, playing some more jazzy études and things, but still basically out of books. And then at some point I was already able to work, because of the war period. I met Lennie Tristano, and he really opened the door to the possibilities of this music for me, and I am truly grateful for what he did for me, and for many others.

Your parents didn't have a piano.

No, they never did.

What did they make of your musical aspirations?

My parents were pleased that I was interested, and they made a sacrifice to get me the instrument. My father loved Artie Shaw's "Concerto for Clarinet," but they had no real knowledge of jazz.

As the youngest of three sons especially, I wasn't able to communicate with my dear mother and father, who had to work hard to provide for us. My interest in music was encouraged but not understood, so I couldn't share this most important part of my youth with them, making me feel like an outsider at home. But I always appreciated their encouragement. They were very good, basic people. Really they were happy that I was doing something I liked, and that I was already earning money at it. They didn't give me the classic "become a doctor or lawyer" alternative of the Jewish family, and probably most families.

So you respected them for that.

I *really* appreciated it. I was left alone very much, so I could practice my craft. I didn't know about "art" as yet.

I left home at the age of twenty to join the Claude Thornhill band, and went to New York. I remember coming back and playing with Warne Marsh and Tristano at a club in Chicago much later, and my parents came to listen. I couldn't imagine what they would be getting out of it. They never really commented. They got the first few touches of my being "famous." A few times they came to hear me when I was playing in Chicago, I think they were proud that I had found a way of life. And I appreciated that. My oldest brother, the natural singer, who had a great sense of humor, was kind of a hero, in some way. But though my brothers and I kept in touch, we didn't really have that much to talk about. Once in a while we talked, but it wasn't that close a relationship. My eldest brother died of a stroke at the age of eighty, and so did my other brother, at the age of eighty-three.

I was always envious of families that were musically involved. I just read this piece on Richard Rodgers, talking about how the parents fought bitterly, but they always went to the theater, and bought sheet music, and stayed around the piano and sang. And when they found out Richard was talented, they encouraged him. And of course the Joneses and the Heaths were the same.[5] My five children never became professional musicians. The oldest boy was kind of interested and showed real talent, but he didn't develop his ability. He works hard for a living, installing heating and air conditioning systems. I never conceived of working that hard; I really respect his decision. He still has fun with music, as do my other children.

Was jazz a way of rebelling against your background?

In some ways. There was something in-groupish about the Jewish people that I saw, that I didn't like—there was always that word *Gentile* which I hated. In my father's laundry and cleaning establishment, black ladies did ironing and things in the shop and they were referred to as "schvarzes."[6] I didn't like that before I knew why, exactly. It just felt like "us and them," and I didn't like that feeling—and I still don't!

Was Jewish music an influence on you?

I never was fond of that music. I heard it—I went to Hebrew school for a short period of time, and went to the synagogue some time, and I never enjoyed that too much. It felt too otherworldly. And my parents were otherworldly, though they weren't strict religiously. They just observed high holidays and some of the dietary things—you don't mix milk and meat, and some preparations I don't really recall. When my parents spoke Yiddish, I was a little bit ashamed that they weren't speaking English more. So I kind of missed out on that cultural situation. I tried, but it didn't really work.

To jump up to the present time, I made a record in May [2000] for John Zorn's label, Tzadik—there's a Star of David on the liner package. He was talking about bringing out my Jewishness. That's one of his missions. He sent me some of the records on his label, and there was a solo record of Steve Lacy, a very nice record. I read the liner notes, and Steve confessed to being a closet Jew. I didn't really know that. And so he felt relieved that it finally came out. I was thinking, "Is that gonna be what I'm gonna do? Let's see, my father's name was Abraham, and my mother's name was Anna, etc. etc." So we made the record, and listened to it later, and John said, "I think we'll put this in the jazz section, do the Jewish one next time"! So it appeared on the DIW label as *Some New Stuff.*

Does he want you to do a klezmer record?

No, he just wants me to do what I would conceive of as being Jewish music, and I don't really know about that. On one occasion someone on the bandstand suggested a Monk tune, and I quickly remarked that I only play Jewish composers!—meaning George Gershwin, Jerome Kern, etc. That's Jewish music to me, that's what I prefer to play.

Without Jerome Kern, I might be in the laundry business!

When I talked about this with Paul Bley, he said he'd "concealed his eth-nicity" from you.[7]
Like hell he did! He's Jewish all over. When you're Jewish it's hard to keep it a secret. Steve Lacy did. But I don't broadcast it. If someone asks, I tell them my heritage, but I don't practice "Jewishness"—except with the jokes!

❡ Interview with John Zorn

Born in New York's East Village in 1953, and raised there, **JOHN ZORN** *is a unique creative figure whose work straddles many scenes: hardcore rock with cult bands PainKiller and Naked City; jazz with News for Lulu and Spy vs Spy; and Jewish music through his two books of Masada com-positions. As an improviser he has performed with every major figure on the international scene, and his legendary game pieces are performed reg-ularly by renegade groupings. His classical concert music is performed by ensembles worldwide, and he has scored music for many independent and underground films. A firm supporter of the music and musicians he believes in, he started the Tzadik label in 1995 and has edited and pub-lished a volume of musicians' writings,* Arcana.

Lee is one of my very favorite saxophonists. I love his tunes, and coming up as a young sax player I memorized *all* of them, playing to his records every day for ten years. His compositions are some of the most beautiful, complex melodies in jazz history. Lee has a very independent creative mind and doesn't take any shit. I respect that. Lennie Tristano was a Svengali in many respects, with a very specific agenda, but Lee was one of the few that broke free and went their own way. Here's a guy that blew Charlie Parker away—for sixty years this guy's been kicking ass on the saxophone! The sound he had when he was with the Kenton band in the early fifties, when he used that hard reed—I don't think anyone ever sounded like that on the saxophone. What a tone, what an incredible sound—certain notes were so intense they became almost visual to me.

So when I started the Great Jewish Music series on Tzadik, to celebrate the contributions of Jewish composers to world culture—we did the music of Burt Bacharach, Serge Gainsbourg, Marc Bolan—Lee was one of the first people I thought of. The scale used in his tune "Kary's Trance" always had a real Jewish feel to me. Eventually I dismissed the idea of doing a project of other musicians doing Konitz tunes and asked Lee directly if he was interested in making a CD of Jewish material. Lee wanted to make a CD of originals, with original chord changes. What he said to me broke my heart—that when he records for other labels, they never want his originals—they just want him to do standards! What I was hoping for, I guess, was a CD of tunes that dealt with Jewishness in some way—perhaps like "Kary's Trance." Other musicians of his generation, Steve Lacy and Borah Bergman for example, made beautiful recordings for Tzadik dealing with Jewish scales, themes, and subject matter. What Lee brought in was a fabulous batch of new tunes, but they just didn't feel particularly Jewish, so with Lee's approval we transferred it to the Japanese DIW label, and it was released as *Some New Stuff*. If Lee ever wanted to revisit the Jewish challenge, I would be delighted—he's one of my all-time heroes.[8] 👈

It's important to realize that Konitz started playing saxophone before the advent of bebop in 1945. His earliest influences, therefore, were musicians from the Swing Era. He now discusses their influence, from before the time he met Lennie Tristano and listened to Charlie Parker—leaving for later discussion his principal mentor from that era, Lester Young.

Apart from Benny Goodman, which clarinet players did you admire?
I admired Artie Shaw and Lester Young. I was very sorry that Artie decided to give up playing completely. He actually tried to absorb bebop, and he did a much better job than Benny Goodman—who just made a half-assed attempt and didn't really get it.

I loved Artie Shaw's bands and his playing. I had preferred Benny Goodman early on, for his sound. But as I continued to listen over the years, I pushed Benny aside—he was a great clarinet player, but Artie was a great *musician*. On Artie's later recordings with Al Cohn and Zoot Sims, and Shorty Rogers arrangements or whatever, he's really playing a different kind of line—it's not somehow as sensational as he was before, with all the high notes, but it was very musical.

What made you change from clarinet to tenor sax and later alto?
It was partly pragmatic—in order to work in a band, you had to play the saxophone. When I picked up the saxophone, I used the clarinet embouchure—I had a very tight jaw musculature to get that sound, and I just brought that to the saxophone. I think that's partly responsible for the sound I ended up with. I preferred that somehow. Over the years I've tried every sort of embouchure to loosen up. I haven't kept up clarinet at all; I used it as what they call a double, in Claude Thornhill's band, and that was about the end of it.[9]

I went from tenor sax to alto because I had an offer to play in a nightclub, in a show band, and they needed an alto player. I also worked with Jimmy Dale's big band. I liked the alto sound, and it became my instrumental choice.

It's been said that in the early forties the Chicago scene was depressed, because the major players had moved to New York.

No, it was very active, there were many places to play. As a teenager I was playing in cocktail lounges and ballrooms. It was a very exciting time for me. The leading player at that time was Roy Eldridge—he was the hero. He played at the Three Deuces, but I never heard him there; I was still too young to get in. But sneaking in, I remember hearing [trumpeter] Red Allen, [alto saxophonists] Pete Brown, Don Stovall, [trombonist] J. C. Higgin-botham—that was very exciting.

I think Roy was one of the hottest trumpet players—one of the hottest players of any instrument—in all of jazz. I loved his sound, his feeling, the note selections. Basically, he was playing as a singer, a great opera singer. I loved the records he made with Chu Berry, like "Body and Soul," and "I Can't Believe That You're In Love With Me" with Benny Carter and Cole-man Hawkins. And with Artie Shaw's band, and with Gene Krupa, "After You've Gone" and "Let Me Off Uptown"—just everything he played was great.

After hearing him, Chet Baker with that pretty sound was hard to take—and Miles too, at the beginning, when he was playing that very subtle vibra-toless sound. I mean Roy let it all hang out—a great emotional vibrato, and a great buzz when you wanted it.

I just had a nice recollection of working in a club in New York [in the 1950s] with my "Tristano student" quartet—Ronnie Ball, Peter Ind, Dick Scott—opposite Louis Armstrong. What a bill—the Lee Konitz group open-ing for "Pops"!

During his act he was singing a song that was anti-bebop—making fun of it to the crowd of Louis Armstrong admirers—and I didn't appreciate that. But Trummy Young [the trombone player] invited me during the break into the back room, with Louis, bless their hearts. Trummy took out a cigar-sized joint and passed it around. I tell you, that was some powerful shit—I had trouble finding the bandstand afterwards!

During that set I looked around the room after playing one of my mas-terful extemporizations [laughs]—and there was Louis leaning on the rail-ing, listening to us. Don't know if he loved it, but there he was. He might just have been standing there looking at a pretty lady—you never know with these guys!

So it was a generation of swing players that influenced you before you met Tristano?

Yes. Johnny Hodges was a definitive influence on ballad playing per se— Phil Woods and John Coltrane loved Johnny. His hot playing, which was virtuosic, wasn't really my favorite concept, but his ballad playing had a very deep effect on me. Every saxophone player loved Johnny Hodges, till Charlie Parker came along and they dropped him! I loved the way he played so sweetly. Now I find it a little schmaltzy, but I still love it. It was just so beautifully done. He was able to glissando down an octave—on "Passion Flower" he did that, at the end of the bridge.

And that's very difficult.

It's impossible! I've been trying to do that since then, and I still can't do it smoothly.

That was a real hallmark of his style.

Yes. When I did that tribute to him recently for the [Jazz at Lincoln Center] Hall of Fame [in New York, 2005], I played these ballads, but I never bent the notes. I've heard Phil Woods play with the kind of bends that Johnny Hodges used, but I didn't want to do an imitation of him, I just wanted to play a very straight, sweet-sounding melody.

Do you ever bend notes?

Not if I can help it! It doesn't appeal to me. But I do have a feeling sometimes to slide around a little bit.

As well as Johnny Hodges, Benny Carter was an inspiration also, especially one record that he made on Commodore, "I Can't Believe That You're In Love With Me," with Coleman Hawkins and Roy Eldridge.

He was thought of as a cool player.

Yes, very much so. No one really thought of that term then, but he definitely was. A lot of times he sounded a bit schmaltzy to me, in the sense of not having the most sophisticated phrases or developments. I always admired him, though, as a great saxophone player, and that one solo—I'm sure there are other ones, but I didn't know all of his records—really got it. It wasn't a long solo. If we start with the premise that Charlie Parker turned the whole scene around with sixteen bars on "Whispering"—which "Groovin' High" was based on—it doesn't take that much to make a point.

Willie Smith has also been mentioned as an influence on you.

He was a fine player who was playing—I was told—absolutely written-out solos. He never improvised in those contexts. But he did it very well, and I liked his sound. He sounded a little out of place in the Jazz at the Philharmonic setting with Bird.

Many people have said it's a good discipline to say what you can in six-

teen or thirty-two bars on a three-minute record, but it is a limitation.
I agree with that. I admire Sonny Rollins being able to play for forty-five minutes and keep it interesting and high-spirited, but sixteen bars is often enough. My longest solo is probably on the solo record I made. I did a forty-minute version of "The Song Is You," and then tried one other tune, "Cherokee" for twenty or thirty minutes; eventually the forty-minute version appeared on CD.

> One of Konitz's first jobs, in 1945, was with Jerry Wald's band—in the sax section, not taking solos—in the Chicago area and on the road. When Konitz left Wald, he worked in the Chicago area with pianist Lloyd Lifton, with whom he made his earliest known (noncommercial) recording. He also played in Teddy Powell's orchestra, in which, as he explains, he took the chair of tenor saxophonist Charlie Ventura, whose "Bop for the People" band later in the decade tried to popularize bebop.

I was with Jerry Wald's band just a couple of months. Jerry was a very fine clarinet player in the style of Artie Shaw. It was a very good dance band, nice and loose, and I played third alto—I didn't play any solos. I wore a uniform. I was able to read and get a blend in the section, and just enjoy some good players. Also that year I played a month with a very fine band—Teddy Powell's. I actually took Charlie Ventura's chair on tenor and really was not qualified to do that then.

I used to hear Charlie Ventura with Gene Krupa's band. He played the altissimo [highest] register very well, and nice augmented [chord] arpeggios. He played very passionately. His concept was a little bit in between someplace I didn't love—elements of Ben Webster, Lester, and Bird, but the final mixture was, I guess, sentimental ballads and virtuosic playing on faster tempos. When I took his chair in Teddy Powell's band, as a teenager, his parts had chord symbols written in concert key. I had very little experience with chords, much less written in another key. I had to play the tenor and the bass clarinet, which I wasn't that familiar with. The first time I played a solo, Teddy banged his head on the wall of the stage in disbelief or whatever. There was a nail in the wall—served him right! A lot of people had left the band for some reason, so I guess they hurriedly got replacements. But it was an experience to play with a good dance band.

Jimmy Dale had a band of Chicago musicians including Gene Ammons and Lou Levy. The only gigs I remember were in the Pershing Ballroom. He jumped up and down in front of the band, pretending to be Lionel Hampton. Harold Fox was his real name, he ran a tailor's business, making band uniforms. He was really a club-date trumpet player—a nice guy and a good friend, but a little bit out to lunch.

By this time Konitz was studying with Lennie Tristano, so before discussing his career with the Claude Thornhill Orchestra and then Miles Davis, it's necessary to backtrack a little to discuss the beginnings of Tristano's dominant musical and philosophical influence on him.

2 ❧ Formative Influences

Lennie Tristano, Charlie Parker, and Lester Young

Konitz's totally individual style on alto saxophone came out of a mixture of influences, whose exact proportions are hard to determine. He says later in this chapter that he was already studying with Tristano when he first heard Charlie Parker, and the same may be true of his first hearing Lester Young. But though Konitz avers that Tristano steered him away from the influence of the bebop master, and the consensus is that Konitz's style is independent of Parker's, in fact his influence on Konitz's tone runs deep, as Gunther Schuller argues in his interview at the start of chapter 8. Even if Konitz is not in any sense a disciple, his distinctive sound is a modern jazz saxophone tone that comes out of Parker. Nonetheless, the influence of Parker and Lester Young was filtered through the teaching of Lennie Tristano, a very dominant musical personality.

Tristano was one of jazz's most remarkable innovators. A charismatic influence on a generation of mainly white players, the blind pianist had a remarkable technique and fertile musical imagination. His work was respected by many leading figures including Charlie Parker. Tristano was widely recognized as a compelling teacher, who demonstrated, against the accepted view up to that time, that jazz improvisation could be taught. His name is a constant point of reference throughout these conversations. Konitz described him as a "musician-philosopher," and the school of young musicians around Tristano became known as a cooler modern jazz alternative to bebop, or at least as an extension of it.

Tristano was born in Chicago in 1919. He had weak sight at birth and was completely blind before being placed at the age of fifteen in the Illinois School for the Blind. There he learned piano and also clarinet, alto and tenor sax, guitar, trumpet, and drums. He began to work professionally at age twelve, and entered the American Conservatory of Music in Chicago, becoming a highly schooled musician with a grounding in classical music as well as jazz. By 1943 he was teaching at the Christensen School of Popular Music in Chicago. His strongly held ideas on jazz improvisation, especially the need for rigorous construction over the creation of overt emotional effect, became the basis of the Tristano school. But although Tristano and Charlie Parker had a strong mutual admiration, critics soon began to contrast the former's music as more cool and cerebral.[1]

Konitz's reminiscences paint a portrait of Tristano as a magnetic but troubled personality whose influence was a source of the saxophonist's great originality, but which he eventually had to escape at some personal cost and with unresolved tensions. The studies with Tristano are discussed in this chapter, followed by discussion of the influence of Lester Young and Charlie Parker. Konitz's participation in Tristano's groups and recordings, and his analysis of the pianist's music, appear in the next chapter.

I first met Lennie when I was playing with a dance band at a ballroom on the southwest side of Chicago. A friend of mine—a pianist named Joe Lipuma—was working at a pub across the street, the Winkin' Pup. When I finished working I went over to hear him. The second band there was a kind of Mexican band, and Tristano was playing with them. I sat in, and spoke with him.

What struck you about his playing at that point?
He was playing a lot of locked-hands things, in the style of Milt Buckner—very interesting lines, really a very special conception. It didn't quite fit the Latin context, but it was very hip!

When Tristano first heard you, you were playing tenor. He recollected that your playing was "horrible, atrocious." He told you, "Forget the tenor, play alto."[2]
I don't remember him suggesting that. To criticize me so strongly because I wasn't cultivated yet, doesn't sound right to me. Maybe it's a way of saying what a good teacher he was, to take a completely untalented guy. Whether he really made that quote or not, is another question.

I think a lot of these interviews in the 1940s and 1950s—which quote you, or Charlie Parker, for instance—put words into the musician's mouth.[3] As you say, if you were playing so horribly, why would he be interested in teaching you?
Well, he was earning his living from teaching, though I presume I was one

of his earliest pupils. I was already improvising, without much knowledge. That's what he liked about me, the fact that I was an improviser. The way I was playing then could be closer to the way a free improviser would play. I wasn't sophisticated about changes, or things like that.

What did studying with Tristano involve?

It was very basic theory. We went through the scales and chord sequences, and talked about music. He was a saxophone player originally, though no longer actively, but he understood how the saxophone worked. Most of all, he encouraged me to become familiar with the great players. It was my own sound that I developed first—though the sound can't really be separated from the notes, it's integrated with what you're playing. But sometimes I could get a sound but not play an interesting phrase.

I really looked forward to those weekly sessions. It felt like I was getting into another world, one that I wanted to get into. That was my first opportunity to really find out what it felt like to improvise, and that's what Tristano was encouraging. Then I was able to play some situations in Chicago with him. The cocktail lounges, as we referred to them, had a lot of good music. I remember one place that had a revolving bandstand. There was a lurch in the stand, so every time we came to a certain place there was a little accent. I think I altered my phrases to accommodate that lurch!

What would a lesson be like—an average lesson, if there was such a thing?

It would mean playing arpeggios of all chords, plus inversions, through the major and minor scales, and playing on a tune, and talking about and trying different sequences to experience different rhythm patterns—tapping 3 over 2, or 4 over 3, or 5 over 4. Learning harmonic theory, and conceptual training. Nonlegato and legato articulations; accents; dynamics. Listening closely to the people who were serious players—I had to sing recorded solos, play them, and write them down and analyze them. We talked about what was involved, besides hard work, in developing a meaningful expression.

Tristano played the tenor early on, like Chu Berry, he said. I never really heard him play it, except just briefly once. And he played Dixieland clarinet. Earl Hines was one of his heroes, and Art Tatum—the great pianists. He never talked about Louis Armstrong—he always started with Roy Eldridge, Charlie Christian, and especially Lester Young.

[My composition] "Subconscious-Lee" began as one of the weekly [written] exercises.[4] Tristano didn't dwell on harmonic subtleties with me because I wasn't that responsive—I didn't play the keyboard at that time, I was a "one-note" guy. Warne [Marsh] started out on the piano.

Did Lennie suggest you should learn the piano?

I don't remember that he did.

Was the lesson a set length?

It was an hour's lesson, pretty much, every week. Very frequently I sat around with him past the lesson time, unless he had people waiting outside for their turn. I think later on, when he had a lot of students, it was half an hour or even less—just to hear what you're practicing and saying "keep it up."

So he struck the right balance between criticism and encouragement?

I think so. The idea is that when you find an inspirational character like that, all you need is to know that you can see him for a few minutes each week as a steady impetus, working productively—just to walk in and see him was an inspiration. Half an hour or an hour with him, and you'd go home and practice with an increased intensity.

He was making his living from teaching, but he charged me very little. The lessons went on for a few years [from 1943 to 1946], with pauses for travel, and then resumed again when I came to New York in 1948.

You knew about chord symbols?

To some extent, yes. But I was basically improvising on melodies, just playing variations. It was pretty intuitive, I would say. I still do that really. I like to think of playing from a melody first, rather than a chord structure. But of course the harmony is included.

It was unusual at that time for a jazz player to be taught more formally, rather than just hints and suggestions.

He was one of the first to get something together, to offer a course of study. Guys used to get together to practice, and share their ideas; but this was kind of formal, and Tristano was the first to do that. As he mentioned in interviews, he learned how to teach through trying to communicate with the students. They gave him ideas, and in that sense I felt I was sharing in this process with him. I then started to teach quite early on, so I was also doing that, formally, before it was the thing to do in the school programs.

Later, Muhal Richard Abrams functioned in that way as an inspiration to the young people in the AACM group.[5] Barry Harris became a guru, and Sun Ra. Monk was also a guru to the people he played with, though he didn't teach formally—and this was after Tristano.

In that situation, a great teacher is someone who has a strong creative vision, which they want to impart, but who recognizes the individuality of the student.

That was something he could do very well. Even though it was called a cult, none of his students really played alike. It was the opposite with Charlie

Parker. No one really studied with Bird directly, but they all tried to play exactly like him. Bird's phrases were so musical and so strong, that it was hard to vary them too much—for his imitators, it was satisfying enough to go through the motions.

The fact that Tristano was blind, what effect did that have?

The communication with a blind person goes through a higher level in some way. I was able to look in his eyes—he didn't cover them—but there was just something extrasensory about it. Plus he was a great communicator, he really could make his points! He was very articulate, very well read, and *very* opinionated, with a great sense of humor.

Charismatic?

Yes. That's where the cult idea came in, because people were really inspired by this man—parading around, feeling they were kind of esoteric and special, which in part was true, since they shared his vision too. A group of us were devoted to Lennie, and his example—the way he lived his life, the way he played, his great ability to hear and direct each of his students in a meaningful way.

What was the opinion of the bebop players about Tristano and his students?

They were curious—Bird certainly was curious, and Dizzy. Mingus would hang out with Lennie. They could hear something of importance. Lots of people came to study with him to find out what he was talking about—Bud Freeman, Phil Woods, and later Alan Broadbent, Dave Liebman, Richie Beirach.[6]

There was a feeling that he was the "witch doctor," as Al Haig put it.[7]

A lot of people caricatured him in one way or another. People who knew him casually, or didn't know him at all, just judged him on the basis of his students' behavior. Warne and I were not exactly show people—none of us were really—and we must have looked and sounded weird!

You didn't look like a hip bebop combo—you looked geeky, nerdy.

Yes, compared to all the hippest black musicians. I had my thick, horn-rimmed glasses, and Lennie was blind . . . Warne didn't look weird.

We were last on that opening night at Birdland [December 15, 1949], after Bird and Lester and a whole long list of bands—we were supposed to be the most modern, and we were, I guess. I'd love to hear that whole program again!

The impression I've got from you is that Tristano was also quite a difficult man.

He certainly was not difficult for me to get on with during the course of

Birdland poster, 1949

my student and playing relationship with him. It got difficult after I left, a little bit.

Tristano was such a strong personality, there's a danger of being dominated.

Yes, I felt that in many ways, with Tristano as a father figure. That's what I really had to get away from eventually. But he certainly convinced me that, if I could deal with it, music was an honorable pursuit.

He provided a necessary corrective to an even more influential figure, though—Charlie Parker.

Yes, probably so. But there was an identification with a white Italian-American rather than an African-American—that had something to do with it. I never felt like I fit in that area. Generous and hospitable as Miles Davis was, and Charlie Parker was always great to me, I didn't really play with those guys that much, regrettably.

Since that time with Tristano I've hardly studied formally. In all these years, I've felt that was enough information for me to continue to review, and try to absorb—which feels strange to me when I hear about all the formal studying that some people do. Compared to them I'm basically an autodidact.

It's a paradox. Tristano taught formally, and yet the students didn't play like him; Charlie Parker never intended to teach anyone, and yet his followers all played like him.
Bird's ideas were taken really literally, and Tristano's were more suggestions that could be developed in different ways. I can only think that the opportunity to speak about the music would have something to do with that.[8]

Lester Young

Through Tristano's teaching, but also independently, Konitz became open to two other crucial influences—Lester Young and Charlie Parker. Konitz loves Lester Young and admires his playing—at least from the 1930s—without reservation. Young's work with Count Basie, and especially with Billie Holiday, provided a cooler alternative to the dominant rhapsodic tenor saxophone style of Coleman Hawkins. Young was the consummate jazz hipster and a highly sensitive artist. After World War II, despite his increasing popularity, he played in a darker style that found little critical favor; by the late 1950s he was in decline due to alcoholism, and died in 1959. His influence on modern jazz was immense, an inspiration both for Charlie Parker and for cooler saxophonists from the 1950s.

Young's supple rhythmic sense was a precursor of the rhythmic complexity of Tristano, Marsh, and Konitz himself. Konitz has commented that "it's possible to get the maximum intensity in your playing and still relax . . . [Lester Young's work with Basie] is a perfect example of the essence of what I'm trying to do. He never sounded frantic, nor did he sound as if it were an effort to play. He sounded as if he were sitting back and putting everything right into the groove where it's supposed to be. It was very pretty and at the same time, it was very intense."[9] Rhythmically, Young's approach was totally original—as Konitz has said, it is "complex in its simplicity . . . polyrhythmic."[10] The tenor saxist's feel is constantly varying, with an inspired use of space between phrases. His eighth notes are more even than the strong triplet feel of Coleman Hawkins's, and this smoothing out became characteristic of modern jazz. Konitz elaborates on Young's influence here.

I had a very strong response to Lester Young which I've never lost. I think he's probably my favorite, ultimately, for that small body of playing with Count Basie. I first heard him on record, then I saw him at the Regal Theater in Chicago. I didn't really know about his music at that time, but I was immediately impressed with this man standing, holding his horn sideways, and making this gorgeous sound. I was reacting to the excitement of the band—the sight and the sound. Later, when I was with the Jerry Wald band, a very fine Lester Young–influenced tenor player named Stan Kosow had Lester Young records with him, and I heard him then really for the first time. And, as proof of how good a work of art this is, I still hear him in a fresh way each time.

What was the immediate attraction?

The first thing that pulled me in, like many people, was the sound—it was just extraordinarily interesting. At the first hearing I was impressed with the melodies he was playing. They were so good that I could listen to them for sixty years and never tire of them. But the sound—it's so much part of the music, it's not a separate entity. It's all coordinated, and very beautifully molded. Great selections of notes, and great time-feeling—he swings effortlessly. And don't forget, in that context he was making a unique sound. Coleman Hawkins's Romantic sound was the real thing at that time.

You were presumably already familiar with Coleman Hawkins.

I enjoyed some of Coleman's work very much. Of course, "Body And Soul," and then the sides with Oscar Pettiford and Shelly Manne—"Sweet Lorraine" and "The Man I Love" were special. I remember Warne and I listening to him many years later, admiring how he was really trying to play the modern eighth-note line with an even feel, though it was still bouncing along a little bit, dotted eighth/sixteenth.

Somehow the vibrato was a little bit too much sometimes, and some of the substance of the music was not as interesting to me as Lester's. It was a kind of operatic sound-projection—Coleman Hawkins was a fan of opera, and he gets that robust, powerful kind of sound, with a pronounced vibrato, in contrast to Lester Young's more intimate sound, though it was full in the most pure sense.

I hadn't thought about it like that—as a sort of declaiming, a different kind of "operatic tenor."

Oh yeah—Luciano never sounded like that!

If you think of Miles Davis's sound, compared to Louis Armstrong, or Helen Merrill compared to Carmen McRae or one of the more lusty singers—the operatic singer really has to have a powerful voice production.

A lot of the early jazz masters were influenced by opera—Louis Armstrong knew lots of arias.

It sounds like it. He was trying to get the maximum sound out of that instrument, as a great singer would do. Harry James, corny as he could be sometimes, really made a sound.

You like to hear a horn player with a strong tone, in some sense.
Yeah, when I heard Charlie Parker play a phrase, it was like an opera singer in that sense—the maximum expression possible at that moment.

But where do you fit into that?
Well, I tried for that. I continue to try to project a sound, loosening up my embouchure as much as possible, using my breath more.

Did you ever meet Lester Young?
I met Pres once at the Royal Roost. He said, "How ya doin', Pres?" [as he always did]. I said, "Hello, Lester," and that was it.

What did you think of his clarinet playing?
It was beautiful! He didn't play clarinet very much, but his playing was just so musical, with—I was told—a metal clarinet that had a very unique, primitive sound in some ways. But it was just lyrically beautiful. He wasn't a virtuoso in the ordinary sense, but in the real sense he was a total virtuoso. That term really has to be defined over and over again. I adjudicated a saxophone competition in Montreux [during the 2002 festival], and I heard guys who could play circles round me in virtuosic ways, but I still had to determine the quality of what they're playing as best I could. My view is that a good solo doesn't care who plays it! I heard Chris Potter last night—there is a virtuoso, but very musical also.

Being able to play a lot of notes very fast might not be musical.
"Virtuoso" for me means a mastery of the expressive means of the music, and in that sense Lester Young was a virtuoso clarinet player. It was totally beautiful music, to me.

Your favorite is the 1930s material, with Count Basie?
Yes, unquestionably—it was short and sweet! That period, that rhythm section, those arrangements, they really inspired him. Also, the lovely small groups with Nat Cole. His later music, in the 1950s, could be sad. But because he was so musical, I just appreciate it for the lovely expression and the feeling behind it. It's like the last vestiges of a great energy and imagination. He was disillusioned and, as a result, in bad health.

But can you explain how his tone changed in the way that it did? From some of the things he said, it was deliberate.
I think it was in a way. But as his health declined, and his energy levels slowed down, he played music that expressed that condition.

People are talking about my changed tone, and how I've slowed down and all that, but I'm a different person now after seventy years of playing. I feel that I've essentialized rather than slowed down. I can play faster than ever—I was practicing "Cherokee" in all the keys just now, with a Jamey Aebersold record.[11] I can whiz through that pretty good, much better than I could in the early days. But I choose frequently to think more about the individual notes, and really trying to get in tune, and all those subtle details—that satisfies me, and can be very, very challenging. To play simply and creatively is some achievement.

Your tone hasn't changed in the way that Lester Young's did.

No, I think he was sick, physically and mentally, and couldn't really feel his music with the same kind of intensity as in the early days. I played a session with Zoot Sims—he was not well, and he was trying to play as he did when he was in good shape, and to me it didn't sound real in some way. I appreciated his pushing himself to get where he used to be, but it's not going to work. He died shortly after that. He was a beautiful musician, and a great saxophone player—one of the best of the Lester Young–inspired players.

[We listen to "Shoe-Shine Boy," Young's first recording from 1936, with Jones-Smith Incorporated.]

Lester really vibrates on that! He's always referred to as not using vibrato—yet he uses it all the time, very emotionally.

That's so familiar to me, yet it's like hearing it anew each time, because it's so substantial. Just hearing how he and Jo Jones "miss" on the bridge, which is kind of prepared sounding—they obviously played it pretty much that way. His playing was just so sweet, and not sentimental like Ben Webster could be.

Did you learn that solo quite early on?

Yes [he starts to sing it]—I haven't sung it for a while! And part of my study plan is to get back and repeat that. I knew Charlie Parker's solo on "Koko" pretty well, but I tried [to play along with the recording] recently and it was flying right by me.

Charlie Parker and Bebop

The bebop revolution marked a turning point in the history of jazz, the moment when the music became self-consciously artistic. This hard-edged, frenetic music was developed chiefly by Charlie Parker and Dizzy Gillespie—the breakthrough came in the *annus mirabilis* of 1945. At his peak, for a few years in the late 1940s, Parker was probably the most phenomenal improviser jazz has ever seen. His tone on alto sax was radically new, and Konitz must have been affected by it. As Carl Woideck writes, "Critics of it considered it shrill and edgy, while adherents found it fittingly stripped down and unsentimental."[12] In comparison to Swing Era predecessors, notably Duke Ellington's alto saxophonist Johnny

Hodges, Parker used vibrato sparingly and attacked most notes on-pitch, without bending them, leaving them stable. The classic "Parker's Mood" was the essence of the blues, expressing Parker's remarkable synthesis of the earthy and the complex. Although his released recordings after 1950 are restrained and commercial, live recordings issued years later show him reaching new heights of creativity and exploration. But his behavior was increasingly erratic due to personal problems and heroin addiction. He died in 1955, aged thirty-four.

Like all players of his generation, Konitz was obliged to respond to Charlie Parker's omnipresence in the music. But because he developed his own personal style apparently at some distance from Parker's, it's not generally recognized how saturated he became in the latter's music. Tonally, as Gunther Schuller emphasizes in the interview in chapter 8, the two players had much in common. From around 1945, Konitz became intimately acquainted with Parker's work, and like other young players, learned Parker's solos from the records. He's said that Parker's music "was more intense than I was able to identify with at the time, but eventually I decided that [attitude of mine] was all ego and I was missing the greatest alto player who had ever lived."[13] In a radio interview in 1956, Tristano asked Konitz how it felt to play Parker's solo on "Yardbird Suite," which Konitz had memorized and practiced: "I feel that I have to use every ounce of energy in my body to play this properly. . . . I learned this solo off the record . . . because it's perfect music to me. And through playing the notes, I was able to absorb some of the essence of the feeling that he used."[14] But despite this intimate acquaintance with Parker's music, and at a time when almost all his contemporaries were imitating the altoist in tone and melodic and rhythmic conception, Konitz developed his own individual and highly intuitive approach. He has no interest in pursuing what he regards as Parker's "compositional" approach of developing a vocabulary of motifs—a difficult issue discussed in chapter 6—and although he recognizes Parker as a genius, he is also in some ways ambivalent about his music.

I was already studying with Tristano when I first heard Charlie Parker, on a ten-inch acetate recording on Guild, a red and white label. The tune was "Groovin' High." Phew! I pricked up my ears. I really listened, but didn't quite get it the first couple of times—whether it was the complexity, or the sound. After listening to Johnny Hodges, that was a shock. It was an extremely intense music. But soon after, I started to realize how great it was.

What did Tristano think of Parker?

He thought of him as a master player. But he pointed out that it could be too tempting to gravitate to that place, so he encouraged me to develop what I could do of my own invention. I think he heard that I enjoyed starting improvising from the first note, a bit more intuitive maybe. Charlie was really a great composer; he played very specific things very well. His music developed very spontaneously, but he retained his best phrases, and attitudes.

You've been quoted as saying, "I tried to play bebop, but it was too hard."

I said that half tongue-in-cheek. I can play many of those solos of Bird's, and they were certainly difficult to really duplicate. When I first heard him I was already formulating a style. My point really was that I didn't want to play like that; to actually duplicate a solo was a great experience, but I didn't want to play in that style. I seemed to have formulated enough of a sound, and a line that was personal to me—but I was far from absorbing the relaxation, and the ability to hear and work with other people that I've been working on all these years.

Because I was associated with Tristano, and going in that direction, I wasn't totally pulled into Bird's influence. It was very fortunate that I started with Tristano before hearing Bird—I would have gone the way of all the others, the imitators. Bird was the man, unequivocally.

Also, bebop was a little bit too sensational for me, *too* intense, I guess. So I didn't identify with it right away. I was listening to Johnny Hodges and Benny Carter, Coleman Hawkins and Lester Young. When I heard Charlie Parker the first time I was really amazed, but I wasn't pulled in yet. It took a little while. And then as I studied his playing I couldn't avoid being fascinated by this master musician playing my instrument. One night, at Birdland, he was having a problem with his alto, and asked to borrow mine. I listened with amazement at what came out of that instrument! When he gave it back, I said I would appreciate it if he left some of that great stuff in the horn for me!

There was some ego involvement too, in not wanting to sound like Charlie Parker. Everybody that I heard was influenced so directly by him, with every phrase and every inflection, and that wasn't natural for me. But studying and playing his solos I found out how great he really was. I've not denied his influence; when a phrase [like one of his] comes out, I just enjoy doing it, but for the most part I never adapted his vocabulary. I was playing more intervallicly, rather than scalar—when I was able to be free, it was more in terms of going from one interval to another, rather than from one scale or chord to another.[15]

Do you think that people don't recognize how saturated you are in Charlie Parker's music?

Not the people who really hear the music—they hear things [in my playing] I heard Charlie Parker do.

But you're thought to have an opposed style.

People who think that can find evidence to support it. White/black, technical and compositional dazzle compared to a more "random" kind of playing because of the lack of specific vocabulary, and things like that.

I hate that word *bebop*. It was a kind of cutesy definition of a serious music.

What was your feeling about flatted fifths, which were a kind of hallmark?

The use of the flat fifth was an addition to the vocabulary. Some people milked that interval to make a musical point, and it could be a kind of melodic gimmick. It was used in a kind of clever, cutesy way, frequently, that I didn't care for. But it figured in many strong melodies that identified that music.

There's this idea that Charlie Parker was harmonically very sophisticated, but in fact he was just incredibly melodic.

Right. [His trumpeter] Red Rodney was quoted as saying that he didn't think Bird knew the changes that well! He never heard Bird discussing them, and whenever Red would ask him what the change was at some point, Bird would make a kind of Zen comment; he would never tell him. So I wonder. He certainly knew elementary harmony. But Dizzy, I think, was the one who was really harmonically sophisticated, and was cueing him into that—as has been stated before.

I had considerations about Dizzy's playing—his sound, his pitch. Great ideas, but they got clichéd quickly. In the early years, Dizzy was doing "spectacles" on his trumpet—fast, new, high—and never sounding as real as Charlie Parker, who was capable of spectacular performance but was still dedicated to the music. Dizzy never played so good, before and after playing with Bird, that I know of.

How far did you identify with the hip ethos of bebop?

I was trying to play jazz, and I wore the zoot suit with the big shoulders, and the peg pants. But I didn't think of myself as a bebopper, ever, and I always hated the behavior of the hippies, with the drugs and all that. I didn't identify with the black people's lifestyle—I felt pretty much like an outsider, actually.

I had a few opportunities to travel with Charlie Parker, or I'd meet him someplace, and he was always very friendly.[16]

Did you think you were like the beboppers, rebelling against the swing players?

I didn't feel that I had a mission, I was just learning how to play the music. When I heard the black expression—anger for the past and so on—I felt the Jewish oppression, I'm sure. But basically I just wanted to learn the music. I wish I was more motivated socially, that way.

Part of the beboppers' motivation was that they objected to white players ripping off black music.

I could identify with that, because that was what was happening. I was copying Lester Young and Charlie Parker, but I acknowledged my love for their music.

I was politically indifferent, just a young guy smoking a little dope, and wearing yellow socks and brown suede shoes with my tuxedo!

You're not politically indifferent now though.

I'm aware of the dishonesty and tragedy that results from inhumane government actions. And I hate corporate control that you find in the pop world.

It would be hard to package your music, like pop music is packaged.

It's like Jim Hall said—he was asked, "How come you never sold out?" and he replied "Nobody ever asked me!" And nobody ever really asked me![17]

◥ Interview with Phil Woods

PHIL WOODS, *born Springfield, Massachusetts, in 1931, is one of the leading alto saxophonists in modern jazz. He studied clarinet at Juilliard, and worked with Charlie Barnet, and from the middle to late 1950s with Kenny Dorham, Dizzy Gillespie, Buddy Rich, and Quincy Jones. In the 1960s he toured the Soviet Union with Benny Goodman, and worked as a studio musician; in 1968 he moved to France. After a period in L.A., he moved to the East Coast in 1973 and formed a quartet with Mike Melillo, Steve Gilmore, and Bill Goodwin, and in the 1980s a quintet with Tom Harrell on trumpet and Hal Galper on piano. Here he gives a characteristically trenchant interview.*

I've known Lee since before Vaseline! We both studied with Lennie Tristano, and when Tristano died, Lee came to my gig and we commiserated about the death of a great teacher. We've always been very close. A couple of years ago we recorded in Umbria; we did four albums in five days. We did a thing called *Alto Summit* back in the sixties, with "Pony" Poindexter and Leo Wright, but we'd never really played just the two of us together. As two survivors, and as in a way two of Charlie Parker's children, to play together was a dream. We did a series of duets, some-times two altos, Lee played piano and I sang, and he sang and I played piano. Get the record set!

I only took four or five lessons with Tristano—I was sixteen years old, I wasn't really ready. I learned that I had a lot more to learn. But he intro-duced me to Charlie Parker—this was 1946 or 1947. We went for a les-son and Mr. Tristano said, "Are you kids coming down to Fifty-second Street tonight? I'm opening for Charlie Parker, perhaps you'd like to meet him." We said, "Yeah!"—we'd always wanted to meet God! After the first set, Arnold Fishkin, the bass player came, and took us—I wouldn't call it backstage, it was a little holding area, the Three Deuces was a remodeled speakeasy, just a bar and a bandstand. And there was Charlie Parker sit-ting on the floor with a big cherry pie. He said, "Hi kids, would you like a piece of cherry pie?" I said, "Yes, that's my favorite kind of pie, Mr. Parker!" So he gave me a big slab. That's one thing Tristano taught me—that jazz musicians are pretty nice people.

People say I came out of the Charlie Parker school, but the first saxo-phone player I listened to was Benny Carter, then Johnny Hodges, and then Charlie Parker—the triumvirate. When they say the Tristano play-ers were intellectual and unemotional, I don't listen to that bollocks! It's not my job to evaluate audiences, or journalists. Charlie Parker loved Lennie Tristano. That's good enough for me.

I think Lee is one of the greatest improvising artists the world has ever seen. He's a master, he's always searching for something, he never settles. He's a real artist, and in jazz, you see a lot of businessmen, but you don't find many genuine artists. As we move to the head of the line, the time is limited and the work isn't finished. We're septuagenarian gladiators. I think people respect that.[18] 🖋

3 🎵 Working with Tristano

The story of the Tristano school of players is an extraordinary one. Jazz was a small area within popular music, bebop was a small arena within jazz, and the Tristano school was an enclave within bebop. Tristano avoided the theatricality of beboppers like Dizzy Gillespie entirely, further limiting his audience. (As Konitz says in this chapter, "Whatever audience bebop got, which was certainly a small, limited audience, had to do . . . with that kind of dynamic [showbiz] expression.") Tristano's players were producing a high art music within an environment of club entertainment. It was a paradox that Tristano himself resolved by withdrawing more and more into a world of teaching and practicing, while Konitz went out into a wide variety of playing situations in the hope of communicating with a wider audience—thereby incurring the disapproval of his teacher. Tristano's recordings are few, but of superlative quality and originality. Konitz, a player of equal artistic integrity, has one of the largest discographies in jazz.

In his early career, Konitz worked mostly with Tristano's groups, and in this chapter he discusses how studying and playing with Tristano helped his own style to develop. He began performing occasionally with the pianist during 1946 at Chicago venues. Tristano then left for New York. When Konitz followed him in 1948, he found the modern jazz scene on Fifty-second Street very exciting, and heard Charlie Parker, Coleman Hawkins, Roy Eldridge, and Dizzy Gillespie's big band. He soon began to acquire a reputation as the leading stylistic alternative to Parker for modern jazz alto players.

Reunited with Konitz, Tristano's group expanded into a quintet, and then a sextet from 1948 with the addition of a new pupil, tenor saxist Warne Marsh. After some club appearances, the group had its first recording session in January 1949, which featured highly intricate original lines on standard material, including the first appearance of Konitz's composition "Subconscious-Lee," based on "What Is This Thing Called Love?," and Tristano's "Judy," based on "Don't Blame Me."[1] Then in May 1949, a few weeks after recording with Miles Davis's Nonet, Konitz was a member of Tristano's sextet for the historic first recordings of free jazz, subsequently released as "Intuition" and "Digression."[2] Later in 1949 Tristano's group toured the Midwest and performed at Carnegie Hall. They appeared on the opening bill at Birdland, the club named in honor of Charlie Parker, on December 15, 1949, in a show called "A Journey through Jazz," and stayed there for five weeks. However, between 1949 and 1955, while Konitz was becoming a prolific recording artist, Tristano and Marsh made few recordings, even fewer of which were issued at the time. Tristano's sidemen included the great modern jazz drummers Roy Haynes and Kenny Clarke.

In 1951 Tristano opened his studio at 317 East Thirty-second Street in New York, meant to be the start of a music school, but it closed in 1956. There he made his first experiments in overdubbing, "Pastime," "Ju-Ju," and "Descent into the Maelstrom," precursors of the better-known pieces on *Lennie Tristano* (Atlantic), which Konitz discusses below.[3] In 1952 the quintet performed a concert in Toronto, and then Konitz left to join Stan Kenton. He rejoined in 1955, and the live recording at the Confucius Restaurant, New York, was released, together with some of Tristano's multitracked pieces, as *Lennie Tristano*.[4] Tristano's later career can be briefly outlined. He did not play in a club again until 1958–59, when a quartet and then the quintet with Konitz and Marsh was reformed at the Half Note. They were recorded there in 1959, but with Bill Evans substituting for Tristano, and worked at the club again in 1964—Konitz's last collaboration with Tristano. During the 1960s Tristano devoted himself to teaching, and played in public less and less. When he did so, it was either solo or with Sonny Dallas on bass and Nick Stabulas on drums. *The New Tristano* for solo piano, Tristano's last major recording and a further radical development of his art, appeared in 1962; in 1965 he toured Europe playing solo, and appeared in Berlin in a televised "Piano Summit" with Bill Evans, Earl Hines, and others. In the 1970s he became ill and reclusive, and died in 1978.

In this chapter Konitz teases out the implications of the critics' charge that the Tristano players were too "cool" and "cerebral." He insists that their music had an intensity just as real for being more subtly expressed, and defends Tristano's distinction between feeling, which is necessary, and "emotion" (emoting), a distraction from the really felt music. After Konitz and I had this discussion, I came across a quote by Tristano that nicely sums up Konitz's argument: "If what I play were intellectual it would have to be all premeditated and it isn't."[5] Konitz goes on to discuss his later relations with Tristano after he ceased to be a pupil, and finally analyzes Tristano's playing style, especially his rhythmic approach and attitude to drummers. He shows some ambivalence toward his great teacher, who from the 1950s onward, along with disciples such as pianist Sal Mosca, criticized him for playing in a wide range of situations. As Konitz explains, this difference in outlook was largely responsible for their eventual falling-out.

Tristano encouraged an approach different from the beboppers—more of a continuous flow with subtle rhythmic inflections.
I think we were less "obvious" in many respects. The feeling for the musical line was very legato, with accents, breath or tongue, to flex it as much as possible. But it was as strong and intense as we could make it at any given moment. It wasn't my goal to be subdued, laid-back. I wasn't trying to establish that kind of a mood or anything. On a ballad, you know, the tendency is to get more into that kind of an area. But for the tempo pieces, I intended to play as intensely as possible.

This music gave us an opportunity to express ourselves. All the secondary considerations between black and white, hot or cool, rich or poor or whatever, happened after the fact that we were given a gift to work with, and were trying our best to do it well.

You've objected to the word *cool* as a description of your style.
I feel that in a positive way that's a great description. If you're talking about cool, you're talking about Louis Armstrong, Lester Young, Charlie Parker—all the people who could really play unaffected music. When it became affected—trying to be emotional, or funky, trying to be something other than natural—then it became "hot." But the real music was cool and really thoughtfully felt. The negative connotation is what was really used on us, as white unpassionate players. I didn't appreciate that.

So *cool* was meant to imply a lack of intensity.
In the negative context, it definitely meant that—as opposed to Charlie Parker, and Art Blakey, and whoever played the so-called black hot music. As a band, we were referred to as "The Six Blind Mice" sometimes—that was about as negative as you could get. We were trying to play the tunes that Charlie Parker was playing, standard tunes usually, and we wrote lines on those progressions—that's all we played with Tristano. It was in the tradi-

tion of bebop, but hopefully an extension in some direction—longer lines or more harmonic additions, and rhythmic differences.

You think that *cool* is a reverse racist putdown?

Surely. [*Hot* and *cool*] are loose terms. I'm not trying to play cool, I'm trying to play as hot as I can—and as cool as I can, as full of feeling as I can.

It's often said that your music is "cerebral."

I reject that entirely. I'm playing very intuitively, at best.

Can you be an intuitive cerebralist, or cerebrally intuitive? If you're intuitive, that means you're not using your thought processes in some way.

When people say that your playing is cerebral, what do you think they mean?

They mean there's no deep feeling. It's thought out and mechanical.

But if you ask these critics, "So you think the playing isn't spontaneous?," I'm not sure what they'd say. It doesn't make sense really. They must think, "This guy isn't feeling anything, because he hasn't got sweat pouring off him, and he's not making a lot of noise or moving around a lot."

But you can feel intensely, without giving all these manifestations of it.

"Thoughtful" is more of a positive observation, "cerebral" sounds negative. But I sweat sometimes, too!

People seem to believe that either you're someone who thinks deeply, or someone who feels deeply, you can't be both. That's wrong.

I hope so! The great players were very deeply in touch with their thoughts *and* feelings.

So you *can* be "cerebrally intuitive"!

"Intuitive" means you don't really have a plan—starting to play, and with intense concentration putting one note after another.

I really want to make that clear about my approach to this music. Because sometimes it's embarrassing for me to admit this, but I don't have a plan, usually. It's become so habitual, I guess, that I just pick up my horn every day and start to play. And the process of playing will suggest things, and I'll proceed from there.[6]

Cerebral suggests a lack of feeling, and also conscious planning at every stage.

So that criticism always seems kind of strange to me. I was frequently inhibited in my playing, I can hear that—but then I was feeling frustration, or anger, or sadness.

You mean like on *Live at the Half Note,* when you didn't feel you could play after Warne Marsh.[7]

Yes—being afraid of high intensity. The fear of not being able to come up with something. I think that's why a lot of people were surprised that I was able to play with Elvin Jones, because they didn't think I could play with that kind of intensity. Me neither, I guess!

That might be a consideration. In fact there's a further irony, because your music sounds "cerebral"—there's no florid feeling—precisely *because* it isn't consciously planned. Still, it's going to take more effort from the listener.

This was definitely a showbiz consideration, in terms of communicating to an audience who might not know about the music. The fast tempos of bebop and very sensational double-time, etc., would attract immediate attention. I mean that music was so highly sophisticated, it wasn't like prostitution of the material certainly, but I always felt that sensational kind of aspect, and I realized the necessity for it. Whatever audience bebop got, which was certainly a small, limited audience, had to do in part, I think, with that kind of dynamic expression.

It's striking how people are swayed by what they can see, the emotion in the player.

Of course. But you gotta do something when you're up there. You've got to sweat, or gyrate, or play beautifully, or whatever you choose to do.

Charlie Parker didn't move a muscle when he was playing; he was like a statue. You'd see the little fat fingers just lifting up a little bit off the keys, and this dynamic stuff was pouring out of him. I never noticed him tapping his foot, or anything. There was no wasted motion. That's the most desirable way to me. But dance to your own music if it's good music; that's okay. You see Keith Jarrett going through those ridiculous gyrations, and playing great sometimes. Certainly when he does a concert, two thousand or more people come out to hear him. If singing along or standing up in the middle of a phrase helps that, fine. But he can play great, that's the most important result.

I'm not thinking of expressing sadness, or some picture-idea, or some way to make an emotional effect. When I play, I'm just thinking of playing a melodic succession of notes, with as accurate a time-feeling as possible. I don't *feel* very poetic. I hear of people seeing colors, or images, or some spiritual motivation. I'm just playing the music clear, warm, and positive—that's really my motivation.

I think that's an important point—you're not trying to create a mood.

No, not at all. When I play a ballad, and it sounds dead-ass or sad, I'm just trying to play a nice melody without forcing. When I hear Miles [Davis] play that kind of thing, I think he is trying to make an effect.

I just heard some early ballads that I did, that really sound very plaintive and melancholic. And I would bet that was one quality that Miles liked in my playing, that he also possessed.

Though as you said, he was aiming at that and you weren't particularly.
Yes, I was just trying to play, and that was the way it came out. I wasn't trying to package it and sell it.

Was there actual hostility to Tristano's music, or just indifference?
There was hostility *and* indifference. The criticism that it was like white European classical music wasn't just from the writers—a lot of musicians were critical too. Those that were critical were maybe the ones that Tristano was criticizing, who were out in the marketplace so to speak, being commercial, or trying to pay the rent.

Why do you think that Tristano didn't get his due recognition?
Well, he was very critical and people criticized him in turn. And he was very petty, I think, about other people who were trying to do things differently. I remember him walking out in the middle of a Bill Evans solo in a little club in New York once. He stood up and we were obliged to stand up with him and leave. So there were ego problems there, and whatever else, he was a human being with frailties. But those that loved his music, and there were many, gave him his due recognition.

He was very strong as an influence on me. But I was obliged, finally, to go out and think for myself, and I found out that I had to reexamine everything in some way.

You mean reexamine the way Tristano had influenced you.
To use the insight that he gave me to tap a more substantial place in myself, to find out what I was really hearing and not just doing things that I thought were the thing to do. But most of what he taught is still relevant to me.

But you drew away a little from your earlier style, in a way that Tristano didn't like?
I left that situation to go and test my wings. I was no longer actively part of the group. And instead of encouraging me, they were putting me down for trying to do my own thing, which I was very disappointed about. That is supposed to be the last stage in the process—go off with blessings.

Do you feel you were belatedly finding things in Charlie Parker, that you were drawing on bebop more?[8]
Not really, I was just trying to find out what felt comfortable to me. Playing with Tristano and Warne Marsh called for a certain discipline that I tried to accomplish. But left to my own devices, I was looking for what was more natural for me. I wasn't trying to "break free" from Tristano as such, I was just trying to play what I could hear or feel. A lot of it meant getting more basic, and I'm still working on it every day, trying to find a phrase that sits in the right place and reverberates properly, comes from someplace and goes someplace. That's a daily undertaking.

Tristano was very critical of most of the people that were out trying to perform, for good reasons sometimes, and not so good reasons other times. But he wasn't out there where people could appraise *him*. He was home safely, studying and learning how to play. And he played great, you know. But he wasn't willing to share it too much, except on a few records. I had the good fortune to work a lot, but Warne Marsh and a lot of his students were emulating him and not going out to work much, just practicing and teaching. And that's not really where it's at, I think. They were criticizing me for going out and playing with different people, and I thought, "Wait a minute. I'm out playing and they're sitting home and criticizing me. There must be something amiss here."

I've had to think about this quite a bit because of my respect for Tristano. Sal Mosca has followed Tristano's way pretty much, as far as I know. I took some piano lessons with Sal. He gave up public playing for the most part in order to be a guru. He was a great player, I think. He criticized me for playing so much, with whomever. And I thought, "Am I prostituting my music by going out and playing it for people, and getting money for it? I'm playing the best way I know how to play, and trying to share it with others." That's still the name of the game.

It was an introverted kind of school.

Sure, ivory tower. But studying with Tristano and playing with him, I got a peek at what this world of jazz improvisation was really like, and how serious a procedure it is. I had no idea that so much was involved. And suddenly my life took on a very definite viewpoint that I've been able to follow to this day. I attribute that to the encouragement from Lennie. Finding a personal voice, so to speak, is the ultimate goal.

You're really the opposite of Tristano in that you work in a huge number of situations, and he worked in very few.

Or not at all. So I go out and work with Italian musicians, with French musicians, and German musicians, and they can play pretty well these days, and I'm completely challenged. Obviously, over the years I haven't had a feeling to have a band and travel with it, like Phil Woods has. I'm more lazy maybe! And this is a very easy way for me to work. I just go by myself, and join these guys, and spend a nice time playing with them, and getting paid afterward, and I love it.

Your later relations with Tristano became difficult.

There was enough of the cult thing that seems inevitable with a strong leader, and I couldn't identify with it. In the early sixties I left New York—I was living in Tristano's house—and went to California for a couple of years, with the intention of getting out of that environment, and seeing what was left after those years of being influenced by his very strong points of view. That's when I started to feel the friction, that I was like a traitor in some way. The encouragement that a student should have was not there at all. I heard that someone called Tristano once to get my number and he said, "We don't mention that name here." That was a very unfortunate reaction from him— I expected more than that.

I think he was putting me down for leaving—like I broke up the band. But there was no band, we hardly worked. It was the art-for-art's-sake path.

So what did he think you should do—teaching?

Well, that's the only other thing you could do. He knew that I had a family to support.

After you played with him for the last time in 1964, did you meet him again?

No. I spoke to him on the phone, one time in the seventies, after not having communicated for years—about how George Wein wanted to devote an evening to his music, in Manhattan. Recently I discovered, from Connie Crothers, that he told her afterwards, "You'll never guess who was on the phone!" He was smiling and happy. When she told me that, I just wept.

George Wein wanted the whole group. First Lennie said we'd have to rehearse for a couple of weeks, and I said fine, and then he decided he couldn't do it. I found out later that he just hadn't been playing—he wasn't well.

Was he jealous of your success, maybe?

Well, I saw that he had an ego problem. But I don't think he was jealous. I think he was as close to being a purist as you could be, and what I was doing was not purist to him.

So he thought that you should only work with people that you were really compatible with, and only in ideal situations—if there weren't any, then you shouldn't work.

That's what he did, so I presume that he would think that other people should do the same.

Was he on good terms with Warne Marsh throughout?

Yes, they were very tight. Though I think Warne had to break loose from Lennie eventually, also.

Because they were quite similar in their attitude to working in the music.

They both were teachers, and played with their students.

But it's often a difficult relationship, when the pupil starts to assert him- or herself. Tristano is such a strong figure, and what people are interested in is how you were able to create your own voice.

That's what a great teacher should encourage and inspire.

You've expressed some irritation at having to talk so much about Tristano—presumably by people asking questions like, "And was he dressed in his pajamas at all hours of the day and night?"—though was he, actually?

[Laughs.] Well, in the later part of his life, when I wasn't associated with him, that's what I heard. My last association with him was in 1964, and then he was as I knew him—very straight-ahead, very productive.

The only time it bothers me to answer questions about the past music and people is after I've played an inspired concert, and the first remark I get is, "I sure love the way you played with Tristano"!

Could you sum up Tristano's most important influence on you?

Tristano demonstrated for me the seriousness of trying to really play some personal music. When he was really playing his best, it was very inspiring. But his music was a little bit over my head in a way. I tried to get with him, but I didn't feel that comfortable, frequently, playing at that intensity and those long lines that came out of the written kind of things that we did.

I was very pleased to have discovered my profession, and have it recognized early on. I thought it was going to continue to grow, but it went its way after a few years. My feeling during that time was very positive, that I had chosen the right profession. But sticking with it over the years, I've had pretty full satisfaction, and I'm still going strong.

⚐ Interview with Ted Brown

TED BROWN, *born Rochester, New York, 1927, is a tenor saxophonist and student of Lennie Tristano. In 1945–47 he played in army bands after learning clarinet and saxophone from an uncle, then moved from Hollywood to New York City, studying and working with Tristano and working with Konitz and Marsh. He co-led a quintet with Konitz in the mid-1970s and led his own quartet in the late 1970s. He recorded again with Konitz, Joey Baron, Marc Johnson, and John Abercrombie in the late 1990s.*

I moved to New York in September 1948 to find a good teacher and, hopefully, become a part of that scene. My first night in town I went down to the Royal Roost, and Lee Konitz was playing there with the Miles Davis nine-piece band—later known as the Birth of the Cool band. I didn't know it then, but that was the only gig that band ever played in a club! They sounded great, especially Lee—his choice of notes, his clean sound, his use of unusual intervals. I was in the army with Warne Marsh and [trumpeter and Tristano pupil] Don Ferrara, but I had no idea that Lee studied with Lennie Tristano. A few weeks later I attended a private session held by Lennie at a rented studio in Manhattan. I started studying with him and continued for seven years. Lee and Warne were dedicated to really knowing their horns inside out, through all the keys. Learning great solos by Bird and Pres, but using them as a tool to develop your own concept, was further strengthened by Lennie's insistence that you write out thirty-two-bar solos the way you would like to play—which evolved into some of those great lines, "Subconscious-Lee," "Marshmallow," "Sax of a Kind," and so on.

Lennie would say "OK, write a chorus on whatever tune you like, and bring it in next week." The following week you'd play it with him, and then he'd make you memorize it. I did that every week for a couple of years. He was trying to get you to really hear what you were playing, and edit out the garbage. When you're improvising, it all goes by so fast that you barely have time to get out what you're really intending. Writing forces you to go through it in slow motion, and you'll eventually hear where each phrase will logically lead to. In the beginning I'd have the horn in my hand as a reference point, and I'd improvise on the tune for ten or fifteen minutes. If I came across a phrase that was a good starting point, I'd jot it down. Eventually I didn't need the horn, and it came out better, because I wasn't using what was under my fingers, but what was in my head.

Once in a while, Lennie would say, "I like that line." I wrote a line on "You'd Be So Nice to Come Home To" which became "Featherbed." That's how Lee's and Warne's lines came about, too, I think. I know Warne did a high-register exercise on "All the Things You Are," which became "Dixie's Dilemma." That's why these lines sound like improvisations. Lennie didn't teach everybody in the exact same way, of course—maybe what he was stressing with me, he didn't have to with Lee. There were other exercises he would have me practice—certain phrases going through all the keys. He would suggest sometimes that you might put this phrase on a certain kind of chord change—but playing in a session someplace, when it came to that spot in the tune, I took my chances. When you're playing, you don't have time to really think, and Lennie didn't want you to. Practicing and playing are two different things—except for those prepared players, where they're the same thing!

I think Lee in his early years was one of the hippest players in jazz. He was a main component of the avant-garde in 1949–50, and I remember many nights at the original Birdland when his sound, sense of phrasing, and choice of notes were just unbelievable. He sounded great with the Kenton band, as well as on those records with Gerry Mulligan and Chet Baker. In 1959, I was one of the five saxes on *Lee Konitz Meets Jimmy Giuffre*. We only had one rehearsal and most of the tunes were done in one or two takes. I was amazed to see how easily Lee was able to improvise his melodic line around Giuffre's arrangements, just as though his ideas were also written.

In the beginning I could always tell where Lee was in the tune—now sometimes I can't and it's frustrating. Lennie used to go out of the key temporarily and then come back to it—he used to shift up a half-tone and play three or four bars, then come back down again. But sometimes Lee will not come back down for a while—in his desire to play "free" he can alter the basic chord progression or abandon it completely.[9] Also, Lee now will sometimes play all alone for one or two choruses—mostly at the beginning of a tune—and he may not give you a clue where he is until halfway through! There was one gig at Birdland where he played on [his composition] "Thingin'" all by himself, and lost me completely—then he starts to play the line [the theme] and I came in a bar or so late. After the set he asked, "What the hell happened to you?" I said, "Man, you've got to give me a clue if you're going to go that far out. Nod your head or something!"

We had a different problem on a gig at Stryker's in 1976. The bass player, Chin Suzuki, was Japanese and didn't speak much English, and when Lee called out the first tune, he said he didn't know it. Lee called another tune—same thing. Lee gave him a little notebook with chord changes and we started playing. By the end of the first chorus it was obvious that he really knew the tune and played it great. But Lee had to go through that routine before each tune. The next night, Lee called out a tune and he said he didn't know it. Lee said, "What do you mean, you played it last night!" He knew all the tunes fine but none of the titles![10] 🎵

Tristano's Playing Style and Approach

Tristano's playing style was complex, and the demands he made on rhythm sections were high. His attitude to drummers became notorious, seemingly reinforcing familiar objections to his music as cold and uninvolving. The normally perceptive Don Heckman, who recognized the pianist's rhythmic advances, commented that "sometimes . . . his quasi-Baroque use of regular eighth notes [is] boring."[11] In fact, Tristano's polyrhythmic intensity played off one meter against another, for example

7/4 against 4/4, which created demands on rhythm sections that requires discussion. It's often thought that Tristano wanted a simpler approach from them, to set his own complexity in relief. In a *Down Beat* interview, he explained that "contrary to the general belief, I love to play for people. If I could get a reasonable facsimile of a rhythm section . . . My problem has always been to find a bassist and a drummer who can play together. See, that's the word—together. But nowadays there are no sidemen left. Everyone is a soloist."[12] These remarks suggest that Tristano wanted rhythm sections just to keep time, so that listeners could focus on the soloist. But in an interview in 1964, Konitz put a different gloss on the matter: "People say that Lennie wants an 'old-fashioned' rhythm section, but that's not it at all. . . . Most drummers seem unable to feel the subtlety of Lennie's pulsation. It's weird. They're just not good enough to play with him. . . . The drummer should be able to improvise as freely as anyone else in the band, to fulfil his function in terms of group improvisation. But what seems to happen is that he either falls into a rigid pattern or else is seized with anxiety and becomes too boisterous in his playing."[13] In a 1973 interview, Warne Marsh explained this subtlety by commenting, "There was no [accent on] two and four in the way Lennie conceived of playing. [With drummers] that was a constant problem. . . . I can get along with about the same drummers Lennie can: Jeff Morton, Kenny Clarke, those two." When asked, "Any others?" Marsh replied, "Not really, man."[14] However, Konitz was more critical of Tristano in a 1966 interview with Ira Gitler: "I think that a great part of Lennie's trouble [with rhythm sections], besides the obvious part of his being a very subtle player—and most rhythm sections not being subtle and just not hearing what he's doing—is that Lennie doesn't go to them. . . . he's never—at least that I can hear it—made too big an effort to find out where they're at, to get with *them*."[15]

In fact, it's likely that Tristano asked drummers to play "simple" only if they were not good enough to play in a more complex way without losing their sense of time. As Larry Kart argues, Tristano's polyrhythmically based accenting wouldn't rule out interventions by the drummer—"one need only think of Charlie Parker to realize that such a claim would be false," he writes, and Konitz agrees.[16] Thus Tristano's ideal was not a "simple" rhythm section—he just had high standards. (The question is discussed further in Eunmi Shim's book *Lennie Tristano*.) In the following pages, Konitz discusses Tristano's rhythmic approach and his attitude to rhythm sections, the classic sides from the Sing Song Room in 1955, and the multitracking experiments on *Lennie Tristano*.

Did Tristano point out recordings of his own that he really liked?
I remember he played "Line Up" for me—I was living in his house at that time—and he was very impressed with that. But when I said, "Gee, how did you get that sound?" he was a little disturbed. "Why do people have to know how it's done all the time?" he said. Why, because it's not a traditional piano sound—it was great, but what was involved? On these tracks, Tristano recorded just the bass and drums, then turned to half speed and recorded his own line—then turned the whole thing to full speed.[17]

[We listen to "Line-Up" from *Lennie Tristano* (Atlantic), based on the chords of "All Of Me."]

What you hear, through technical manipulation, is a most extraordinary accenting—he's all over the bar line, starting in every conceivable place, and articulating in the most extraordinary way. It's *impossible* to play like that in real time, I think. But he was trying to demonstrate what that could sound like—rendering the lines with that kind of flexibility, to be able to accent any note in the phrase. The next record he made [*The New Tristano*], he was able to do that more—to play at a faster tempo with that kind of articulation, with no adjustments [in recording].

[Konitz sings the opening phrases of "Line Up"] There's no rest [between the phrases], that's the point. The first phrase is seven beats long; the next phrase starts on four, and it's seven beats long. He's really playing in 7/4 time there, for a couple of bars.

Or you could say it's like a polyrhythm, because the backing plays 4/4.
That's the idea. Bartók would have written two bars in 7/4.

But Tristano didn't want it to be known that it was technically manipulated?
I don't think so. Overdubbing and doubling the tempo was thought to be scandalous—he was really put down for that. I'm surprised he even tried to do that for public consumption, knowing that it would be ridiculed by the cognoscenti.

I think it's fascinating. I just hear it as it is. And when I have the facilities to listen at half-tempo, it's very musical at that speed also.

And then it sounds like a piano.
In the low register, yes—a great piano.

Dave Douglas and others are playing in 7/4—and Dave Brubeck gets the credit for playing in 5/4, which is easier, and it's not in polyrhythm.
They're all doing that. Brad Mehldau is a genius at playing "All The Things You Are" and many other tunes in 5/4 and 7/4. It's spectacular the ease and control he has with that. But Tristano always did it in polyrhythms; he never played in 5/4 or 7/4 per se, that I know of.[18]

This Italian guy invented a kind of electronic metronome, called a tri-nome. I went by his apartment to hear it. It was a big black box with three levers that you could set, to get three simultaneous rhythms. You could get 3 against 4, 4 against 5—it helps to practice with it. I haven't really worked so much on those things lately—I'm still enjoying good old 4/4![19]

That's a very Tristano thing to have.

It's part of the discipline of accurate subdivision—swing at its best.

Various people have said that the point is not to have fancy time-signatures, but to play in a rhythmically complex way in 4/4.

Well, that's what Tristano was doing—and Charlie Parker and Lester Young and all those players.

What he frequently did was to play a phrase in 3/8 time—"*dee*-dee-oh-*dee*-dee-oh." But this example [from "All The Things You Are"] is in 2/4 time, very unsyncopated, starting on the down beat each time.

It's not lyrical.

What is lyrical?

Something that's easy to sing, maybe.

I can sing that whole improvisation on "Line Up."

But most people would find it hard to come out of a concert singing something that Tristano did. It's complicated and that makes them think it's "cerebral."

I think so. But he sounds very swinging to me, and very loose. It's very intellectually and emotionally conceived. That's the goal of the playing composer. When he was feeling inspired, he was awesome!

What do you say to the criticism that Tristano played lines of even eighth notes, and didn't use space like Monk did, for instance?

Well, I can understand it. But that's the way he heard it—a very long, intense line. I mean, McCoy Tyner played even eighth notes, in his modal playing, though it was a different kind of concept. And when Keith Jarrett winds up and plays a long line at a rapid tempo, he's playing even eighth notes, certainly. At a fast tempo a line of eighth notes, which is usually the basic rhythmic subdivision, would be fairly even or else risk sounding awkward. Bud Powell played even eighths also, at a bright tempo—there's no other way, I think. Monk was another kind of player.

Was it neurotic, Tristano's concern about drummers speeding up and slowing down?

He was difficult to play with. One time we were working in Toronto with Roy Haynes as the drummer. Roy was a little late, and so I sat down to play some time. And I really was surprised, it didn't feel comfortable at all. He was all over the place, with his feeling for the phrase—he was playing very odd phrases, accents and things, that made "ding-ding-a-ding, ding-a-ding" not too easy. But I am not a very accomplished drummer, to say the least!

But slowing down or speeding up really bothered Tristano.

That was part of his concern, trying to start at a tempo and keep that tempo. As all of us do, he liked a good feeling for a steady tempo. One time, he beat off a tempo [Konitz claps it off] . . . and the rhythm section didn't hear him—started to play, and they were in a different place and he never changed. They had to come with him. I thought proving his point like that was rather insensitive of him. He was sitting with his back to the rhythm section, and he had to turn halfway round to snap it off [with his fingers], and the fact is, they didn't hear him.

Lennie's concept was first to get a rhythm section playing very basic, so that what he was doing would be in clear relief. And with the rhythm section playing straight time, with not much rhythmic counterpoint [cross-accents from the drummer], his lines were really clearly articulated. Just to start out with straight time was what he liked. In a band situation he was busy but strong, and he heard what we were doing and responded. When the music started to open up and it was really swinging, then was the time to really play together—the tune would become free for a while, and the drummer was accenting and doing all the things that you do when you improvise. That was very welcome—though I didn't hear it happen too much with Lennie and Warne. Everyone was listening too hard, maybe.

His favorite drummer was Kenny Clarke, at that time, and he was a great traditional drummer. Tristano was maybe impatient with drummers, but not with Kenny Clarke. And when he played once with Charlie Mingus and Elvin Jones, I didn't hear any complaints about that. I wonder if someone has a recording of that, that will pop up some day.

As a teacher, Tristano was trying to develop people to get a good loose feeling, and then stretch out as far as you could go.

Why did he like Kenny Clarke in particular?

I only heard him with Kenny playing brushes on a telephone directory, and Bird, at Lennie's studio. We never discussed Kenny, that I recall. But he had a great time-feeling—he was a swinging drummer.

Although Kenny Clarke was a bebopper, he didn't play many cross-accents or "bombs."

He could sympathize with a good soloist, and swing like hell! When Lennie played his music, it was very intense, and Kenny responded full force, I'm sure.

Do you also not like very busy drummers?

Well, I heard Brad Mehldau and the fine guitar player Peter Bernstein in

New York some weeks ago [in 2002], playing with a young bass player and drummer who were playing very straight time. And again I was reminded—because most of the rhythm sections are not playing straight time—of how effective that makes the soloist sound. The rest of the stuff is very frequently distracting, if the soloist is really doing something interesting. This was like a real traditional rhythm section. I don't know if they were advised to do that, or if this was the way they heard the music that night. But I think that's pretty much what Tristano had in mind.

So you're bothered by busy drummers?

Elvin Jones was one of my favorite drummers to play with, so obviously I'm not. I loved playing with Elvin, and Philly Joe Jones, and Kenny Clarke, et al.

Are you bothered by rhythm sections speeding up or slowing down?

No, I'm bothered by rhythm sections not listening! Speeding up or slowing down is inevitable. As long as there is some good positive energy, I'm satisfied.[20]

Turning to your recordings with Tristano, how did the 1949 date come about?

I was supposed to make a record with Tony Fruscella, the trumpet player. I didn't know him, but he came by my apartment to try some things. I made some suggestions and offended him, somehow, and he didn't want to do it. So I asked Lennie, Shelly Manne and Tristano's regular bassist, Arnold Fishkin. I was very pleased with the results. Later I made some things on the same label with Warne Marsh, without Lennie—they were with Sal Mosca. Warne plays beautifully on these first records for both of us [together].

What was your feeling about the live sides with Lennie from the Sing Song Room in 1955?

I was happy with those sides, to an extent. There were five tunes on the original recording, and more on later reissues.[21] I thought it was some of Lennie's loosest playing. And I really had to congratulate Art Taylor and Gene Ramey for being so *simpatico* with Lennie. It was a great rhythm section. They really played a good strong beat, and very simple I thought—just straight-ahead. I really respected Art Taylor for not making it more intricate like he would do with the beboppers.

Sometimes [Lennie] felt too busy for me. Almost always he was leading the rhythm section, and they were accompanying, in a very traditional way. I wasn't entirely comfortable with that situation. I just wasn't ready, I'm sorry to say. But I can enjoy listening to it.

Tristano was calling out tunes on the bandstand and Gene knew every tune perfectly—he'd been around for a long time, playing standards, I'm sure. We did a steady few days a week at this Chinese restaurant. It was a small room, and you smelled sweet-and-sour pork in between phrases, which was a bit of a drag.

Was the audience attentive?

Very—between mouthfuls, I guess.

¶ Interview with Kenneth Noland

KENNETH NOLAND, *born 1924, is one of the leading American abstract expressionist painters from the generation after Jackson Pollock, Mark Rothko, and Barnett Newman. With his friend Morris Louis, he adopted the technique of allowing acrylic paint to soak into unprimed canvasses. He is best known for his paintings of targets, and later focused on hard-edged chevron- and stripe-based designs. He has had a love of jazz, and in particular the Tristano school, from the earliest days.*

I first heard Lee around 1948, when he was playing with Lennie Tristano and Billy Bauer—Warne Marsh wasn't there yet. I had heard a record or two, but the first time I heard Tristano and Lee live was at a little club in Washington, D.C., where I was living. A friend and I went to hear them. It was a black club, and we were the only two people that showed up that night! So we got in conversation with them, and particularly with Lee. The next day I took him to my studio to see my work. He liked it, and I gave him a painting. From that point on, we kept in touch.

They played quite a lot at a club in Hudson Street in New York—it was really incredible playing.[22] The Tristano group played very fast. Lee could play incredibly fast, he doesn't play as fast now, and he plays more chromatic. God no, it wasn't unemotional! Because it flowed, and had that lilting, kind of floating rhythm, I think people thought it was "white" music—though Miles [Davis] certainly played the same way. It wasn't as punchy as Bird and the black players. Just about all of the jazz musicians I ever met could be called cerebral—they certainly knew what they were doing. It was hyperskillful, and there was a broad spectrum of playing that allowed a lot of creative improvisation.

I thought of them as fellow modernists—I don't know that we used the word *avant-garde*. I had quite a few artist friends who were hip to modern jazz—David Smith and I used to go to the Half Note, and Herman Cherry was a fan. Bruce Nauman was a fan of Tristano, I've learned. Clubs in New York used to stay open till five or six in the morning, and you could go from club to club—it was really wonderful.

We used to go and hear Bird and Thelonious Monk—we really were very *au courant* with jazz at that point. I produced a Gil Evans record, with his orchestra—I put up the money to have it made. And about fifteen years ago, I made a video with Steve Lacy's music. It took me three years to make. His music was the background, and the foreground was abstract. This was a labor of love. We were good friends too.

The clubs are gone—but then culture has just about gone! The creative flow of the forties, fifties, and sixties is not there any more—the arts have become a kind of entertainment. But Lee is still up there playing, and wonderful too.[23] 🖛

4 ⚑ Early Collaborators

Miles Davis and Warne Marsh

Aside from his work with Tristano, Konitz's most important early work was with trumpeter Miles Davis. In 1947–48 he was a member of the Claude Thornhill Orchestra, whose dreamlike Impressionist arrangements by Gil Evans prefigured Davis's groundbreaking nonet of 1948–50. Konitz's first commercial recordings, made with Thornhill in September 1947, revealed a cool paradigm on alto sax, though the compositions that the nineteen-year-old altoist solos on— a sixteen-bar solo on "Anthropology" and a twenty-bar solo (including four-bar introduction) on "Yardbird Suite"—were both composed by Charlie Parker. These solos attracted attention for their pure tone and legato phrasing that seemed such a contrast with Parker's. Thomas Owens, for instance, writes that at this point Konitz was a player "almost completely untouched by Parker's idiom, though later some similarities in phrasing developed"—a view contested by Gunther Schuller in chapter 8.

Konitz's tone was an essential element in the Miles Davis Nonet, later known as the Birth of the Cool band, which created some of the most distinctive sounds in modern jazz. In the minds of many jazz fans, Konitz is still most closely identified with these sessions. The chamberlike arrangements by Gil Evans, Gerry Mulligan, Miles Davis, John Lewis, and John Carisi marked a break from big-band writing of the 1930s and 1940s, and featured instrumentation unusual for a jazz band—notably the use of French horn and tuba as melodic instruments. The reduced ensemble produced a light, floating sonority that avoided the Swing Era juxtaposition of brass and reed sections. Konitz's alto sax figured as a mobile voice in the lead parts, and he solos on "Israel," "Rouge," "Moon Dreams," "Move," and "Budo." He worked with the band in its short engagements at the Royal Roost in 1948 and at the Clique in 1949, appearing on the live broadcasts in September 1948 that were recorded and released, and on the studio recordings for Capitol in 1949–50.[2] The week after the nonet played at the Royal Roost, Davis led a quintet there with Konitz, John Lewis, Al McKibbon, and Max Roach, plus vocalist Kenny Hagood—though Konitz has said that he was ill prepared to play in that bebop combo. This group's radio broadcasts were also recorded. The nonet reassembled the following week, and the final week featured the quintet with Konitz again. Konitz and Davis were highly compatible partners, throwing ideas off one another, for example on the nonet's version of "Move," and on the small group recordings they made in 1951.

Despite his identification with the *Birth of the Cool* sessions, Konitz has shown ambivalence toward them. In *Jazz Masters of the Forties* he commented, "As much as I enjoyed sitting there and playing with the band and as lucky as I was to get a couple of good licks on the records, I felt I wasn't as completely involved as I would liked to have been." In the present interviews, Konitz is more positive in his judgment of the recordings, although his main commitment is to improvisation rather than interpretation of written scores. With his own nonet in the late 1970s, he attempted to re-create something of the sound of the *Birth of the Cool,* recording several albums including *Yes, Yes Nonet* in 1979, which reinterpreted the original Gil Evans arrangement of "Moon Dreams." In this chapter, Konitz discusses Davis, Marsh, and other collaborators.

Tristano went to New York in 1946, and I wanted to move there too. The next year I was asked to play with this beautiful band of Claude Thornhill's. They were playing in Chicago or nearby, and I don't really know who recommended me for that job, because I hadn't been out of Chicago yet, and I was only twenty years old. Maybe it was Gil Evans. I was very pleased to join, but basically I wanted to get to New York. I could have walked faster than the ten months it took me to get there with the band!

That was a very special band. Gil Evans traveled with them quite a bit, teaching them how to play bebop—there were a lot of older swing/dance-band players, and he taught them how to accent the eighth notes on "Anthropology." Of course, through that situation the so-called Birth of the Cool evolved. Gil Evans was a very friendly, big-brother figure in my life. He was very laid back and philosophical.

He was looking to find an alternative to the high energy of bebop.
Compositionally he was attracted to Charlie Parker's music. But he also had a very Romantic, Impressionist notion of orchestration.

Your first commercially recorded solos were with Thornhill. What were the first recordings you made that you were really satisfied with?

The Claude Thornhill things were still very formative. "Anthropology" and "Yardbird Suite" were tunes I was already playing so I knew how to phrase the lines—I just had a problem improvising a solo. I was still trying to stick in my intervals of a fourth, or whatever, and the rhythmic feeling was very tense and unsettled. Barry Galbraith, a fine guitarist, played a nice solo, but it was the same one every night. I think that's the smart thing to do!

After that, I liked all sorts of things that I did. I feel good about the Stan Kenton recordings, though there was too much corny vibrato sometimes.

In an article from 1948, Barry Ulanov refers to your "year's sojourn with the sweet nothings of [Thornhill's] polished organization."

Well, it was a dance band, not a concert-performing jazz band. We played mostly in ballrooms. So compared to Ellington, or Basie, it was pretty sweet. I don't know about "nothings" though! It was a beautiful ballad band. Claude was a fine musician who knew how good Gil Evans and Gerry Mulligan were, and they provided the fine arrangements that we enjoyed playing, and which were very danceable and listenable.

❦ Interview with Kenny Wheeler

KENNY WHEELER, *born Toronto in 1930, plays trumpet and flügelhorn, and is a composer and bandleader. He studied trumpet at the Royal Conservatory there, and in 1952 moved to London. In the late 1960s and 1970s he performed and recorded with Tubby Hayes, Ronnie Scott, Tony Oxley, Anthony Braxton, and Dave Holland, and led his own bands. He has made many recordings on the ECM label, with Keith Jarrett, John Abercrombie, and Dave Holland. These recordings include* Angel Song, *which featured Konitz.*

The first time I ever saw Lee was when I still lived in Canada. I was seventeen or eighteen—this would be 1947 or 1948—and the big bands used to come through Niagara Falls, Ontario. He was in the Claude Thornhill band—I think Red Rodney was also. On "Anthropology," he had a solo, but he didn't play anything in the middle eight—the rhythm section were all playing. So afterwards, I went up to him and said, "Excuse me, Mr. Konitz, but why did't you play anything in the middle eight of your solo?" And he said, "Well, I couldn't think of anything!" It was an "I Got Rhythm" chord sequence—he would have known it quite well—so as he said, he just couldn't think of anything. I was very interested in jazz then. I knew about Lee—that's why I went to see the Thornhill band.

I've always tried to listen to him, and I've always liked his playing. He's looking for a melody all the time—he never plays any hot licks. Over the years, whenever I've had any problem with my sense of direction, I'd go back and listen to his records. That puts me on the right path. *Birth of the Cool* was a great record, and I love *Motion* with Elvin Jones. I never bothered with the critics' descriptions of bebop or cool or whatever. I liked Tristano's music very much—I realized how difficult it was, though. The themes were even more difficult than bebop. I've played odd gigs with Lee over the years, but *Angel Song* was probably the first time I really connected with him. I know he likes to stand in front of a band, shut his eyes and not read music, but I didn't really want to play standards on that recording, I wanted to play originals. And he plays very well. Also, I did a week at Ronnie Scott's with him a few years ago—he didn't like it much, but I did warn him that people do talk there![3] 🎜

Kenny Wheeler's story rings true because if you couldn't think of anything to play, you wouldn't play something meaningless.
Well, one night I was playing with the Thornhill band at a dance, and I was stoned a little bit. I got up for my chorus and the rhythm section sounded so nice that I just stood there preparing to play, for thirty-two bars! I looked at them, and smiled, and nodded, and looked liked I was preparing to play. Claude was probably laughing. I thought of that as one of my best solos!
Was Miles Davis, like you, someone who "tried to play bebop and couldn't"?
I don't think he really wanted to. He already had a lyrical sense, and was pretty sophisticated theoretically. He didn't have the chops to play bebop at that time. He tried to model himself after Dizzy Gillespie to an extent, but he was always very personal in his way.
Did you get on well with him?
Very well. I used to call him "Blocks," which is part of a mile, ten blocks to a "mile" in America, but I don't think he ever got it! I didn't know him that well, but he was always very friendly to hang out with.
How did you come to be involved in the *Birth of the Cool* project?
It was Gil and Gerry Mulligan's suggestion to Miles. I was in the Claude Thornhill band, with Gil and Gerry, and Miles was hanging out when we played in a hotel in New York. Miles was the focal point of the group; he

could get the gigs and he had the sound that they wanted for the ensemble. Gerry Mulligan was more active in organizing the *Birth of the Cool* sessions, but Gil was the guru figure. They felt that my sound would fit with them. Charlie Parker would have outblown the whole outfit. They were talking about Sonny Stitt, but that would have been a similar situation. Later on there was talk about the choice of me being questionable, but Miles said he didn't care if I was green, he liked my sound!

That was a great time, with interesting people. There were many meetings and rehearsals, and then the recording. I was just one of the voices, the arrangers were the main men in that group—Gil, Mulligan, Miles, Johnny Carisi, and John Lewis. It was really their baby.

Did you feel at the time that these might become classic sides?

It's not too likely to think as you're playing something, written or improvised, that it will become a classic. I felt this was very interesting chamber music, and I was very happy to be part of it. The title was a little bit off-center—that's not the *Birth* of the Cool. Frank Trumbauer and Bix Beiderbecke might have been the "birth of the cool," Benny Carter, then Lester Young and all his influences, Charlie Parker, and Tristano and his friends. Bird was "cool" when he played "Yardbird Suite."

The Birth of the Cool band had a short life before the recording, and I don't remember that we played any gigs after the recording—amazing!

Were you sorry that the band folded so quickly?

I was—it could really have developed into something special.

You said that you weren't as completely involved as you'd have liked to have been.

To be completely involved in a chamber music situation would be to compose some of the music, and have more solo opportunities.

Did you offer some compositions?

No—I've never been an orchestrator. Lines, I write all the time, but somehow I can't get to the next step in the process.

At the time my main interest was with Tristano's music.

You enjoyed it enough to do projects like *Yes, Yes Nonet.*

Actually that was suggested to me by someone else, but I thought it would inspire me to write. I wrote a little, but never orchestrated really—just lines. Sy Johnson was a very prolific writer and arranger for that group.

I really enjoy an ensemble but haven't had many opportunities to play in such a special situation. In the last few years I made CDs with big bands playing arrangements of my tunes. I don't think they will become classics, but they're nice, though.

❧ Interview with Mike Zwerin

Trombonist and writer **MIKE ZWERIN**, *born in New York City in 1930, was a member of the Miles Davis Nonet, and has kept in contact with Konitz ever since, interviewing him in recent years for the* International Herald Tribune *and other publications. He toured with Claude Thornhill in 1958–59, and with Earl Hines in the Soviet Union in 1966. He has lived in Paris since the late 1960s.*

Miles heard me jamming with Art Blakey at Minton's and asked me to a rehearsal the following day at Nola's. Later, in his autobiography, he said: "J.J. [Johnson] was busy so we got this white cat." I was eighteen and very impressed, but basically it was just an unexpected good gig. I was only hired for the gig at the Royal Roost—I was not on the record and had not expected to be. I never felt [the gig] was historical or classic or important in any way, other than that I had been "discovered." I was sorry but not surprised when the band folded. I went back to the University of Miami.

"Cool jazz"? Call it what you like. It was the beginning of a new style of ensemble playing, with less vibrato and behind the beat. Lots of black cats did not like the *Birth of the Cool* for that reason. But it was the thing to come, and whatever you call it, we helped give birth to it. I am against classifying music along racial lines. Everybody jokes about it, and there is even some truth to it. Black people do tend to swing more, but it is a stereotype basically and ought not to be encouraged.

I don't see how anyone in the world of jazz could be criticized for playing music that is "too cerebral"—it's meaningless. Since I first heard him, Lee has gotten better, more mature, deeper, with a better musical sense of irony and ambiguity.[4] ❧

❧ Interview with Hal McKusick

Composer and alto saxophonist **HAL McKUSICK**, *born 1924 in Medford, Massachusetts, plays most saxophones, clarinets, and flutes. He was a member of the orchestras of Boyd Raeburn, Claude Thornhill, Woody Herman, Benny Goodman, Dizzy Gillespie, and Charlie Barnet. In the later 1950s he made recordings with George Russell, Art Farmer, Al Cohn, Manny Albam, Jimmy Giuffre, Gil Evans, among others, and appeared on the 1959 album* Lee Konitz Meets Jimmy Giuffre. *From*

*1958 to 1972 he was a staff musician for CBS in New York. His composi-
tions for Boyd Raeburn, his own groups, and others show an original
avant-garde sensibility. Today he teaches and performs on Long Island in
New York, and makes fine handcrafted furniture.*

I left Buddy Rich and took Lee's place on the alto chair in Claude Thornhill's band in late 1948. Danny Polo died [the next year] when we were
in Chicago, so Claude had me playing the lead part on clarinet, too, and
all the alto solos—he couldn't find anyone else to do that tour. I left in
1950, at the end of that whole big-band regime. Most of us held on even
with a cut in salary, because we loved the band so much. We were mostly
playing dances, not clubs—playing Gil Evans's orchestration of "Donna
Lee," and Gerry Mulligan's "Five Brothers," a really nice tune, but the key
of D put the altos in the key of B, which is five sharps. Jazz players didn't
play in D concert those days very much! The band was always a great
challenge and most satisfying to play with—the intonation and dynamics
were superb, and it always swung in a beautiful way.

Lee lived in Queens with his family at that time, and so did I. We
played for hours together, just two altos. I had a style before I got to
know him—I was very much influenced by Bird, and by Davey Schild-
kraut, who did a bunch of albums with George Handy for RCA Victor
which have never been rereleased. They're incredible. But I was very
much influenced by Lee Konitz as well. He's one of my heroes—one of
the most sensitive, brilliant, thoughtful players I've known. We recorded
an album under his name, with five saxes—*Lee Konitz Meets Jimmy Giuffre*. We often worked at the same venues, but at different times.

I thought the Tristano school was fantastic. I didn't study with him,
but later I studied orchestration with the classical composer Paul
Creston and with Hall Overton. Warne Marsh and I were especially
close. I lived in California in 1945–48, and I'd been playing jam sessions with Warne. I knew he wanted to come east, and I got him into
the Buddy Rich band. Buddy said we needed a third alto player, and
Warne was already playing in the altissimo register, so I thought he'd
work perfectly—I transposed the third alto book to tenor. Buddy
wasn't crazy about him in the beginning; he liked macho guys. Warne
always had a light sound, an alto or C melody sound on tenor.

Lee's a true artist. I always thought he had an extremely warm sound.
Warne's sound was the cooler kind of thing—highly technical and highly
evolved in a harmonic sense. I think Lee's expression has become even
warmer, and he's refined his whole approach. Every statement he makes

is meaningful, there's nothing wasted. You can't pay a bigger compliment to a jazz musician.[5] 🎵

In March 1951 you led a date with Miles Davis.
Miles recorded a few tunes with me on my Prestige album. He came by the studio to rehearse one of my lines, "Hi Beck," on the chords of "Pennies From Heaven." He ended up not playing it, but he was really interested in trying. He had a heroin problem at the time, and came to the date without a trumpet and had to borrow one. He had to play some very difficult music of George Russell's—"Ezz-thetic" [based on "Love For Sale"]—and just barely got through it. He was not in great shape. That was a tough date!
    [We listen to the recording of "Ezz-thetic," on *Conception* (Prestige)]
    Phew! It's pretty fast!
Presumably you set the tempo.
Well, George Russell was there, he must have set it. I wouldn't set a tempo like that.
Not even in those days?
No. It's a throwaway at that tempo. I wish it had been a little more relaxed.
You were in the orchestra for *Miles Ahead*, but did you play with Miles on any later occasions?
Miles asked me to sit in at the Jazz Workshop in San Francisco in 1963. Frank Strozier was the alto player at the time, and it didn't feel right to go up there in that situation.
You're not really a jam session player.
Not really. One other time, Miles asked me to join him at the Village Vanguard, with the famous quintet. I think they were playing the blues. I was very nervous—Wayne Shorter was leaning against the wall, and all of that. I might have had a poke. After my third or fourth chorus Miles came in and took over.
    I didn't know where "one" was, so I was probably playing more "out" than they were, without trying! That was a great rhythm section, and I was not ready—too bad for me!
    [We listen to the earlier Miles Davis Quintet with John Coltrane playing "If I Were a Bell," from *Relaxin'* (Prestige, 1956)]
    Miles always had great rhythm sections to play with. Paul [Chambers] really came through very strong, and Philly [Joe Jones]—it was really a professional jazz performance at its best.
    Gil Evans and I were supposed to do a duo on some dates, and he told Miles.[6] Miles asked, "Not using a rhythm section?" He said, "No, just a

duo." And Miles replied, "Get a bass player behind the curtain!" He knew the value of a great rhythm section.

What are your feelings about Miles's soloing on that record?

Well, I have a problem sometimes with Miles—his playing is so stylized in this kind of context. I've heard him do that song so many times, and he's not specially different in this version. He jumbles up some phrases and things. And Coltrane's sound really bothers me—it's very raw on this one, and I don't really love that. When he played brilliantly, I was fascinated. But either the intensity, or the sound, or the approaching hysteria, didn't feel good to me.

But you must love Miles's sound.

It depends what he does with it. When he's really playing, yes. But he's pretty much a performer, so to speak.

So this feeling about real improvisation really affects your listening.

Not if the performance is really good. I just have to do it more spontaneously than some other people. When I hear a great solo, that's it, however it's conceived.

But you said Miles sounds stylized, and you think he'd done it quite like that many times before—and that was a criticism.

In a way, yes. But he knew where his bread was buttered. In this period, that meant setting up the melody very attractively, and then Coltrane could roar, and grind the gears—and the rhythm section was in there every beat, no fooling around. That's set, it's like an arrangement—but they do it great, and it's always nice to hear a band swing.

You haven't worked much with trumpet players. Is that deliberate?

No. Apart from Miles, there was Don Ferrara. He was a fine player, involved with the Tristano school, and I had a few occasions to play with him. He was the one that introduced Warne to Lennie—they were in the army together. I was studying with Lennie in Chicago; Warne only met him in New York.

More recently I recorded a Brazilian CD with [trumpeter] Tom Harrell. Though his chops weren't in good shape that day, he really played nice. He's a very loveable character, but everything he does is at a different tempo [to other people] until he plays—then he's very responsive. I've only made that one record with him, and it was beautiful. We couldn't use one of my tunes because he fluffed the theme. After that date he went to work with Joe Lovano at the Village Vanguard. That's some very difficult music, fast tempos, Joe playing a hundred miles an hour. I called Joe in the middle of the week and asked him, "How is it going?" He said, "Great, except I'm playing a lot of harmony parts by myself!"

Going back to the "Ezz-thetic" date, how did you come to meet George Russell?

Through the Birth of the Cool situation. I remember going to his house once and meeting a friend of his, George André, who was very much into the Schillinger system—it's possible he was an inspiration to George in coming up with the mathematics for the Lydian system.

Did you ever read George Russell's book, *The Lydian Chromatic Concept of Tonal Organization*?

I studied some of his concepts at a summer jazz school, the Lenox School of Music in Massachusetts, in 1958. Gunther Schuller was there, and Ornette [Coleman] came and was encouraged by John Lewis and Percy Heath to pursue his own music.[7] I was hired as a teacher, but I went to George's 9:00 A.M. class out in the woods. Jim Hall and I were there in this beautiful country environment. George asked us to write lines on standard tunes using special scales, and oh man, I remember the funny music that I heard at nine o'clock in the morning!

It was very encouraging to have some more information to work with—he opened up doors to stretching the tonalities. But I never used George's system, as I think Coltrane did. George analyzed a piece of mine in his book—"Kary's Trance." I found that interesting, but I didn't use those scales in writing it.

Gerry Mulligan was also involved in the Birth of the Cool—you had quite a lot of contact with him over your career.

I always thought of him as an ally. He appreciated my playing, and I appreciated his, and especially his writing, very much. I played his arrangements with Claude Thornhill, and Stan Kenton. The occasions that we had together, they were very fruitful.

Was he an intuitive player?

Gerry was a great musician, also a great composer and arranger. My favorite playing of his was with the Birth of the Cool. He also recorded a free version of "Lover Man" with me and a trio with Peggy Stern that was very intuitive and really inspired.[8] He was pretty much an intuitive player, but maybe too conscious of making an impression on his audience—and that means functioning other than intuitively.

We haven't talked about your view of West Coast jazz.

I've been called a West Coast player many times. It was almost a dirty word in New York. The guys [on the West Coast] heard what was going on there—Miles, Lennie, MJQ—and did their own sunshiny versions. Some good things happened, but Shorty Rogers, Marty Paich, and Art Pepper never broke any new ground, with all due respect to their musicianship.

Jimmy Giuffre was one of the most impressive, and Bill Holman is a great arranger.

¶ Interview with George Russell

GEORGE RUSSELL, *born 1923 in Cincinnati, Ohio, is a composer, music theorist, bandleader, and pianist. His book* The Lydian Chromatic Concept of Tonal Organization, *published in 1953, expounds a system that can be used in all genres of composition and improvisation, based on scales or modes rather than chords or harmonies. Russell composed for Dizzy Gillespie, Buddy DeFranco, and Lee Konitz, and his ideas influenced the development of modal jazz, in particular Miles Davis's* Kind of Blue. *In 1958–59 he taught at the Lenox School of Jazz, and in the 1960s recorded with his own sextet, which included Don Ellis, Eric Dolphy, and Steve Swallow. In 1963 he moved to Europe, where he taught in Sweden and Denmark, and in 1969 returned to the United States, teaching at New England Conservatory, where he remains, leading and recording with his own large ensembles.*

Lee would drop in at Gil Evans's basement apartment [in New York City] when a group of musicians used to hang out there—Gerry Mulligan, Miles, myself, sometimes Bird, Johnny Carisi, and others. Gil would organize trips to Juilliard to hear the symphonic conductors preparing the orchestra in Stravinsky, Ravel, and other composers in which these musicians were interested.

I don't think I set up the Prestige date; most likely Lee did. Lee or maybe an Artists & Repertoire man asked me to write a couple of pieces. "Ezz-thetic" is based on the chords of "Love for Sale," and "Odjenar" was the maiden name of my then wife, Juanita. I remember her grabbing Miles by the neck and dragging him back into the studio when he tried to leave the session in the midst of it! I think he was strung out. I heard that recording a few days ago and thought it was much too fast, too; sometimes musicians want to prove their chops by upping the tempo, but who knows what happened in that session? It was many years ago.

I taught at the School of Jazz in Lenox in 1958–59. I believe John Lewis was artistic director. Ornette was a student in an amazing concentration of important jazz figures. George André was a good friend and extremely interesting man, but I was never turned on by Schillinger; my inspiration for the *Lydian Chromatic Concept* came when I asked Miles what his musical aim was. He replied, "To learn all the changes." I knew a musical genius like Miles already knew all the chords, so I reasoned he was saying he wanted to learn which scales relate to which chords. That sent me on my quest. There is a lot of misinformation out there about what the *Lydian Chromatic Concept* is, but the important thing is that it provides all the tonal resources for the musician to use in any way he or she desires. No dos or don'ts.

We analyze [Konitz's composition] "Kary's Trance," along with Bach and Ravel. No one says any of these composers used the scales we used in analysis. "Kary's Trance" is an interesting example of what we call an ingoing vertical melody. Lee is right in his approach to improvisation: the melody of the piece is the most important element of the music.

Lee is one of the important figures in jazz—he endured and did it his way.[9] 🖝

Warne Marsh

Together with Konitz, Warne Marsh was Tristano's most important disciple. Born in Los Angeles in 1927, Marsh fell under the influence of Charlie Parker before becoming a student of Tristano. A highly innovative player, Marsh had no inclination or talent for self-promotion and remained woefully neglected throughout his career. One factor here was that his family was wealthy, and their financial support enabled him to adhere to Tristano's uncompromising artistic ideals. Marsh's playing is some of the most metrically and rhythmically complex in jazz, and his musical constructions show a compelling rationality. Avant-garde saxophonist Anthony Braxton cites these features as a major influence. Marsh died in 1987, following a heart attack at Donte's club in Los Angeles, while performing "Out Of Nowhere." His story is told in Safford Chamberlain's excellent biography *An Unsung Cat*.

It's clear that among all his contemporaries and successors, Marsh is the saxophonist Konitz most admires. The pair had a vital if relatively infrequent partnership that continued up till the 1970s. Konitz has commented that their musical rapport was a kind of "magic . . . really special . . . On a one-to-one basis I can't think of any horn player that I've ever had that kind of affinity with. . . . You had to play at your highest level, or else fall by the wayside."[10] This inspiration also engendered insecurities that Konitz discusses here. With the two players' improvised counterpoint in mind, Marsh referred to "my updated Dixieland,"

and toward the end of his career commented, "The improvised solo coming out of one musician, with others supporting him, is a dead end. . . . In front of us we have many years of the collective improvised effort, the intuitive and adult collaboration between peers."[11] On classic recordings such as "Marshmallow," "Fishin' Around" (both by Marsh), "Tautology," and "Sound-Lee" (both by Konitz), and on *Lee Konitz with Warne Marsh* (1955) and *Live at the Half Note* (1959), the two saxophonists took the art of counterpoint, neglected in jazz during the bebop era, to a new level. Their unison lines were breathtakingly exact, even compared with models such as Parker and Gillespie, and as Frank Tirro writes, on "Marshmallow" from 1949, "the instruments in unison sound like one, until they choose to separate on distinct melodic paths."[12]

When I think of Warne Marsh, I think of the definitive creative player, no theatricality, no showboating, just a true musical improviser. It's a true unexaggerated voice, that's what was so sophisticated about it—without the "bleating" and overblowing that many saxophone players seem obliged to do. So he's very high on my list, as I review all of these people that I love. Just to follow him was inspiring. It worked both ways; I think he respected my approach also. I was getting more public exposure, and he might have resented that in some way. But otherwise I think there was a mutual respect throughout, between the three of us—Warne, myself, and Lennie.

You created such beautiful counterpoint with Warne Marsh. How is that possible when it's not worked out in advance?

I think that two simultaneous lines that are strong will form a good counterpoint. Sometimes it connects magically, sometimes it's just two independent lines, but a chord progression holds it in common.

You would also do very tricky unison lines.

We used to stand around the piano as Tristano would play a phrase, and say, "How do you like this one?" And then we'd play it, and then a second one. We'd learn them standing there, and write them down after the fact.

What is your feeling about your early recordings with him, such as those under your own name in 1949?

I just picked up a bootleg two-CD set of my earliest recordings—no royalties, but a tribute! I liked some things, and didn't like others. I was very tense on the faster-tempo pieces with Warne, "Marshmallow" and "Tautology." Some of the medium tempos, "Sound-Lee" and "Fishin' Around," I like pretty well. I did have a pretty solid sound, but I do vibrate quite a lot to end phrases.

Despite your great musical rapport, reading Safford Chamberlain's biography, it seems it was hard to get close to Warne personally.

There were moments that were intimate, sitting around at Lennie's place, talking, getting high or whatever we were doing to relax together—there were beautiful moments. But overall, we weren't really close friends.

But he wasn't that close to anyone. So he was as close to you and Tristano as he was to anyone.

Well, that's what they say. He preferred to be by himself, I think—but we don't really know.

He didn't talk about his feelings.

No, he didn't. I think there was a form of therapy going on in the relationship with Lennie—not per se, but in their conversations. I don't know if Warne went into the Reichian thing—Tristano's brother was a Reichian therapist, seeing some of the students for therapy sessions in Tristano's house. Lennie believed in that, and they were trying to combine that with learning how to play real music.

I know Peter Ind was into it—he built an orgone box, and was very much involved in it. You're supposed to sit in this little box and accumulate a certain kind of energy. I guess it works. But I never had any sessions.

Tristano never suggested you try.

No.

So he thought you were "normal"!

I don't think so! [Laughs.]

Warne Marsh found it hard to break free of the Tristano influence.

I think, finally, he wanted not to be referred to only as Tristano's student. I don't mind being known as that, because Tristano gave me my musical inspiration.

Safford Chamberlain writes that "Warne Marsh refused to rely on a conventionally 'pretty' tone as a substitute for ideas. . . . As one listener said, it's as though the sound is not happening in the horn, but in Marsh's head."

Wow! There was a time when his sound was not really developed, but what ultimately comes through the horn is a totally balanced and proportionate music. Great sound, great selection of notes, great rhythmic articulation, ingenious melodies—and a great intention to be truthful.

Warne was able to use all the materials of the jazz tradition in a most direct development. No really revolutionary changes in harmonic, tonal, rhythmic, or melodic ingredients like Coltrane, Ornette, Dolphy, or Cecil Taylor—but in a most ingenious way, each element was stretched a little further. I think that Warne really absorbed what Lennie was talking about, the rhythmic ideas that he was trying to convey—about playing more broken-up odd rhythms in the line.

So he took that aspect of Tristano's playing to a possibly even higher pitch.

Yes, I think that was very important for Warne's concept. He had an extraordinary rhythmic sense. I never heard him play like that, but he remarked that when he first came to Tristano, he was playing more like Charlie Parker. I hadn't gotten into Bird then—he was already very strongly oriented that way.[13]

So he was a more mature player when he met Tristano than you were?

Yes, I think so. And he was a pianist also.

His family background was completely different from yours. They were well-to-do, and I was reading that they had three servants.

Maybe so. I stayed as a guest at Warne's place for a few days, in the 1950s—we were working someplace. There was nobody there but his mother, whom I never saw; and Warne was always in his room. It was like a Charles Addams place almost.[14] It was a very quiet old Hollywood mansion, with an empty swimming pool, and as beautiful a place as it was, there was very little warmth being shared. It was a house of very introverted people. Warne was not very sociable with me, and I was just left to myself. But his parents were very creative, and that rubbed off on Warne, obviously. His father was a leading Hollywood cinematographer.

I guess the people who really love jazz know about him. But do you feel it was tragic that he was so unsung?

Warne was not a popular figure and in that sense he was unsung, but the guys who knew his playing had the deepest respect for him. Rereading Safford Chamberlain's biography, I'm reminded of what a talent he was and how he was really so ignored. Dan Morgenstern wrote about the tenor players and gave a whole list, including Richie Kamuca and Bob Cooper—and Warne isn't even mentioned! He was at his peak then, playing at his most brilliant—how that can escape the attention of so-called music lovers is amazing to me. One of my favorite records of his is the Atlantic record—just four tunes—with Paul Chambers and Paul Motian.[15] That trio is just beautiful together! But Martin Williams reviewed it and put it down completely "because they never got together." And I thought, "What is he listening to?"

Later, I didn't know exactly what he was doing, but I kinda felt that he wasn't going public very much. I guessed he was living his life as he wished to, and I didn't give it that much thought. But whenever it was pointed out that he was not being acknowledged as a great player, I thought that was regrettable.

For the people I was associated with, the music was the prime interest. We never made it [commercially] as a group, though we actually bought uniforms and took a professional studio picture to try and sell the Sextet. But we were playing all those strange kind of lines, Bach Inventions, free form or whatever. I was really the first one, and the only one to begin with, that went out and did different things, because I was trying to play, and support my family. And when Warne got a chance, he went out too. But Lennie tried and it was too difficult for him, I think because he was blind—that had a lot to do with it.

But Warne's music can be difficult.

Not when he's *on!* Very subtly complex maybe, but never difficult in a melodic way, to me. When he was in good spirits it all came out in seemingly perfect form—maybe more than seemingly.

It's strange that when he did get a little more attention, it was because he was in Supersax, playing arrangements of Charlie Parker.

It was basically that he wasn't out and playing for people. And when he went out he played with local guys; he never tried to play with guys of his caliber. Of course, I guess that's what I did much of the time—playing with local guys, but all over the world.

I think that Tristano advised Warne not to play with Supersax anymore. That point was well made, because on the records that came out, he wasn't given any solos. On some [private] tapes that a friend of mine made, you could hear him play some great solos with that group. He was the only soloist [in the group] that was really extending what Charlie Parker did—Conte Candoli and Frank Rosolino didn't really do that.

If a player is into Warne Marsh—like Mark Turner for instance—that tells you something about their musical intelligence.

Mark Turner, and Joe Henderson and Wayne Shorter, knew Warne's playing. Joe Henderson and I were playing with the George Gruntz big band in Los Angeles, and after we finished, Joe asked me to join him and go to a club where Warne was playing. I couldn't go, but the next day he said it was great. Mark was more willing to talk about him publicly than many others; he's really the first of the black players who came out with no reservations. He just loved Warne's music.

I recorded a tribute to Warne Marsh in Tokyo with the alto saxophonist Gary Foster—who played with Warne—and a rhythm section that had probably never heard of him![16] Earlier, I had played with Gary at the Jazz Bakery in Los Angeles, with a fine rhythm section who had played with Warne—Alan Broadbent, Putter Smith, and Joe LaBarbera.

[We listen to "I Can't Give You Anything But Love" from *A Ballad Album* (Criss Cross, 1984).]

That's a lovely arrangement. Warne just sounds so gentle—a non-schmaltzy kind of sweetness. Nothing is forced at all, it's just so effort-lessly played. It sounds like a direct result of what he heard from Lester Young, more so than from Charlie Parker. He doesn't have to shout or play double time to gain momentum—he gets it with a sweet, great time-feeling.

It's amazing that in that decade, the 1980s, he was playing so well, and yet so few people were paying attention.

Well, it's not blustery, it's not self-conscious. It's real music. Every time Warne got up to play, he was improvising. And there's a different feeling between an improviser, and one who has an ability to improvise but feels it wiser to make a plan before he goes out in public. Warne wasn't naive, he had a plan in some way—his plan was to improvise in the best possible way.

Warne and Hank Jones had never worked together before, and yet on *Star Highs* in the 1980s they were playing counterpoint like old friends—Mel Lewis and George Mraz helped too.

Your 1955 album on Atlantic, *Lee Konitz with Warne Marsh,* is one of my all-time favorites.

With Oscar Pettiford and Kenny Clarke—plus Billy Bauer and Ronnie Ball, and Warne and me—you've got the beginnings of an interesting music. It sounded promising. But I was uncomfortable that day, so I didn't really love the way I played. I didn't feel comfortable musically because I didn't feel comfortable personally. The problem, for me, is that it was my date, and I was not feeling like a "leader," I guess.

You felt, "I don't know if I'm good enough to be leading a date with these great players"?

Something like that, yes. Somehow, I was not experiencing the kind of confidence that happens when you enjoy the sound you make when it's your turn to play. But I'm glad you like it—I do, too; overall.

I'm also reminded of the feeling that it was impossible to get close to Warne, with eye contact or whatever. He was in another place. And I was, too—high, probably—and I couldn't relate to what I was hearing.

I must make the point that that stuff works—marijuana, I'm talking about. I never did anything else. Marijuana puts everybody on a delicate bal-ance, somehow—for me it was like turning the volume up.

I mean it's possible to break loose from daily concerns and get deeply into the music. Everybody was doing something to get high, to get away from the daily thought-process. There's intense physical and emotional awareness that can happen with pot smoking—I was hearing more acutely, touching the keys felt special, and so on. When I decided to stop doing it, I was very pleased to realize that I could still enjoy playing. But that "ecstasy" is not there without the drug, usually, for me.

Does being high accentuate the state you're in?

I think, for me, all the senses are amplified, for positive or negative. I did tend to play mechanically in the early days, and I continually work on that problem—smoking pot was the way I tried to avoid that terrible tendency. But since it's better to make a strong effort to relax and just play, I stopped the smoking dependency years ago. I still have fond memories of ecstatic moments, but I like consistency and responsibility more.

I've never smoked pot, but isn't it like alcohol in deadening your sensibilities?

Being interested in jazz as you are, you've never tried? You ought to try it once to get that insight—you might become a viper![17]

Pot is not at all like alcohol for me. Alcohol is stultifying—it just makes me heavy and insensitive. Pot makes me supersensitive.

But is that an illusion?

It's true for the moment. It's been described as a magnifier of your feelings—everything is more intense. I've felt clearer, in many respects, with the pot. It was said that if you played great on the night before with a smoke, and it was recorded, the next day you had to have a smoke to listen back!

But at that date in 1955, I had the feeling that I was almost there by myself—I didn't know quite how to relate to anybody that day. Very strange—Oscar [Pettiford], Kenny [Clarke], Sal [Mosca] . . . everyone was busy with their own responsibilities.

I read that playing at the Half Note with Warne in 1959, after one of his solos you felt you couldn't compete.

Competing is probably the problem. At times when it was my turn to play I didn't feel like it, it felt complete. And sometimes after smoking pot, I could get very paranoid. Listening to Warne and Lennie, I figured that the music had hit a high spot and I couldn't add anything. In *An Unsung Cat,* Sonny Dallas is quoted as saying that I was actually stopped from playing on the bandstand after Warne and Lennie played—that's how deeply it affected me. I'd feel that I couldn't participate in the music at the moment—which is a devastating feeling for a player.

You are very self-critical.

To an extent, yes. But still I can listen to most of the records I made and enjoy them very objectively. People who say they never listen to themselves, I don't believe. If so, they're really missing an important ingredient in knowing their musical tendencies on a more objective basis.

The point of playing with others is to commune with them. If one's attention is basically on one's own reality, that's not going to work. And the strong players frequently intimidated me. I felt not up to it in some way. It was swinging, and I said, "Oh shit, can I really do this?" Getting stoned could emphasize that tendency, or it could make it easier; it depended how I reacted to it. If I got the confident part of being high, I could thrive on it; but the paranoia and all the negative things that could very easily happen were devastating. That's what made it necessary to stop.

Paranoia for me was becoming conscious of what was going on in the music, at the moment, and somehow, getting embarrassed by the process—it was too intense, too intimate.

So you stopped smoking because of this feeling of paranoia.

That was one thing—and waking up the next day without that intense insight. A painless hangover, compared to alcohol, but painful in the sense of having had an insight and not having it anymore.

But you didn't like the dependence.

I was never that dependent on it—as I mentioned, I never smoked a lot. One poke was enough to open the door for me. I knew that it was a problem drug, and I never got that involved with it.

It's addictive—psychologically, and neurologically, I believe.

You want me to put this in?

I think it's important to mention these things. I want to talk about my involvement in that, and in general, my curiosity about what condition different players were in when they played great. Just about every writer, musician, and painter got high somehow or other, with mind-altering substances. Was Bird on heroin when he made "Don't Blame Me" or "Koko"? That's of interest to a certain degree, but the final product is what we're left with, and we can just be thankful he manipulated whatever he had to, to get that, for Christ's sake.

I mean there's only one person who could play like that, and he had to do what he did, to reach it. So we can thank him for that, and regret that he only lived thirty-four years.

Does it bother you, the connection between jazz and drug-taking? Do you feel . . .

A stigma? By this time, musicians are probably using drugs less than doctors, and lawyers, and professors, and ordinary people! I read something recently where all the dopers were outlined—Sonny Rollins, Sonny Stitt, Thelonious Monk, Charlie Parker . . . I thought, "Oh my God, it's like a police lineup or something." I hate to go in for that. But it's necessary to acknowledge what a positive part drug-taking could play.

We're called on to be creative at nine-thirty on Tuesday night in Verona,

Italy, and then at ten on Wednesday night we have to be creative in Rome or wherever. And how do you turn that on without turning on—that was the rationale. You're supposed to be well practiced, well rested, well fed, and in a positive frame of mind, like a musical athlete—to be in good shape. But the easier way was an instant high.

Why didn't you go down the road of so many, with heroin?

Because it was frightening to me. The needle itself was a total turnoff. And when I saw people that were high like that, they looked like they were close to death. The pot was the only thing that appealed to me.

Did that lack of confidence disappear by the 1960s, so you felt you could function with other great players?

It depended. The opportunity to play a lot, that's how you build confidence. But I could still be intimidated. It's much less now; I feel much more confident. But the insecurity, I guess it can be called, also comes from really trying to play from a clean slate. The guy that knows what he's gonna do can walk in pretty confidently. If you're not feeling good, if the acoustics or whatever are not good, or the people you're playing with—that's the chance we take, trying to improvise.

Did you ever feel like showing off your technique?

Yes, I did that when I realized that I could play double time. But I got past that, finally.

It is surprising to hear you say that on a classic like *Lee Konitz with Warne Marsh*, you weren't ready.

Of course, I have a set of standards that are different from yours, though I appreciate yours. If I was able to play good enough to satisfy your standards, I feel that's very important. But it didn't satisfy mine, and that's still more important for me.

You still have a lot of unreleased recordings with Warne.

We worked a week in 1977 at the Jazz Showcase in Chicago with Wilbur Campbell and Eddie De Haas. Six nights of very special quartet music were recorded on the cheapest quality cassettes, but it's swinging like hell, with very fast tempos. With technical help from Mark Levinson, the music was transferred to CD with much improved sound quality. Eventually maybe some of this nice stuff will be available to the people who love that music.

❧ Interview with Clare Fischer

CLARE FISCHER, *born Durand, Michigan, in 1928, is a pianist and composer. In the early 1950s he studied at Michigan State University and wrote arrangements for the U.S. Military Academy Band, and in 1960 was arranger for Dizzy Gillespie's album* A Portrait of Duke Ellington. *From 1962 he performed with bop and Latin jazz groups including Cal Tjader's. His compositions include "Pensativa." He continues to freelance in the Los Angeles area.*

How did I get to Lee Konitz, when everybody else was doing Charlie Parker? The sound, for one thing, the notes that he played—man, it just knocked me off my feet! When Lee was first playing, God he was inventive! I worked out so many solos of his off the records, from when he began recording with Tristano and Warne Marsh in 1949. I listened to Charlie Parker but I was not a fan—he was repeating himself too much. That's why when Lee came along, God suddenly arrived! I loved Lester Young, and Coleman Hawkins, Don Byas—not so much the piano players. I could see that Tristano was doing complicated things, but I never got the feeling from him that I got from them. Tristano was too contrived for me; he sounded *terribly* planned. Lee is *very* intuitive. With him I had a feeling of free-flowing inventiveness. One of my proudest achievements was when I finally got to play the saxophone well enough that I could improvise on it. I aimed to have a tone like Lee Konitz—but I don't necessarily think I got there!

I transcribed the solo that Lee took with the Gerry Mulligan Sextet on "Lover Man" [in 1953], and when I had my big band, I wrote that out for six saxophones. But I've lived in California since 1958, and Lee wasn't around much on the West Coast. I played with him at a place in Hollywood called Shelly's Manne-Hole, where I was working with my group on Monday nights, I think it was, and also we did an afternoon concert at the Lighthouse in Hermosa Beach. When I had a big band in the late 1960s, though, Warne and I were working quite a lot together. Warne would be turning time around, and dealing with cross-the-bar structures, and starting phrases in odd places—his intuition was really far out! He was one of the greatest players *ever.*

[Konitz and Marsh] were not looking for a publicity buildup. They were always interested in the music, and that was what was wonderful about them. The average listener—even the musicians themselves—what are they interested in? Pyrotechnics!—compared to someone like Lee, or Chet Baker, who's thoughtful, intuitive, and meaningful. I find Lee's focus on standards a very strong point. It means you're handling materials that you're really acquainted with.

Lee at one point decided that he didn't like it if he had some things that started repeating. I played with him once [in the 1950s] and on one of the faster tunes he waited *twenty-seven bars* before he played a note! That's like saying, "I'm focusing on intuition, and if it doesn't come out that way, it's not going to come out at all!" I believe in intuitive improvisation, but in his case, he threw away what he recognized he'd used, and that left him with a lot of bare spots. We are all related to a vocabulary of some sort—even in spoken language. Most jazz players got involved in becoming a duplicate—of Charlie Parker, or Dizzy Gillespie, or whomever. As a young man, on "Wow" and those things, Lee was blazing trails. But then he started thinking about it too much, I think. I don't mean to be critical of that. But when he was playing, originally, I'd have hairs standing up on the back of my neck![18] 🎜

Other Tristano Players, and Tristano's Legacy

🎜 Interview with Billy Bauer

Guitarist **BILLY BAUER** *(1915–2005) was a key member of the Tristano groups. He began playing banjo and switched to guitar in the early 1930s. He worked with Woody Herman in 1944, then Benny Goodman and Jack Teagarden in 1946. He was on the sessions that produced the early free jazz pieces "Intuition" and "Digression" with Tristano. Konitz recorded duets with him in 1950–51 ("Indian Summer," "Duet for Saxophone and Guitar," and "Rebecca"), and he appeared on* Lee Konitz with Warne Marsh *from 1955. He recorded with the Metronome All-Stars during 1947–53 alongside Charlie Parker, Dizzy Gillespie, Miles Davis, and Tristano. In 1950–53 he played with NBC staff orchestra, and taught at the New York Conservatory of Modern Music. He freelanced in New York City in the 1970s and 1980s and taught privately. When I interviewed him in 2002 for* Jazz Review *magazine, he provided a fund of anecdotes from which these remarks are taken.[19] Billy Bauer died in 2005, aged eighty-nine.*

From what I heard, Lennie used to make all his students write lines— take a progression, and write an original line.[20] One of them became "Subconscious-Lee," and so on. I wrote a couple of tunes, but not under his guidance. When I hear talk that Lee, Lennie, and Warne used to play free music up in his house, I wasn't in on that. The only time I did it with them was in Birdland, and on the record date. There was no real time, you'd just take a phrase. . . . I think it was a breakthrough. [Tristano] had a tough time releasing the record.

After he came to New York, that's when I met Lee. He had a floating style. It wasn't biting like Charlie Parker, he didn't have that kind of forcefulness, but he had another kind of a thing. One of the write-ups that he got for a record date without Lennie—I was there, it was the one with "Rebecca"—said, "Lee finally comes into his own." That's the first time they recognized that Lee had his own thing, that he broke away from the flavor of Tristano.

At that time Lee was using me quite a bit. I don't know where he got the idea of just the two of us, but one of the first duets we made was in a little room, a guy's living room, and he had a little acetate machine, the old discs, not a tape machine. We played about two takes and Lee wanted to make another take, and the guy said you can't, I haven't got any more acetate. And they released them. ✒

Billy Bauer was not a pupil of Tristano, but a bandmate of ours. He lived in Long Island, New York and into his late 80s was still talking a mile a minute like he always did, still full of plans and ideas. He was a totally unique guy. He loved to talk, and he had a very special sound and vocabulary, full of enthusiasm and interesting anecdotes. He issued a book, called *The Sideman*.

I only know him through his playing with Tristano—did he retire from the music?
Well, teaching was a big thing with him, and I think he played occasionally. A few years ago, I actually asked him to play a couple of tunes on a record, and he thought about it, and the next day he just said it would be too difficult to travel into Manhattan.

He's said that he didn't feel he had a style, that he was a perpetual sideman. You worked with him quite a lot—what did you like about his playing?
Basically his accompaniment ability—he was a very exciting and inspiring accompanist. His solos were never really that great, he was very insecure about that, and very much encouraged by Tristano to play. But he just had a way of pushing you with his accented chords, and the quality of the sound he made. And when we played as a duo, without the need to swing, he was very effective, as an original voice. Harmonically and melodically he had a very unique conception.

Sal Mosca was studying at the same time as you. He was an interesting player.

Very interesting, the most interesting pianist after Tristano, very much a spontaneous player. And very devoted to Tristano—you could recognize Tristanoisms in his playing, but it was very unique overall.

He went the way of Tristano, teaching and not playing in public.

Yes. There's some nice stuff available, if you can find it. A recording with Warne at the Village Vanguard has some really special playing on it.[21] I really enjoyed playing with Sal. When we got stoned, and played together, sometimes the tempo got slower and slower—which is a characteristic of people who get high sometimes. He spends most of his time teaching, but I haven't talked to him in many years.

I heard that after a serious illness, he recently started to play gigs again. . . . He's a more original player than Ronnie Ball [another Tristano student].

Ronnie Ball was a fine player, in the Bud Powell–Lennie Tristano style. But Sal had great originality in all respects, harmonically, melodically, and rhythmically.

❧ Interview with Sal Mosca

Pianist **SAL MOSCA**, *born Mount Vernon, New York, in 1927, studied with Lennie Tristano and also at New York University and New York College of Music. From 1949 to 1965 he worked with Konitz, and recorded as a leader in the late 1950s. During the 1970s he performed with Konitz and Warne Marsh, in 1971 releasing an excellent largely duo album with Konitz,* Spirits, *as well as giving solo concerts in New York. In the late 1970s and 1980s he led groups with Marsh. After his recovery from recent illness, his career has undergone a renaissance. He is also an active teacher.*

I like Lee's playing, of course. But I especially liked his early playing—from '47 up to about '62. I didn't think it was so cerebral. It was the only original music going on, on alto saxophone, beside what Bird was playing, because everyone was imitating Bird. And Lee was told by Lennie not to play that way, but to stay in his own style—and therefore he would make a name for himself rather than just be another Charlie Parker imitator. After 1962, he started playing with all these other people—people who were as good as him, people who were worse than him, and people who were sort of indifferent to him. And when you expose yourself to a lot of different musical situations, eventually they weaken your own individual concept.

Lee I think does play polyrhythmically, but he doesn't stretch out as much with it as Warne did. But rhythmically he's not what I would call a simple player. I think he's sophisticated.

I used to feel that I wasn't part of the main black tradition of the music. But then I was thinking, "I've had a lot of bad experiences, I had a rough childhood, I had health problems—so I gotta right to sing the blues too, even though I'm white." I don't think Tristano thought he was setting up a white tradition in jazz. If he did, he was wasting his time, because he was influenced by black players himself—by Art Tatum, Lester Young, Charlie Parker, and Roy Eldridge.[22] 👈

Do you have much to do with the so-called second generation of Tristano players, such as pianist Connie Crothers and tenorist Lenny Popkin?
Lenny Popkin studied with me for a couple of years, and Connie did too. I sent Connie to Tristano, and Popkin eventually went to Tristano too. He's a fine tenor player, very much in the style of Warne. There's a few records of them—Lenny Popkin and Connie—and they're very unique, together and separately.

Did you have less to do with them because you grew away from Tristano?
I just didn't have occasion to see these people. I got a little closer to Connie Crothers the last few times I was in New York, and I appreciated being able to talk to her about Lennie, and found out some things I didn't know about him and our relationship that were very good to know. She doesn't get to play as much as she wants—so, again, teaching is the path we have to take. She likes to play very free—not playing on structures and tunes—and the best playing that I've heard her do was in a duet with Max Roach.[23]

When I'm working in New York, there's an alto player that used to study with me, and plays with Connie, called Richard Tabnik, and sometimes he comes in and we talk for some time. But I didn't identify with that group after I left.

Alan Broadbent was a pupil of Tristano in the late 1960s. He was one of the most interesting of the later pupils.
Yes, he's a great writer, and a marvelous pianist. He and I did a duo session a couple of years ago.[24] They're some of my favorite recent recordings, and we agreed that we enjoyed playing together. He even told me that he enjoyed playing with me more than Warne—and that was confounding to me! But I was a little bit disturbed at how much of Lennie I was hearing,

when he did his bass line and eighth-note kind of playing. It was very well done, and musical, and he did such interesting things with his chords. But psychologically, it felt a little weird.

I hadn't realized, till I heard those albums with you, how close to Tristano in some ways he is. He's not interested in re-creation and museum pieces, he really thinks that's a valid way to play today.

Yes, and it is very valid. I think probably playing with me brought more of that out. I didn't get so much of that impression hearing him with Charlie Haden's group [Quartet West]. I really do like him and I should be more vocal about it, I guess. I'm filled with doubts about my own playing, and I'm not able to express anything to the people I play with!

◥ Interview with Alan Broadbent

Pianist **ALAN BROADBENT** *was born in Auckland, New Zealand, in 1947. He studied at the Royal Trinity College of Music there, and at Berklee in 1966–69, at the same time studying with Lennie Tristano. Pianist and arranger for Woody Herman's band from 1969, he also composes orchestral and chamber music. He later recorded with Bud Shank, Warne Marsh, and Gary Foster, and since 1987 with Charlie Haden's Quartet West. Two duo albums with Lee Konitz appeared in 2003,* Live-Lee *and* More Live-Lee. *He has recorded several trio albums, and a fine solo piano CD for Concord Records in the* Live at Maybeck Hall *series.*

It's the young Lee Konitz I was influenced by—I came to know the older man when I was an older man myself! He was what I aspired to as an improviser. When I studied with Tristano in the late sixties, Lee was no longer around, and Warne had left to go to L.A. I never knew him till I got to there myself. I heard Lee Konitz at the Jazz Workshop in Boston, when I arrived at Berklee in 1966. Lenny Popkin was sitting in. I started playing with Lenny Popkin, and he said, "Why don't you call Tristano?" I ended up going every week for a lesson, for two years. Lennie never forgave me for going with Woody Herman, because Woody had insulted him—he'd written some chart for the band that Woody hadn't used. In that two years I sang Lester Young solos, did the chord progressions that he had for the left hand, and the slow scales.

    Lennie always talked about Warne—he didn't mention Lee as part of his circle. Warne knew it all—he had a condescending attitude, at least to me, and I never really felt close to his playing. I never got close to

Warne's time, it was always dragging to me—though he was one of the greatest of all improvisers. But there's a searching quality to Lee's improvising that moves me every time. Lee changed somehow in the mid-fifties. His sound changed, and he became more introverted, and that intrigued me too.[25] To this day I have deep self-doubts about my playing—it's a struggle to even listen to myself, some of the time. Warne and Lee are Liszt and Chopin, if you want, and I prefer the Chopin of Lee. Warne was detached, at least when he played with me. Lee is completely dependent on who he's playing with, which is the way it's supposed to be. But then there's the question, "Who are you, to be criticizing Warne Marsh?"

Lennie Tristano used to have me sing Lester Young [solos], and in those days you could put the LP onto half speed, down to 16 [rpm]. Lennie's idea was that with Lester, at half speed you didn't lose any intensity, in fact you gained intensity. In those 1938 Basie things, each note goes to the next in full value—and slowing it down, you understand it deeper. Not that you're copying Lester, but you're divining the personality that produced the notes. But when I put some of Lee's tunes on to copy, and listened at double speed, somehow these slow lines made such beautiful sense—the reverse of Lester Young! Tristano absolutely emphasized being an intuitive player. What he was trying to get me to do with Lester, by slowing everything down, was becoming involved in the creation of each note—the note-to-note process. To be aware of *every* note, full value, the tone you're making, with the metronome at sixty. If you're learning a Chopin piece, you have at most three sets of fingerings that'll get you through the passages—with improvising note-for-note, you have to have your fingers ready for any note which comes up.

Lennie's ideal of that note-for-note process was Bud Powell—in his cleanest, his healthiest state. There are recordings where even if Bud plays a sixty-fourth note, you have the feeling that it's "that note, to that note"—it's not a run. At the Three Deuces, when Lennie had a gig opposite Bud Powell's trio, he spent his entire break underneath Bud's piano— yes, lying on the floor—and he told me that's what changed his life. The intensity of Bud's time, that's my ideal.

On our duo recordings, sometimes Lee is searching, and I'm trying to figure out, "Is it me? Maybe I fucked up a chord there, or got in his way." It became like walking on eggshells. But I found my way after a while, to be a part of his expression. It didn't occur to me that he was having the same feelings about himself. But in one of those faxes he sent afterwards, he said, "I wouldn't be playing with you, if I hadn't got something from you!" I love his beautiful time. There's a preconception of how you're supposed to play with Lee Konitz—as a "cool" player—instead of listening to the moment. Most drummers have energy, but Lee has another energy to draw from, and it requires listening. It's frightening for drummers—or pianists—to listen to that intensity of the note-to-note process—the emotional intensity. This is what moves me in the music—that this guy is so damned vulnerable. It takes a lot of guts to play that way and to live your life that way. Warne was never vulnerable, to me—though it took a lot of guts to be Warne Marsh too!

Lee mentioned that being with him brought out the Tristano side of my playing—if he's talking about the bass lines, though, they're a very difficult thing to do. When Tristano did the *New Tristano* album, he was actually re-creating that jazz tension between the soloist and the rhythm section, but between his right hand and his left hand. It's not Dave McKenna or Earl Hines, or that stride feeling. It actually is two different times, the solid rock in the left hand, and the Chopin rubato over the top. That's a joyful thing for me to be able to do—what Lennie called a "life force"—and I don't get too much of an opportunity to do it. *The New Tristano* is the greatest solo jazz piano album bar none.[26] 🎵

There's something I would like to know. . . . This conversation inevitably goes back to that period with Tristano. It's true that it was a revolutionary period. Still, it begins to seem like a paper written on Lennie Tristano, Warne Marsh, Bud Powell, and Charlie Parker!
Well, the material from the forties and fifties was really groundbreaking—nothing in jazz could have that kind of influence now. And writers keep coming back to Tristano, when they talk to you, because *cool school* is a definite label they can apply. The standard history of modern jazz is bop, then the cool school, then hard bop, which was a reaction to this "cerebral" music.
Tristano was a very creative force in music, and in my life and a lot of people's lives. I love all of the records that I made, but I don't think any of them were as "historic" as *Birth of the Cool* and the Tristano records that I was part of. I may feel, "Oh God, have we got to talk about Tristano again?" but we do. He was a very important character that people still want to know another detail about. And if I can provide it, I will.
Would Tristano have had the name that he has, without the pupils? He would have been a very interesting piano player like Dick Twardzik . . .
No, no—if he hadn't had the teacher stigma, he would have been more accepted as a pianist, I think. Sometimes he was thought of as a teacher first, and a player second. But he was a player first, a great pianist. It seemed like

they preferred to talk about him being a Schoenbergian influence as a teacher. Which would make me Webern or Berg. They were a very special triumvirate.

Which would you rather be?

Well, I know Berg better than Webern, so I would say Berg.

So that would make Warne Marsh into Webern, which seems quite appropriate.

He wasn't that economical! . . . These composers are all great. But I don't identify at all with their kind of genius.

This is something we haven't talked about really—the reasons for Tristano's reputation.

Yes—I haven't expressed that before, really. To play that good and be so little acknowledged just seems strange to me.

To those who know the music, he's a master. But there's not that many recordings.

There's enough to hear how the man plays, for Christ's sake. People seem reluctant to talk about him as a piano player. I can't believe it's because I was so close personally that my perspective was distorted.

Maybe it's because he was too "cerebral"!

Cerebral? He swung his ass off! The concerts we played sometimes were very exciting. The recording from the Sing Song Room is some of his most relaxed playing, but I didn't play that well myself, and it's not a good example of how the quintet played, or the sextet. With Billy and Warne Marsh, sometimes we hit some extraordinary moments. Not too much of that was recorded, unfortunately.

The stigma of being an intellectual in jazz, maybe that's part of it.

Sometimes it takes a long time for a real perspective to develop.

Endnote: Cool Jazz

Following the discussions with Konitz, I'd like at this point to draw together some of the issues surrounding cool jazz, and try to define it.

Konitz is often regarded as one of the architects of the "cool" style in modern jazz, in contrast to the "hotter" style of Charlie Parker and the modern jazz mainstream. Those at the cutting edge of jazz in 1945 were dominated by Parker—the term *modern jazz* usually means "jazz inspired by, or produced in the shadow of, Charlie Parker"—and Konitz was probably the first alto saxophonist in modern jazz to forge a style recognizably distinct from his. From the beginning Konitz's tone had a consistent purity and an understated, chamber-like quality, that proved ideal for Miles Davis's Birth of the Cool band. This tone, essential to Konitz's unique style, has been widely misunderstood. His phrasing tends to be legato, but as we've seen, his tone is not uninflected or vibratoless. With the Claude Thornhill Orchestra, Konitz's playing is original but immature, and Thomas Owens comments that "Rebecca" and "You Go to My Head" from 1950, "nearly devoid of rhythmic complexity and pitch inflection and played with his characteristic thin tone and slow, narrow vibrato, are sad and lonely pieces."[27] But in Paris in 1953, with musicians from Kenton's band, Konitz recorded some beautifully lyrical performances, especially two versions of "These Foolish Things."[28] During the 1950s his tone became richer and warmer, and he developed an increasingly rhythmic punch. His most lyrical playing has been in the last decade, but a sampler of Konitz's work would reveal a great variety of moods.

Konitz's typecasting as a cool player is an issue that recurs throughout these interviews, and we've noted how the distinction between hot and cool is often oversimplified. Hot playing involves displays of instrumental virtuosity, hard-driven swing, a bluesy or vocalized tone, and—in the case of the avant-garde—multiphonics and other extreme techniques. Hot players sweat and emote on stage, and are inclined to work out their inner demons through music. Cool jazz, in contrast, as defined by Mark Gridley in the *New Grove Dictionary of Jazz,* is "perceived as subdued, understated, or emotionally cool. There was some implication that performers in this style were emotionally detached from their creation." As Gridley also comments, most saxophonists of the cool school were disciples of Lester Young, and many of them played in the big bands led by Woody Herman and Stan Kenton during the late 1940s or early 1950s. Apart from Konitz, the most prominent were Stan Getz, Art Pepper, and Zoot Sims. The style of Miles Davis was the basis for a number of cool trumpeters, including Chet Baker and Shorty Rogers, who used almost no vibrato, and in contrast to bebop emphasized simplicity and lyricism, avoiding the upper register. However, as Gridley notes, the term "cool" seems to contradict the high degree of intensity in Tristano's work.

Miles Davis's Birth of the Cool nonet was the classic larger ensemble of cool jazz. Arrangements by Gil Evans and Gerry Mulligan distilled the style, and both Evans and Mulligan led or recorded bands during the 1950s in which it evolved. Despite a great disparity in their approaches, groups of the 1950s and 1960s such as the Modern Jazz Quartet, George Shearing's quintet, the quartets led by Dave Brubeck and Gerry Mulligan, and many ensembles led by Jimmy Giuffre, have all at one time or another been described as "cool." The work of Bill Evans, who was specifically influenced by Konitz and Tristano, could from 1959 onward be seen as a descendant of cool. West Coast jazz of the 1950s is categorized as cool, but the style was mostly restricted to white jazz musicians working there. Many cool players revived improvised counterpoint as practiced particularly in New Orleans jazz—John Lewis with Milt Jackson in the MJQ, Dave Brubeck with Paul Desmond, Bob Brookmeyer with Gerry Mulligan, and Jimmy Giuffre in his groups, as well as Konitz and Marsh with Lennie Tristano.

André Hodeir, in his classic *Jazz: Its Evolution and Essence,* provided a more philosophical definition of the cool style, as "a striving towards a certain conception of musical purity . . . it contributed . . . a kind of modesty in musical expression that was not to be found in jazz before. Even when the performer seems to be letting himself go most completely (and cool musicians . . . cultivate relaxation), a sort of reserve, by which we do not mean constraint, marks his creative flight, channelling it within certain limits that constitute its charm. . . . jazz becomes an intimate art, rather like what chamber music is in comparison with symphonies. Analytically speaking, their conception shows three principal characteristics: first, a sonority very different from the one adopted by earlier schools; second a special type of phrase; and finally, an orchestral conception." Later he adds: "To date . . . the cool sonority exists only in jazz, so there is every reason to conclude that it really is a jazz sonority."[29]

Hodeir is right to emphasize the "orchestral conception"—an emphasis on classically influenced writing was a major factor in the development of the cool school. However, his account is wrong if it suggests that a cool conception had not been found in jazz before 1945, since there has always been a strand in jazz opposed to emoting. It was present as far back as Bix Beiderbecke and Frank Trumbauer, and exemplified by Lester Young, who criticized his own band members for "showboating."[30] King Oliver objected to trombonist Clyde Bernhardt's "fast stuff" when he started working for him in the early 1930s: "Son, you don't have to do all that shit to impress me. You got a good swinging style and all them snakes you makin', loses the flavor. It don't mean a damn thing."[31]

In fact, as Gunther Schuller says in his interview in chapter 8, "the best players are in a way everything from hot to cool." Compare Ben Webster on "Cottontail" to the ballad playing on which his later reputation rests, or conversely, Coleman Hawkins on "Body and Soul" as opposed to his up-tempo playing. Lester Young's "Lady Be Good" and many of his Basie sides could be regarded as "hot." And as we've seen, it would be wrong to conclude that cool players are unemotional and lacking in intensity. The finest of cool players show a relaxed, as opposed to a "hot," intensity. The Tristano school provides the most obvious illustration of this.

Konitz objects to the description *cool* as applied to Tristano and himself, because of this association with criticisms, which began early, that their playing was "cold and cerebral." Even Stan Kenton, who hired Konitz, described Tristano as "a good musician, but very cold and utterly lacking in emotional communication." Later he said: "You can criticize Tristano for the same thing for which you can criticize Schoenberg. Music is created because of the people and *for* the people . . . there's too much of a feeling of wanting to shut yourself away in an ivory tower, and create, because you were born a hundred years too far ahead."[32] In his autobiography, Dizzy Gillespie commented: "There was no guts in that music, not much rhythm either. They never sweated on the stand, Lee Konitz, Lennie Tristano, and those guys."[33] This line of criticism persists, for instance in Robert Gordon's book *Jazz West Coast,* where Tristano's music is described as deliberately unemotional. Tristano's playing is passionate in a way that makes these criticisms absurd, and it also challenges Hodeir's account of the cool style. As Schuller puts it in *The Swing Era:* "Tristano's early work pulsates with the vitality of invention, luxuriates in warm sensuous harmonies, revels in a richly varied pianistic touch, and pleasures in the contrapuntal independence of two hands. If that be mere 'intellectualism' . . . it is much more likely that it is only so in the ear of the beholder."[34] Mark Gridley argues that Tristano and Konitz were "passionate players who do not fit the characterization of being 'cool': detached and subdued in their work. Their music is quite intense."[35] Tristano and Charlie Parker had a strong mutual respect, and recorded together in 1947, 1949, and 1951, and Parker affirmed, "I endorse his work in every particular. They say he's cold. They're wrong. He has a big heart and it's in his music. Obviously, he also has tremendous technical ability. . . . He's a tremendous musician." Tristano commented, "Behind what I do there is a very comprehensive emotionality." In the same interview he made the vital point, which Konitz develops in his discussion, that "If what I play were intellectual it would have to be all premeditated and it isn't."[36]

This intensity separates the Tristano school from other manifestations of the cool style. Lennie Tristano is often regarded as affiliated to—indeed possibly the founder of—a white "cool school." But his ideas are unique, and it would be better to refer simply to the Tristano school. The racial designation is also questionable. Miles Davis is rightly identified as the leader of a group that launched the style, which also included Max Roach, J. J. Johnson, and other noted black players, all of whom were leaders in hard bop—one reason it is wrong to say that hard bop appeared in reaction to cool. The Modern Jazz Quartet were important exponents. Tristano is closer to these players, but very different from what most jazz listeners identify as the "cool sound," exemplified by musicians mostly from the West Coast such as Stan Getz, Gerry Mulligan, and Chet Baker. The sound of Konitz and Marsh is not as ingratiating as these players', who tend to be more easygoing and less challenging, and less "cerebral." Among them, perhaps only Chet Baker is a real improviser in the way that Konitz is—someone who accepts the challenge of the moment, and the demand to be spontaneous, and aims to create wholly new variations through responding to the ideas of their fellow musicians.

The preceding chapters have shown how the Tristano school was more a development of bebop than a reaction to it, as the received history says. Gunther Schuller described Konitz as "fusing the musical conceptions of Charlie Parker and Lennie Tristano," a view he develops—although Konitz questions it—in his interview in chapter 8.[37] Although much cool jazz of the 1950s was indebted to the Basie and Lester Young groups of the late 1930s, cool musicians had assimilated bebop. Indeed, Parker, Tristano, and Konitz had a common influence in Lester Young. Young's sound—often, like Konitz's, mistakenly described as vibrato-less—has long been recognized as the basis for the cool tenor saxophonists of the late 1940s and 1950s who reacted against the stylistic model of the "hotter" Coleman Hawkins. More recently, however, it has been recognized that Young was also a major influence on Charlie Parker and other "hot" players. Konitz recalled in an earlier interview how together with Parker he was on tour with Stan Kenton. He was "warming up in the dressing room—I happened to be playing one of Lester's choruses—and Bird came noodling into the room and said 'Hey, you ever heard this one?,' and he played [Lester Young's] 'Shoe Shine Boy' about twice as fast as the record."[38] The "hottest" tenor players of all, Dexter Gordon, Sonny Rollins, and John Coltrane, repeatedly said in interviews that Young was their initial model—but then again, Young himself had switched to a "hot" style by 1944, when these younger players were just starting to develop. It's also interesting to note that bebop was at first described as "cool"—for instance, Tristano commented, "Swing was hot, heavy, and loud. Bebop is cool, light and soft."[39] And in his interview in chapter 8,

Gunther Schuller refers to "the hot, loud, brash jazz that had particularly been played all through the war. That lingered on with the big bands, until bebop cooled things off." One should probably conclude by reiterating, with Schuller, that the best players, including Parker, were both hot and cool.

There has been no real Konitz school of cool saxophonists, though he is often held to be an influence on players such as Paul Desmond and Art Pepper. Desmond, the saxophonist with Dave Brubeck's commercially successful group of the 1950s and 1960s, was born in 1924, three years before Konitz. His light sound was influenced by Lester Young, and he played more "motivically" than Konitz, but not in the way Parker played motivically in order to create a compositional mosaic. Desmond is identified with Brubeck's group, and his first commercial recording with the Brubeck Octet in 1948 has clues to his later style. There's some evidence of influence on Desmond, and Konitz is a much more original figure whose style has evolved more than Desmond's did.[40] But there is little evidence of influence on Art Pepper, who was born in 1925, two years before Konitz, and came to prominence before Konitz or Desmond, playing with Benny Carter and Stan Kenton as early as 1943. He was a much hotter player, but no Bird imitator: "They'd copy these things off the records and practice by the hour Bird's solos and his licks. Everybody sounded like him with the same ugly sound. . . . I didn't want to play that way at all, but I realized that I had to upgrade my playing and I had to really learn chords and scales. So I didn't copy anyone."[41] More plausible claims of influence by Konitz include players such as Bud Shank, Gary Foster, Arne Domnérus, John Tchicai, Lars Gullin, and Anthony Braxton. But as Paul Bley puts it in his interview in chapter 9, "The most important thing about Lee is what he doesn't do. The fact that he doesn't sound like a Blue Note bebopper, and the fact that it's possible to have a whole career without sounding like a Blue Note bebopper, already is refreshing to young jazz musicians."

With Lloyd Lifton (vibes) and two others, Chicago, 1946. (Courtesy Institute of Jazz Studies, Rutgers University.)

With Tristano and Joe Schulman (bass), ca. 1949. (Courtesy Lee Konitz.)

Konitz with family, late 1950s. *Clockwise from lower left:* Stephanie, Lee, Karen ("Kary"), wife Ruth, Rebecca, Josh, Paul. (Courtesy Lee Konitz.)

Konitz as baby (Courtesy Lee Konitz.)

(upper left) Miles Davis, Konitz, and Gerry Mulligan at the Miles Davis Nonet recording session, 1949. (Courtesy Lee Konitz.)

(middle left) With Stan Kenton and Orchestra, 1952. (Courtesy Lee Konitz.)

(lower left) With Charlie Parker, on tour with Kenton, 1953. (Courtesy Lee Konitz.)

Konitz in the United Kingdom, 1957, while on tour with Jazz at Carnegie Hall. (Courtesy Tony Cryer.)

With Phineas Newborn (piano), Oscar Pettiford (bass), and Kenny Clarke (drums), probably Jazz at Carnegie Hall Festival, 1958. (Courtesy Lee Konitz.)

(*above*) The Marshall Brown/Lee Konitz Quartet at the Five Spot, late 1960s or early 1970s, with John Beal (bass), Ronnie Bedford (drums). (Courtesy of The Institute of Jazz Studies, Rutgers University.)

(*below*) With Dizzy Gillespie (trumpet), Curtis Fuller (trombone), Nice Festival, 1960s. (Courtesy Lee Konitz. Photograph by Lotte Mortensen.)

With Warne Marsh (tenor sax), Peter Ind (bass—not visible), Al Levitt (drums—not visible), Dave Cliff (guitar), Corner House, Whitley Bay, Newcastle, United Kingdom, 1975. (Courtesy Jack Goodwin.)

On tour with Shelly Manne (*left*) at a festival in Europe, probably 1977. Art Blakey (*center*) just dropped by. (Courtesy Lee Konitz. Photograph by Joao Freire.)

With Bill Evans, on tour in the
United Kingdom, 1978. Konitz
says that Evans "looks like a
rabbi delivering a sermon."
(Courtesy Lee Konitz.
Photograph by Lotte Mortensen.)

With Lionel Hampton,
while on tour in the United
Kingdom, 1978, probably at
Middlesborough Football
Stadium. (Courtesy Lee Konitz.
Photograph by Denis J.
Williams.)

(*top*) With Art Farmer, 1979. (Courtesy Lee Konitz. Photograph by Elena Carminati.)

(*middle*) With Kenny Wheeler, Calagonone Jazz, Italy, 2002. (Courtesy Agostino Mela.)

(*left*) At Barga Jazz, 2003. Konitz now has a street named after him in the small hill-top town in Tuscany. (Courtesy Enrico Stefanelli.)

5 ✒ The 1950s

Stan Kenton and Early Projects as Leader

In August 1952 Konitz joined the orchestra of Stan Kenton and stayed for over a year. Working with a commercially successful big band solidified his reputation, and its European tour gained him an international audience. But as he explains, the Kenton orchestra was an unlikely setting for the saxophonist to operate in. Kenton had formed his first band in 1941, and his "Artistry in Rhythm" orchestras, featuring vocalists such as Anita O'Day, June Christy, and Chris Connor, became increasingly brash, gargantuan, and popular. With the decline in big bands, Kenton broke up his organization in 1947, but reformed in 1950 with a forty-piece orchestra that included strings. He brought together excellent soloists and imaginative arrangers, including the rather avant-garde Robert Graettinger, but his bands had the reputation of being too massive to swing effectively. Many of Kenton's altoists at that time—such as Art Pepper, Lennie Niehaus, and Bud Shank—had a "cool" tone, but Konitz was the most original.

Konitz's period with Kenton marked his independence from Tristano, and brought his work to a wider audience on features such as "In A Lighter Vein" and Bill Russo's arrangement of "Lover Man." He left Kenton in 1953 but rejoined him in early 1954 for the Festival of Modern American Jazz, a rival to Norman Granz's populist Jazz at the Philharmonic tours. Konitz and Charlie Parker joined the revue at the same time and toured the East Coast, the Deep South, and the western states; Konitz commented on their troubles in the South.[1] As well as touring with Kenton, Konitz also made a trip to Scandinavia in 1951, his first visit to Europe, where he met the great Swedish baritone saxophonist and composer Lars Gullin. He recorded with Gullin several times from the 1950s to the 1970s, and in 1983 recorded an album of his music.[2]

As Konitz's style matured, his tone became richer and more expressive; his lines became smoother, and his rhythmic conception diverged from Tristano's overt complexity. In recordings with Billy Bauer in 1951, for instance, he still plays polyrhythmic phrases derived from Tristano; after that, he favored a less overtly complex approach. Konitz was now recording prolifically. In 1952 he recorded a proto–Third Stream project with Charles Mingus, and in 1958, another with Bill Russo. He recorded with Gerry Mulligan and Chet Baker in Hollywood in February 1953. In 1954 he formed his own quartet and played quite often at Storyville in Boston, where his group was recorded on *Jazz at Storyville*. Later that year *Konitz* appeared on the same small label, but the group was poorly promoted and did not endure. Also in 1954 Konitz won the poll for alto sax in *Metronome* magazine, ahead of Charlie Parker; previously he had been runner-up to Parker in the *Down Beat* poll.

As discussed earlier, Konitz appeared on the live Atlantic album *Lennie Tristano* in 1955, first of a series of classic albums for that label including *Lee Konitz with Warne Marsh, Inside Hi-Fi,* and *The Real Lee Konitz. Inside Hi-Fi* includes rare performances on tenor sax with pianist Sal Mosca. A contract with Norman Granz's Verve records resulted in *Lee Konitz Quintet* (1957) and *Lee Konitz Meets Jimmy Giuffre* (1959) with arrangements by Giuffre. One of Konitz's finest post-Tristano recordings, *Live at the Half Note,* from 1959, with Warne Marsh and Bill Evans, has only quite recently been issued. Konitz now discusses his work with Kenton, and then turns to these figures, and others who came to prominence during the 1950s.

Stan called me in 1952. I was raising a family, and there wasn't that much opportunity to work. A lot of the initial interest in me was dispelled, I think, after making the rounds—you can go back a year later to a club in Philadelphia or Washington, or wherever, but that wasn't really enough. The prospect of a steady job at $175 a week was enticing. But that was only part of it. As a kid, I saw his band in a theater in Chicago, and it was a very powerful sight and sound, with Stan as the figurehead. So I was excited by his invitation, and I went there eager to become part of his organization. The opening night, I was featured on a tune on a radio broadcast. He really encouraged us, and exposed us to the audience. I won one of the magazine polls during that period, in *Metronome*.

So that exposure was important in your career.
I think so. It was a fine band, but it was a difficult situation sitting in front of ten brass. It was not easy to play convincingly in that strong environment.

It meant that I had to take a deep breath and blow for all I was worth to hear myself! But the spirit was good, and I got a chance to make some records with him that I like. We did many radio shows and lots of traveling. He tried to play good music, and the hits that he had, "Peanut Vendor" and things like that, were requested, and we played those too. But for about fifteen months it was a very vital experience musically and personally.

Stan was quite a gentleman, and I always appreciated the way he treated all the guys. I wasn't one of the drinking group at the back of the bus. But he was very respectful—just play good and cool it with the drugs, and show up!

What do you make of the criticisms that his ensemble wasn't very swinging and it was much too massive?

Well, I agree with some of that. He loved the bombast he could get from them. He was a Wagnerian kind of character, I guess. It was a powerhouse.

I happened to be part of a band that he was trying to lighten up a bit. But I felt the power that was possible with that instrumentation. We were playing Gerry Mulligan's and Bill Holman's music, which was pretty close to the real thing I think.

An ordinary big band makes a big enough sound!

Sure it does. But "Peanut Vendor" and some of those very brassy things were always very brilliant in some way.

With Kenton I played some good solos, I think—especially on a Bill Holman tune called "In A Lighter Vein." I did play some prepared things on that one. With ten brass hitting the backgrounds, I had to know what I was doing—I couldn't hear new things that easily. You sit in the sax section, playing functional parts, then stand up and play all you know in thirty-two bars!

Did you worry about your hearing being damaged?

I did, yeah. There were times when I stuffed some paper in my ears. But you get used to it and start to just wallow in it. That situation and listening with earphones a lot have given me a tinnitus condition—a hissing in my ears. Thankfully there are days at a time when I'm not aware of it.

Last night someone gave me two CDs that he put together from the radio shows the Kenton band did every week—just the tunes I had solos on. It took fifty-one years to finally hear that! I liked some of the official recordings very much, but others don't sound too relaxed or musical to me now—not in the note selection so much as in the oversentimental rendition, with that corny vibrato, and rhythmic phrasing as a result of tension that I don't like.

I was told by Connie Crothers that Tristano thought of me doing a simi-

lar thing with that band that Lester Young did with the Count Basie band—
if you can make sense out of that! He really liked what I did, and students
copied my solos. I had got the impression that they were all putting me
down for going with this big, loud, commercial band, so I was happy when
she told me that. Lennie didn't say anything to me about it—but he knew I
had to do that, to support my family at the time.

Did you know Bob Graettinger, the arranger?

We played something he wrote for saxes on a standard, "You Go to My
Head." It was very unique. I just met him at the rehearsal, I didn't really get
to know him. He was a very interesting composer, but I guess wasn't able to
take care of himself. Some of what he wrote, "City of Glass" maybe, didn't
have much jazz indication; it sounded like modern classical music to me,
with some saxophones added. I love to hear nonconventional orchestration,
but I feel that it was kind of forced in some way. I haven't listened to that
work for many years—I'd be curious to hear it again, maybe I'd hear it differently.

You had toured Scandinavia before you joined Kenton, in 1951.

Yes, and I was greeted by some very good Swedish musicians who knew the
Tristano lines, and mine—a great welcome for a new visitor! So I felt
acknowledged and eager to play with them. Bengt Hallberg on piano was a
fine player—I think he had studied Lennie's records. There were a few
Swedish musicians who really played well, influenced by my playing and
Warne's, such as Arne Domnérus, Rolf Billberg, and Lars Gullin.

What did you feel about European jazz?

At that time it was very formative, but people were eating up the records.
The biggest problem was with rhythm sections; some of the horn players
were really working at it.

In 1953 I recorded with [baritone saxophonist] Lars Gullin—it was his
date, and he was a world-class player, a concert pianist, and a writer of symphonies. I was in Sweden with Stan Kenton, and some of the guys in the
band—Frank Rosolino, Conte Candoli, the bassist Don Bagley, and Stan
Levey—formed an ensemble, playing tunes Lars wrote. They felt like standards, with nice, familiar-sounding melodies and chord structures. Lars
loved Tristano's music. He was a very sweet guy. He got one of the nicest
sounds, very much influenced by Gerry Mulligan with Miles Davis, that
kind of a baritone sound that's almost a tenor sound. And he carried around
this terrible drug problem. He had much respect from the Swedish government; they were supporting him through the years. I cannot imagine such a
thing happening in America.

Have you ever played the baritone sax yourself?

Once I played a few choruses on a record with Lars Gullin, Hans Koller, and some German guys—I borrowed a horn. I played a duet with Lars, but he sounded much better! If it wasn't so damn heavy, that instrument would be the closest to my voice. If I sing a Charlie Parker solo, I have to go up into that alto register. The baritone—or the tenor—would be in a more natural register to me.

Who were your favorite baritone players, aside from Lars Gullin and Gerry Mulligan?

Jack Washington, the baritone player with Count Basie, would take very few solos, but he played great. He really swung and played really musical lines. I wonder sometimes if Lester was affected by him, or the other way round. Harry Carney was very stylized—with Duke he was very effective, but he wasn't one of my favorites. I liked Cecil Payne—he got a lovely sound out of the instrument.

¶ Interview with Jack Goodwin

JACK GOODWIN *is a British jazz fan from Newcastle upon Tyne who curates the Warne Marsh website, www.warnemarsh.info. The Musician's Union exchange system that he refers to, which largely excluded American jazz players from Britain, lasted into the 1970s.*

The British Musicians' Union would not allow American musicians to tour England unless some reciprocal arrangement was made to have British musicians tour America. So in 1953, the nearest the Kenton band could get was Dublin. *Melody Maker* organized trips for British fans to see the orchestra at the Theatre Royal there. I wanted to see the band mainly because it featured Lee Konitz. Warne Marsh's sound was near that of Lester Young, but Lee's was different from anything I'd heard, and I was instantly attracted to it. "Marshmallow," "Fishin' Around," and "Sound-Lee" from 1949 are sublime.

The special train left from Scotland and traveled down to Holyhead in Wales, picking up Kenton fans in Newcastle, Manchester, and other places along the way. On the front it said "Kenton Special," and all those traveling were avid jazz fans eager to see American musicians, perhaps for the first time. On arrival at Holyhead, we boarded a ferry to take us the seventy miles or so across the Irish Sea to Dublin. The crossing was a nightmare. But we had enough time between landing and the afternoon concert to realize that in Dublin, in contrast to rationing-starved

England, we could buy and eat as many steaks as we wanted. . . . As the stage curtains parted, the musicians walked on, all in silver-gray uniforms, very formal—climaxing with the entrance of "Stan the Man," and the signature tune "Artistry In Rhythm." Every solo by Konitz, Zoot Sims, Frank Rosolino, Conte Candoli, Bill Russo, and others was applauded to the rafters, and the band really swung, propelled by the drums of Stan Levey. But it was Lee Konitz who held me with that magnificent crystalline tone, on "Lover Man" and many other titles.

We had also bought tickets for the evening performance, so it was back to the steaks before the concert began. The overnight return crossing was indescribable. I remember going up on deck to get away from the regurgitated food swilling about in the lounge below, and seeing these huge, almost vertical waves crashing down. Many thought they'd never survive the crossing. The headline of *Melody Maker*'s 26th September issue read "DUBLIN GOES KENTON CRAZY AS 7,000 FANS STORM CONCERT." I thought there were more![3] 🎵

Parker, Young, and the Problem of Imitators

During the 1950s, Konitz began to influence other saxophonists. The problem of responding to imitators is something that he felt as keenly as Charlie Parker and Lester Young, even if there have been fewer in his case. By the 1950s both Parker and Young had become the dominant influences on their respective instruments and had legions of admirers, a fact both found hard to deal with—tenor-player Brew Moore even claimed, "Anyone who doesn't play like Lester is wrong!" In many cases the imitators were white and enjoyed more commercial success. Lester Young was bitter about these imitators, and not just about their greater commercial success, commenting, "They're me. They are taking me. [And] I'm not even dead yet."[4] Tristano condemned Parker's imitators in characteristically colorful language: "[I]f Charlie Parker wanted to invoke plagiarism laws he could sue almost everybody who's made a record in the last 10 years. If I were Bird, I'd have all the best boppers in the country thrown into jail!"[5] Charles Mingus echoed the sentiment in his composition "Gunslinging Bird," subtitled "If Charlie Parker Were A Gunslinger, There'd Be A Whole Lot Of Dead Copycats." Konitz begins by describing how he got to know Charlie Parker when both were touring with Stan Kenton's "Festival of Modern American Jazz" in 1954.

Some time after I left the band, in 1953, Stan called me and asked me if I would come as a soloist, for a series of festivals. I said, "Great, who else is gonna be on?" He said, "Charlie Parker." I said, "What!" I never did find out the reason for inviting me and Charlie. But I was coming back to a very familiar situation, and playing with a band I knew, and Charlie was in new surroundings—and I don't think he was in great shape during that tour. The word got out that this young ofay was cutting Bird.

I got to know Bird a little bit at that time, and he was really a very nice man. He was very considerate. My wife was having a child in New York and I was on the West Coast. He called me and said, "I think you need a friend at this time," and we hung out. Otherwise I never really got to spend a lot of time with him, unfortunately. He always told me that he appreciated that I wasn't playing like him, and I can believe that. I've had a few people trying to play like me. When I first heard Paul Desmond, I wanted to change my sound completely.

But almost everybody played like Charlie Parker. What must he have felt like, this man? Every place he turned was like looking in a mirror. How much he invested to get to that point—what else could he do? Maybe he decided that was enough, and gave it up at the age of thirty-four.

Lester Young was very upset by imitators too.

It's a very strange feeling to hear someone playing like you, duplicating what you've worked on for years. Tristano refused to record for a long time, thinking that he would be imitated. He knew that people would be jumping on it and duplicating it quickly.

Isn't it flattering?

Well it is, but then it gets down to the very basic thing about what you're doing. If someone's already picked it up, that means you've got to go on to new grounds, which is good in a sense. But it gets to feel a bit like a theft of a personal invention. There's no way to patent it!

But you're doing it better.

Just the fact that someone is making a sound similar to me was kind of encouraging, and discouraging at the same time, that it was that accessible. I thought I had something unique. Imagine how Charlie Parker felt when they were really playing his *notes,* and every inflection. Sonny Stitt identified so much that he thought he invented it! That's a very intense psychological disturbance, I think, and obviously Charlie Parker couldn't deal with it ultimately.

You've not had too many saxophonists who are close to your sound.

A few, not many today. These white players, Paul Desmond, Bud Shank,

Gary Foster, the Swedish players Arne Domnérus and Rolf Billberg, were trying to get away from Bird too, so I was an example for them. I think Art Pepper liked my sound and concept to an extent. And, bless him, Gigi Gryce heard us too.

I admired Paul Desmond's playing, but I didn't really love it somehow. It felt very stylized, and kind of pretty—and he had a lot of girlfriends! In fact, when I first heard him I wanted to change my style more, to get away from whatever was pretty in my sound. I've been trying to eliminate "pretty" from my sound and expression.

Did you feel that he was your closest imitator?

Well, he heard me, but I also thought there was some influence from Stan Getz, and Lester Young, and Zoot Sims. I kind of said, "Thank you," but figured that I had to keep going—if it was that obvious for them to be able to get it, enjoy, but let me find something that's new and personal for me.

Hearing you last night [at Coventry in 2002], I wonder if in some ways you were getting more lyrical.

I'm hearing that, when I hear myself play, and it really pleases me. To me "more lyrical" means being as melodic as possible at the moment, but not schmaltzy-pretty. Melody is still my chief concern, with a strong rhythmic underline.

I basically dislike what I call an ugly sound, whatever emotionality it can convey. I can listen to Ornette Coleman now, and not be offended by his tone, and Coltrane too. A lot of guys I still can't listen to. I like Monk's tune "Ugly Beauty" and I know there is such a thing, but I don't like my music to sound that raw!

Konitz now comments on players he was associated with during the 1950s, either as a musical partner or by stylistic affinity: Charles Mingus, Stan Getz, Serge Chaloff, Bill Evans, and Chet Baker. He also discusses other musicians whose work at this time he had a regard for, including Bud Powell, Jimmy Giuffre, Thelonious Monk, and Sonny Rollins.

Bassist and bandleader **Charles Mingus** (1922–79) was generally a supporter of Konitz, but his reactions were unpredictable—in 1955 he criticized him on a *Down Beat* blindfold test for playing "as dead as Paul Desmond"! In 1952 Konitz took part in an unusual session of chamber jazz, in which Mingus recorded four original compositions—"Portrait," "Extrasensory Perception," "Precognition," and "I've Lost My Love"—with vocalists Bob Benton and Jackie Paris and a quintet. Tristano was the recording engineer.

The session was done at Lennie Tristano's studio in East Thirty-second Street. A student of Lennie's, Phyllis Pinkerton, was the pianist, and Jackie Paris, the singer, was involved. I was under contract [to another label] at the time, and I told Mingus I couldn't play a solo [but could only play written parts]. So he wrote one for me on a piece called "E.S.P." He wrote it in the most complicated kind of way—it was a stream of sixteenth notes, as I remember, about one sixteenth note before the down beat. Just to look at it would make you dizzy to begin with. The intention was quite smart—he wanted me to play behind the beat a little bit, which I do anyway frequently, so he didn't have to go to all that trouble!

I haven't heard that record for years. But in the seventies, I was in a big band Mingus had in a Lincoln Center concert that Bill Cosby emceed. It was recorded and called *Charles Mingus and Friends*.[6] At a rehearsal, there were eight saxophone players sitting in the studio—Gene Ammons and Gerry Mulligan were in the section—and he brought out that piece ["E.S.P."]. When we got to that part, you heard eight saxophones going in every direction, and he said "Follow Lee!" And I was more confused than I was in '52, about how to interpret that!

Why did Mingus ask you on that date in 1952?

Well, he was allied with Tristano in some way, so I guess he was hearing us play.

Did you have much contact with Mingus over the years?

Not really. Also in 1952, Mingus agreed to do two weeks with me in a club in Detroit. Al Levitt was the drummer, and Ronnie Ball was on piano. After the first set we were all in the dressing room and Al was talking with Mingus about the time, and Mingus slapped him in the face! After a minute—knowing a bit about his outbursts—I said, "Charlie, could we just play some music and cool it?" or something like that. After that he just played, with no scenes. Then on the last night some of the Detroit cats were in the room—Milt Jackson, Barry Harris, Paul Chambers among them—and Mingus started in on Ronnie, then Al, then me. He just had to show his friends, I guess!

At one point, I met him and he called me a traitor, for having left the Tristano fold. And that kind of took care of that—it was hard to have a discussion with him about the reasons. But he had been very supportive of me. He said things like, "I don't care if Konitz is playing Charlie Parker backwards, I dig it."

But he had an explosive temper and didn't operate on a very even keel.

I just accepted his accusation, I don't remember defending myself.

Was he particularly attracted by your unique tone?

I think so, in the beginning anyway.

That was in a period—the early 1950s—when he was doing a lot of almost Third Stream work. Later, he seemed to reverse that, and rehearsed his band without written music.

Well, I don't know a lot about his career progression. But I know one of the guys that did a lot of his orchestration, Sy Johnson—he's still doing it for the Mingus Band, I believe. He wrote arrangements for my nonet also.

You wouldn't think that Mingus and Tristano had much in common.

Mingus was a thinking man, and he wanted to know what Tristano was thinking about.

Some years later, in the sixties, Mingus asked me to do something with him at the Village Vanguard. It was going to be a sextet, trumpeter Lonnie Hillyer was there. We rehearsed something, and Mingus put his bass down and got very hysterical, talking about calling Bobby Jones, who used to play tenor with him. He didn't feel it was enough with me and Lonnie, he needed another horn. I didn't really know his music, and he wasn't really pleased with what I was doing. The ballads were okay for him, but he didn't like the way I played his faster tempos—and I didn't either!

> **Thelonious Monk** (1917–82), one of the leading pianists and composers of modern jazz, developed at a tangent to the bop revolution. Although Konitz doesn't have much affinity with him stylistically, it's still surprising to find him so critical of Monk as a pianist, if not as a composer.

Tristano was criticizing Monk's piano playing to his dying day, and I thought he was missing the point with that.[7] I don't think anybody thought that Monk was a virtuoso in the usual sense, but how many can get a personal sound out of a fucking piano! My God, that's a hard instrument to sound original on. And there Tristano was, denying him that right. Not to speak of all the tunes that he wrote that were so original. Tristano never wrote an original tune in all the time that I knew him. I remember he tried a chord progression one time, but it didn't work, we never used it. Standards all the time.[8]

But I'm not really a fan of Monk as an improviser. I hear his uniqueness, but it wears off quickly—compared to Keith Jarrett, Brad Mehldau, Chick Corea, Herbie Hancock, Lennie, Bud Powell, Earl Hines, Teddy Wilson.

Is it Monk's sound that's the problem for you?

It's the sound, and the actual music that he chooses to play. His tunes are his definitive talent; his piano playing almost sounds like arranger's piano, like

Gil Evans or George Russell. It's more than that, because he could actually get a personal sound on the instrument, but he plays the same solo, over and over again, I think. I never played many of Monk's tunes, but I enjoyed hearing others play in that style, especially Chick Corea's CD of Monk's tunes. He got it, I think—and added some chops! Really a great version of Monk.

You never played with Monk?

No. It would have been fun, I think. He left a lot of space, and he swung pretty good. I think I would have enjoyed it.

We did go on tour together, however—this was some Carnegie Hall concert tour. It must have been in the 1950s. Warne and I used to play pinochle with Lennie, who had braille cards, and we were playing in the front of the bus, across the aisle from each other. Monk was a few seats back with [his wife] Nellie. For a week or so we never heard a sound from Monk. Every once in a while I would turn around, and it looked like he was sleeping—he had on this Chinese straw hat. When the bus came to a sudden stop, one time, Monk stood up in the aisle and said "Shut my mouth wide open!" That's an old black expression.

Where were you touring?

In America![9] I don't remember if this was the same tour or not, but George Shearing, Al Hibbler, and Lennie were standing by the bus one time, before we got on to leave, discussing who was going to drive that day! They were all blind.[10]

I'm looking at Monk's music now [2003]. Kenny Wheeler and I are talking about possibly doing an album of it, and I'm looking at some sheets I've been given. I've had a problem with that stuff—I characterized it as hip black music, in some way, and stayed away from a lot of it. But some of it is beautiful.

You have recorded some of his compositions.

Certainly I've recorded "Round Midnight" a few times. I love it!

> **Bud Powell** (1924–66) was the leading bebop piano player, and a tormented individual. With Lester Young, he was the basis for the character played by Dexter Gordon in Bertrand Tavernier's film *Round Midnight*. His influence on Tristano was discussed in Alan Broadbent's interview in chapter 4.

I think he was one of the great players—the musicality, and the kind of energy he was able to project was amazing. He was very much out of Charlie Parker, and he transposed Bird's notes—and his own—to the piano. I think he bugged Charlie Parker in some way; on one record they made together Charlie came in on Bud's solo and cut him off. I thought there might have been some personal ego stuff at work there. I think he was great and a mental case to boot.

You have a higher opinion of him than of Thelonious Monk, as a pianist.
Yeah of course, no comparison as an instrumentalist. But I respect Thelonious for what he did, and so did Bud!

Do you see Bud Powell as a spontaneous player?
Not really, no. I think he played pretty much what he knew—and he knew a lot. It's very satisfying to hear someone able to do that—to play at a tempo like that without faltering, and with good lines. But it's impossible to improvise at that tempo, I think. Do your improvising at home, and then put it together to present coherently to the listeners—he's from that point of view.

I played with him in 1948, and it was way over my head in some way. I know something was released that I did with Miles, and I think Bud is on it—live. I didn't really love the way I fit in. I wasn't really playing bebop and I felt way out of context.[11]

Did you know him personally?
I have a very clear picture of sitting with him in the dressing room of the original Birdland, and he was just laughing, like a crazy guy. I said something and he kinda laughed—no communication. Once I was playing with Tristano in Philadelphia, and he came up and tried to push Lennie off the piano seat to sit in; but Lennie wouldn't move out. I also remember walking down Broadway in New York one Sunday, and Bud was standing on a corner asking for fifty cents!

At Birdland, one time in the late forties, the billing was Art Tatum's group, Lennie's group, and Bud's group. When we came off the bandstand with Lennie holding my arm, Bud looked at Lennie and said, "When I listen to you cats, I want to poke my eyes out"!

That same gig, I remember sitting in the booth with Lennie, as Art Tatum was playing "Élegie," one of his classical pieces. He played one of his arpeggios and Lennie looked up and said, "He made that same mistake on the record"!

Serge Chaloff (1923–57) was the leading baritone player in the early years of modern jazz. **Stan Getz** (1927–91) had affinities with Konitz as a cool stylist, while **Sonny Stitt** (1924–82) was a disciple of Charlie Parker.

I did know Serge Chaloff, and I didn't really love his playing that much, but he was one of the minor immortal characters. I don't think he was a great musician, but he had great chops. His mother, Madame Chaloff, taught piano to Kenny Werner and many guys. She was the one to study with in Boston, a highly respected classical piano teacher.

On his classic album *Blue Serge* he has a very full vibrato, and I used to love that. But after talking to you, I don't know what I think about it.

I don't really remember that record specifically. But he sounded very Charlie Parker-ish, kind of rough in some way, and it never pulled me in. I remember we did a Metronome All-Star date, and played a Lennie Tristano line. It ended with a descending diminished scale, and perhaps because he was stoned, Serge never made it. I leaned over to Lennie and said, "Maybe he should lay out." Lennie didn't comment. I think on the record, which I haven't heard for years, he messed it up.[12]

Warne and I had worked hard to learn that line, but Stan Getz practically sight-read the piece, which had many triplets and sixteenth notes. He had perfect pitch, I believe, and a photographic memory—my goodness!

Would you compare Getz to Sonny Stitt in terms of his inventiveness?

He was more inventive than Sonny, and when he didn't try to emote, he really had a great sound. But Sonny never sounded corny to me—Stan sometimes overdid it.

But supposedly Getz didn't like interacting with the band—he would do his thing and the others had to fit in.

He did his thing, yes, but he always had very good rhythm sections, and he played with them very well, I think.

But that doesn't mean that it was all worked out beforehand.

No, but I think he knew what he wanted to play, and played it well. He sounded very musical, and very familiar. His best playing, to me, was with Dizzy and Sonny Stitt—also with J. J. Johnson at the Opera House in Chicago.

His tone was phenomenal.

When he didn't vibrate too much. The vibrato annoyed me, it was too sweet, pretty, schmaltzy. It was very distinctive, and very effective on the bossa nova things especially. Stan could swing hard, but also play lovely Brazilian tunes beautifully, when he didn't milk it.

Sonny Stitt was a very accomplished saxophone player, and a great musician in terms of having absorbed the tradition. I liked him especially on tenor. He had total control of the sound production, and his ideas were also totally controlled—the result is a very clean expression. But the emphasis was on re-creation rather than creation, and he didn't add much to the vocabulary of jazz. When I heard that kind of playing, I understood how good it was and what it entailed.

Fantasy Records sent me a whole set of Art Pepper records, because I recorded with him on some of them. I listened to a couple of sides Art made with Sonny, and Sonny destroyed him! Sonny was really playing straight on, he wasn't showboating or anything arrogant, which he could do. One time in Chicago, I remember he asked to use my horn, and I was really flabbergasted how he could just play on it so effortlessly—unoriginally, but it was very impressive to hear a guy going through the paces, with a great feeling for the time, the line, and the sound.

Again, Konitz has praise but also some criticism for saxophonist **Sonny Rollins**, born in 1930, one of the towering figures of modern jazz, and one of Konitz's few equals as a spontaneous and thematic improviser, and musical thinker.

Sonny is one of the great instrumentalists of all time. I first heard him probably with Miles Davis, on "Paper Moon" and that vintage, when he was really playing closer to Lester Young, and I really loved that.[13] A lot of Sonny's playing, over the years, has been brilliant—with Miles, early on, with Max Roach and Clifford Brown. . . . When he was really *on,* he was extraordinary. I have one tape where he plays "Four" for about forty-five minutes—it's from '68, with NHOP [Niels-Henning Ørsted Pedersen], Tootie Heath and Kenny Drew, at the Café Montmartre.[14] The tempo keeps on getting faster and faster, and he's got a nonstop perfect command of the music—though a lot was already familiar. It was really straight-ahead, and astounding. To make the contrast between Coltrane and Sonny, which generally we're obliged to make, Coltrane created new vocabulary, while Sonny developed the existing material—I think there's a comparison there between him and me.
Did you ever play with him?
One time Attila Zoller was working with him and he asked me to sit in, at the Village Vanguard. There were very few people in the audience, it was the last set.

And one time in the early sixties, in San Francisco, Sonny was late for an afternoon set, and Paul Bley asked me to sit in. I think Henry Grimes was the bass player and Roy McCurdy was the drummer. I was just in the audience, and don't know how come I had my horn with me. So I played a set, and then Sonny came in, and played the most fantastic set you could imagine—nonstop outness! He just played stunningly creatively. It was *very* free, though with a groove.

I had a lot of trouble with Sonny in the beginning. I had a problem with his sound, and his feeling overall. I didn't like his sense of humor, when he messed around with tunes—that was kind of bad taste to me. I think he was trying to be an entertainer and it was not cute to me.

But he tended only to do that with the songs that were schmaltzy anyway—"Toot Toot Tootsie," "I've Told Ev'ry Little Star," "There's No Business Like Show Business."

He did it on many other tunes too—he just couldn't think of anything meaningful at the moment, I guess. The calypso material is not my favorite, but he does it great.

What problem did you have with his tone?

Well, it was in that Coleman Hawkins/Don Byas kind of operatic sound-projection. In the early recordings there was more Lester Young and Bird in the sound.

But it bothered me what he did on the recording with Coleman Hawkins and Paul Bley. I thought that was being disrespectful. Maybe it was necessary for him, to separate himself from Hawk as a father figure. But if he'd played inspired, the way he can, it would have been a great tribute to Hawk, and it wouldn't have sounded like Hawk at all.[15]

What did he do?

He just played very out. But I think Paul Bley [the pianist on the date] can do that for you, by just playing a cluster or two—I've had that experience with him, of just wanting to go out. But why do it when Pappa [Hawkins] is there playing beautifully? Sonny could play beautifully too. He was, and is thankfully, a powerhouse performer. So Sonny, I have to make this point while I still have the floor: Please continue doing whatever you like to do for a long time—we love you!

¶ Interview with Sonny Rollins

In conversation, master saxophonist SONNY ROLLINS *is as thoughtful and rational as are his improvisations—like Konitz, a thinker with gravitas and modesty.*

People said that you were an unlikely person to talk to about Lee, but I think you have a lot in common as spontaneous improvisers.

I'm very flattered to be told I've got something in common with a player like Lee Konitz. I try to improvise spontaneously, with greater or lesser success. I originally heard Lee with Tristano and Billy Bauer and Warne Marsh, of course, and I certainly have a high regard for him. Lee has a great tone, very distinctive.

One obvious point is that he's from the so-called cool school, and you're not in that.

Really? They used to call it the cool school years ago, but I thought it was more apt then than it is now, as a general description. When I heard Lee last week, at the Hall of Fame ceremony [September 2005], I wouldn't describe his playing as cool.

But maybe you're not so obviously a hot player yourself, when you're being ironic.

Well, I've been described as having a certain sardonic wit—some of my material has been unorthodox, and it may explain some of my inner feelings. I do use a lot of obscure song material.

Lee has problems with that though—he wants to be respectful to the tunes, and he doesn't always like the way you mess around with them.

Really? That demands a duel—I'll have to get my guns out and meet Lee at ten paces! We'll have to shoot this one out![16]

He's a real purist about "entertainers."

I can accept his feelings about that. I'm sure there are complex reasons behind my playing—Lee or anyone else may not be aware of them. I know when I was growing up, we used to look down on Louis Armstrong because he was entertaining too much. Then my view of him changed, because there were so many extenuating circumstances involved in his life. I'm not putting myself in the same position, of course. But I find in my own playing, a need to be a little bit more removed from the audience-player nexus than Lee does. I respect Lee and I think it's wonderful to be that much of a purist. I don't quite come at it that way, though I certainly have exhibited serious moments in my playing career. When I was a kid they used to call me the Jester, and I like to joke around. I know Lee admires me, but he may not approve of that aspect of my psyche.

He's got a great sense of humor, but he doesn't direct it at the material he's using, like you do with "I've Told Ev'ry Little Star" and "There's No Business Like Show Business"—the kind of unlikely material you're known for exploring.

We're quite different players in that respect, yet in another respect we are serious jazz improvisers and we have quite a lot in common.

Lee is very critical of what he calls "prepared playing," where someone prepares their solo in detail, in advance.

Well, I could never do that anyway, I'm not that type of a musician.

Everyone has certain licks that they may play at times, but the music is happening so fast, as soon as I interrupt my train of thought to try and remember what to play at a certain place, the moment has gone. So therefore I just try to keep my mind blank. Occasionally a lick will come in, but 95 percent of the time I'm just playing what comes into my mind, I'm not thinking about it. I practice at home to find out the structure of the tune, and then I want to forget that when I'm playing onstage. I don't want to be in an active state of thinking what to play next—it doesn't work.

Maybe the way you look for new material shows that you're a more restless kind of player than Lee. He's found his niche, and is happy to be digging into that, whereas you're always looking for new areas.

I think that probably illustrates that Lee is a much more proficient musician than I am.[17] When I came into music, and started playing with Bud Powell, J. J. Johnson, Miles, and Coltrane, I was always the youngest guy. I got into music a little late, and I never had formal schooling, so I've always felt insecure about my own ability as a musician. I'm always trying to prove myself and trying to improve myself. I'm always searching because I feel I haven't gotten it yet—although I recognize that people who have to search don't always have to do it because they're not musically proficient enough. I have a restless mind. I'm never satisfied with my playing, and that's led me into experimenting with lots of different kinds of things.

Are you keen to explore different keys with a song?

That can change the character of a solo, definitely. That adds a little bit of life to a song, and sometimes I do that.

In your early career, did you make and play transcriptions of Charlie Parker and Coleman Hawkins solos?

To a degree, yes. We had some success in that, and it gave us some idea of the style. I eventually realized that I was not a good enough musician to really pursue that—there's some guys that can really play the solo note for note. So I had to end up just absorbing the other players' styles into mine.

You worked with Paul Bley in the 1960s. Do you agree with Lee that the way that Paul plays, he can make you really go far out—play in a free fashion—just by the clusters that he plays?

I think that Paul is a very unique player, and I would agree with what Lee says. If you listen to what he's doing, I would certainly say that you would end up playing some things that you didn't intend to play originally.

Lee says that if he had just to play one song, say "All The Things You Are," for the rest of his career, he'd be happy to do that.

Well, there are songs that I have played a lot, such as "Long Ago And Far Away." Interestingly, that's another Jerome Kern song. I thought "Boy, every time I play this it's like playing it for the first time." But then it got to the point that I got tired of playing it—though I'd played it a lot before I reached that point.

That's interesting. I can't imagine Lee saying, "I'm fed up with playing 'All The Things You Are', or 'Stella By Starlight.'"

Well, I wouldn't say "fed up," but I felt it didn't present any new challenges for me. I've worked out whatever I can work out of it—which again, could be an imperfection in my own playing, that there's only a certain amount I'm able to do with a certain set of chord changes, or a certain song. I'm trying to make sure that what I'm saying is not in any way a pejorative toward Lee, or toward me. Different people have different ways of approaching music, and it doesn't mean that one way is superior to another. Now I could say this: I might one day want to play "Long Ago And Far Away" again. So I wouldn't say I'm going to throw that song in the Atlantic Ocean. But for the moment I've exhausted what I was able to do with it. So no, I couldn't say that I could wake up every day, and just play "Long Ago And Far Away" and be happy. It doesn't lend me enough avenues of expression.

I withdraw my offer of a duel. I was speaking too hastily. A duo with horns, yes, a duel with guns, no![18]

Bill Evans

Bill Evans (1929–80) was most famous for his brief tenure with Miles Davis, a partnership that produced *Kind of Blue*. He was a stylistic innovator whose Romantic lyricism influenced generations of pianists. His cool approach might appear compatible with Konitz's, and the two had an intermittent partnership. Evans was influenced by Tristano and his disciples, whom he heard "building their lines with a design and general structure that was different from anything I'd ever heard in jazz."[19] Evans was featured on the Konitz-Marsh recordings from 1959 later released as *Live at the Half Note*. Tristano was teaching, and Konitz asked Evans to sit in. In 1977 Konitz and Marsh recorded with him on *Crosscurrents,* and the following year Konitz and Evans played the Nice Festival and toured Europe, with Marc Johnson and Philly Joe Jones. It was a troubled tour:

the pianist was suffering from hepatitis, while Philly Joe Jones on drums was often barnstorming and unsympathetic. Konitz commented that "[Evans] had the tendency to play up on the top of the beat and I have a tendency to try to play in the middle of the beat and sometimes behind. So when people do that I feel like I have to run to keep up because that's not my comfortable feeling. So I was listening to Marc Johnson all the time—he was trying to hold it together."[20]

I just listened again to the playing that Bill did with Warne and me on that date at the Half Note, and it sounded beautiful. But he seemed to be a little uncomfortable, not accompanying me, for example. Listening to the record, I hear that I was sharp to the piano, which was frequently a problem with me.[21] I felt that he probably didn't play behind me for that reason. But they didn't release that record for thirty-seven years, because someone at the controls thought it was not a good representation of Bill Evans, apparently. As is frequently the case, the person who made that decision didn't listen to the music very carefully. It was the same with the Miles Davis *Live at the Plugged Nickel* sessions, released, I think, seventeen years later.[22] Wayne Shorter was fantastic, and the rhythm was great, but it was Miles's date, and he was not in good form those nights.

Though Bill played beautifully at the Half Note, he just doesn't play so much—two or three choruses [on each song]. I think he was intimidated by that situation somehow. He was playing in place of Tristano—very strange, as infrequently as Tristano played, that he would miss a night to teach. But I thought the rhythm section, Jimmy Garrison and Paul Motian, were great, and I thought Warne played especially well those nights.

You worked with Bill Evans on a few occasions.

A very few only. On one occasion, I recall [in 1965], I was supposed to play a few festivals with him, and Niels-Henning Ørsted Pedersen and Alan Dawson. Bill was kind of sick and we didn't really get along too well. So I played in a trio mostly and then we played one tune just to recognize the contract. I played longer solos, since it wasn't the Bill Evans Quartet, and I played very well those nights, I think.

A lot of times I had a problem with his playing. It sounded very tense to me, or else moody in some way. Sometimes when he was trying to swing hard, it wasn't relaxed enough.

That's reckoned to be his main weakness—he's a great ballad player, but wasn't so good on the hard swinging numbers.

At times he was very loose at a faster tempo. He always had great rhythm sections. When Bud Powell swung, it was all there, and Keith Jarrett, and

Tristano—the great players did that. But Bill often sounded forced, the same way that I sound when I'm trying to play a fast tempo and I'm uncomfortable. It feels like I'm hanging on for dear life, sometimes, and that's an emotional and, ultimately, a musical problem.

But it meant that he explored other things deeply.

He played beautifully on ballads, and very personally. He continued to try to play a stronger music, I think, and there were times when it came out more. He had his share of emotional and drug problems and sometimes it was distracting in the music.

Before he started using cocaine, I don't think he had this problem of trying to play very fast, and forced—he did do up-tempo things that were good, like "Minority" on *Everybody Digs Bill Evans,* from 1958.

Well, that's one where I felt this compulsive faster tempo feeling. But I haven't heard it for years, I have to verify that.

But I thought on some of the later stuff he plays very fast, and it's just awful.

What's awful about it? The time-feeling? Because I think that's the basis for anything we enjoy in jazz—how relaxed the rhythmic feeling is.

It wasn't relaxed. Did you find Bill Evans difficult to communicate with musically?

I never really felt like I locked in with him, like I have felt with many piano players. This "locking in" can happen on the spot—a glorious experience— but it usually takes a while getting familiar with each other.

A lot of people would see you as having something in common, because of this idea of the cool approach.

Well, I thought we did. I can usually enjoy listening to Bill, but there's a lot of him that doesn't quite ring bells for me. His playing with Miles was really beautiful. Miles helped guys to play their best.

Saxophonist, clarinettist, and composer **Jimmy Giuffre** (born 1921) is also associated with the cool style. Starting out as a fairly conventional West Coast player, during the 1950s he adopted a more "folksy" style and had a hit with "The Train And The River," featured in the film *Jazz on a Summer's Day.* In the early 1960s he became increasingly associated with the avant-garde, developing a quiet, chamberlike form of free jazz with Paul Bley and Steve Swallow. As a composer he was always innovative, even in his early years. Konitz has had intermittent contact with him throughout his career. *Lee Konitz Meets Jimmy Giuffre* features Giuffre arrangements from the 1950s, and Konitz again recorded with him, together with Paul Bley and guitarist Bill Connors, in 1978.

I thought his music was nice, but "The Train And The River" wasn't my favorite. He was playing in the lower register of the clarinet most of the time. When he was hired to teach at a university, Benny Goodman is meant to have said, "Who's going to teach the upper register?"!

You didn't like the folksy stuff?

I didn't dislike it, though I was listening to Lester Young and Charlie Parker, and I preferred that. But I appreciated the personal intimacy of his music. Jimmy was a beautiful writer and player. He was very affected by Ornette Coleman, and went out for a while, looking for a broader palette to explore.

I always appreciated that he wrote a couple of albums for me. On the saxophone album, Warne Marsh is in the sax section with Ted Brown and Jimmy, and Hal McKusick. He made some very nice arrangements of a couple of my tunes. Then we did some arrangements of standards with six brass and rhythm that were fun.[23]

Jimmy Giuffre was someone who hasn't really got his due.

Well, what is one's due, after all? People have said that about me too, for Christ's sake. We get to play our music, some people love it, we get paid— it's a great life! I got my due, Jimmy got his.

But compared to you he had long periods when he wasn't recording, and didn't seem to be playing much.

I have an impression that he's always been involved in some project—teaching or playing or writing or something. He was a pretty active guy. He's had Parkinson's for some years now, bless his sweet soul.

[We listen to one of Giuffre's later recordings, the title track and "I Can't Get Started" from *Fly Away Little Bird* (Owl, 1992).]

That's pleasant enough. I'm pretty sure it's Steve Swallow, but I can't imagine Paul Bley playing like that.

It is Paul Bley.

It is? There's some nice things there, but I don't particularly love it.

Giuffre doesn't seem to feel like playing. He's kind of standing back and listening. Sounds like both Paul and Steve want to play. I don't know why Jimmy's holding back like that. He's just kind of fetching out the melody without too much conviction. "I Can't Get Started" is one of the traditional pieces that you can dig into, and I miss that.

Still, it can also be very moving to hear someone listening, and not feeling compelled to play nonstop, which seems to be the norm these days.

Steve Lacy (1934–2004) was the pioneer of soprano saxophone in modern jazz. After working in Dixieland ensembles he leaped into the deep end of the 1950s avant-garde with Cecil Taylor. Known for his association with the music of Thelonious Monk, he performed in an immense variety of challenging improvisational contexts. Lacy is a figure whom Konitz much admires. He was another great musical thinker and committed exponent of the process of "real improvisation."

[We listen to "Shuffle Boil" and "Thelonious" from *Live at Unity Temple* (Wobbly Rail).]

Steve took a couple of lessons from me in the fifties. He gets a real soprano sound—I like his clarity. He really plays with a solid, traditional feeling, with a sound that's not forced, just trying to play the music he's hearing at the moment. And of course, playing all by himself keeps it very uncompromising in some way. As soon as you add one more person, you have to start adjusting. I enjoyed that.

I must say that listening to a few minutes of a recording isn't fair to the people. Listening to music is a very fragile situation. A lot of it isn't moving me, and I'm wondering, "Why am I insensitive one time, and receptive the next listen? Am I just getting old and less sensitive?" But when I listen to the things that have already worked for me, to test whether they still work, they always do—Louis, Lester, Bird, Lennie, Warne, Bach, Bartók, Stravinsky.

Chet Baker (1929–88) worked with Gerry Mulligan in his original piano-less quartet from 1952. His quartet recordings for Pacific Jazz, first with Mulligan and then with pianist Russ Freeman, popularized the "cool" style and show great charm and inventiveness. In the course of his drug-ravaged life, Baker's saccharine style evolved into one of great intensity. He and Konitz shared a melodic approach, but like other friends, Konitz experienced the contrast between Baker's warm playing and cold heart.

He was a real improviser. His playing was a direct extension of what he heard. You hear something and you express it with your voice, and then try to transfer it to the instrument. I thought of him as a singing player, and I respected that very much, but he was a little bit too delicate for me at times. **His playing got tougher as he got older.**
Yeah, I think so. *He* got tougher too.
What do you think of his singing?
It was pleasant, but it was never my favorite voice. I heard him scat-singing and that was very musical. I think he could have been in the pop arena, if he had taken care of himself; or, maybe, a more accomplished player.
I get the impression he never practiced.

He had to practice somewhat—you can't play that instrument without doing some kind of warm-up. But he worked all the time—and that's the best kind of practice. He was a full-time minstrel-man.

You worked with Chet Baker and Gerry Mulligan in 1953, and made some recordings.

I was working with Stan Kenton in Hollywood, and Gerry was working at a club with Chet. He invited me to join them, so on the off nights—Mondays—I did. Gerry was very encouraging, and he wrote these very charming arrangements for the three horns. Some very nice pieces resulted. We recorded at the club one evening, and then we went to the home of the bass player Joe Mondragon, and recorded some more tunes. I didn't really want the extended pieces featuring me released—there are some good things in them, in the spirit of "jazz is not the perfect art"—but I loved the organized pieces very much. At the club, Gerry asked me to play a featured tune sometimes, and he and Richard Bock of Pacific Jazz decided to use it on the album. I would have liked to have been able to do that more. It was a very nice combination of instruments, and Gerry was such an ingenious orchestrator—and Chet was the all-American boy!

You liked the freedom of not having a piano—that was quite new then.

Yes—a very musical setup, I think.

Later, in 1974, Chet and I made a record together at Ornette Coleman's loft, with Michael Moore and Beaver Harris. There was a small audience, and I think there's some nice tunes on that record.[24] I remember feeling that Chet was not in very good spirits. I was maybe coming on too strong, frequently playing the first solo after the theme. I do that usually—not with Chet so much, but with technical players like Joe Lovano or Martial Solal. But everybody wants to play first, after the theme, not wanting to stand around for their turn. I remember Joe Lovano got angry with me once, for that.

For a while, Chet and I were looking to see if we could play more permanently together. There was a club across the street from my apartment in New York, Stryker's it was called, and Chet worked there sometimes and I sat in with him. But that plan backfired. He cost me a job at a music school I was teaching at, because he was so crude and rude to the director. I resigned as a result, and that was the end of our partnership. He was really a complex character and I just didn't want to get involved with that. If the music had worked, I would have tried, but it didn't really work anyway.

Have you read James Gavin's new biography of him?

No. I don't think I will. I never read Art Pepper's book either—I prefer to remember their good playing. I hear that Gavin tears him apart, and it's about time, because he could be a mean little motherfucker.

6 ✒ The Art of Improvisation

Konitz is one of the most astute and eloquent commentators on the art of improvisation. In this chapter he states his artistic credo, offering one of the most extended accounts of the practice of improvisation by a jazz musician. Konitz is totally committed to "really improvising," as he puts it, a commitment that he believes few jazz players share. In his daily routine of practicing, he prepares himself "to not be prepared." His distinction between "real improvisers" and what he calls "prepared playing" may come from Tristano, who commented that "I can count on one hand the great improvisers. . . . This kind of improvising you always hear about almost never happens."[1] Konitz contrasts his own intuitive approach with the more prepared playing or "professional performance" of Oscar Peterson or James Moody, who have a routine that wows the audience. He also describes a third approach between prepared playing and intuitive improvisation, the "compositional" approach of Charlie Parker or John Coltrane, which has a more specific vocabulary. Using "compose" in a different sense, he explains how he intends to "really compose, and not just try to perfect what I know," by which he means that he hopes to create an improvisation that stands up to analysis as a piece of music.

Konitz is not denying that Parker and Coltrane are improvising. He is just saying that they adopt a different approach to improvising; with Moody and Peterson he would be more severe. I believe that Konitz's approach, in avoiding licks and focusing on melody, is more purely or more "really" improvisational. These claims must not be overstated, however. The crucial musical issue is not so much whether or not something is composed or invented in the moment, but that it sounds fresh, spontaneous, and natural. Why else would people continue to play classical pieces? This issue is also discussed here.

The present chapter also brings out Konitz's concern with authentic emotional expression and exploration of the music. His stage presentation is resolutely untheatrical, and he rejects "showboating" and emotional display. His improvising practice is in some ways quite austere. In one interview he comments, "As soon as I hear myself playing a familiar melody I take the mouthpiece out of my mouth. I let some measures go by. Improvising means coming in with a completely clean slate from the first note. . . . The most important thing is to get away from fixed functions."[2] In what follows here he is perhaps less severe in rejecting such phrases. He is also concerned to disguise the simple repeating twelve- or thirty-two-bar chorus-structure of the blues or standard song in order to create a unified improvised statement. In an early interview in 1948, Barry Ulanov quotes him as arguing: "Let's say we change the punctuation of the 32-bar structure, like carrying the second eight bars over into the bridge, making our breaks sometime within the second eight and in the middle of the bridge instead of at the conventional points. We re-paragraph the chorus . . . that leads to the next logical point, to continuity and development . . . so that you get not four choruses, but a four-chorus statement." This may be what Konitz does, but he now says, "I've read this three times and it is not making sense to me! I don't think I said that."[3]

In our conversations we approach these difficult issues from various angles, trying to tease out what is distinctive about "real improvisation," the art of "theme and variations," as Konitz calls it. Konitz then discusses composition and the contrast with classical music, how to teach jazz, and the importance of singing for improvisers.

You've said that you thought Charlie Parker was really a "composer." You mean he had a vocabulary of phrases that he'd adapt?
What is a "composer"? One who puts good phrases together. When I came to New York with Claude Thornhill in '48, I went right to Fifty-second Street and listened to Charlie Parker. He sounded great, but very familiar to me, and I was wondering why that was at first. Then I realized he was playing vocabulary that I'd already heard on the records—but it was fantastically played and realized. As a "composer," he conceived of these great phrases, and fit them together in the most logical way, and played them until they came alive—and then decided to depend on what really communicated with his audience.

That approach doesn't appeal to you?
Of course we have to function with a vocabulary in order to speak musically. But because I've had so much experience playing, and had my confidence reinforced and encouraged through doing it, I realized that it's possible to really improvise. And that means going into it with a so-called clean slate. That appeals to me very much. Not to deny the importance of a speaking vocabulary, but having one that's flexible enough so it can be used to reinvent constantly.

Keith Jarrett stated it pretty eloquently on his new record, *Always Let Me Go.*[4] He explained how he had to really withdraw from following through with something that he already knew could work. That's a very important point.

Both Bird and Coltrane had a very prolific vocabulary. It becomes licks and clichés when there's no feeling behind the phrase any more. But you have to have things to play. I have what I think of as a more flexible vocabulary. When I practice and come up with a good combination of notes, I work with it through the keys; different tonalities, rhythmic changes, etc. Then, when I play, that idea inevitably pops up in a most unexpected place.

Bird's phrases were very specific, and it was hard to alter them, for him or [followers such as] Jackie McLean or Sonny Stitt. Mine, and Warne Marsh's, phrases are more like filler material—rhythmic phrases that could be played in many different contexts, connecting one to the other.

I want to try and understand what you're saying here. What exactly is "filler material"?
For example, odd rhythmic phrases—in 5/8, "da-ba-ba-da-ba, da-ba-ba-da-ba," that kind of a feeling, you could play it against any chord at any point. Charlie Parker would play [sings Parker phrase]—that phrase he only did in that key, on that progression. I think Tristano had some specific things that he played against certain chords—I do too, you can't help but find a way of navigating most accessibly through a certain terrain. But as Keith Jarrett suggests, don't look for that security!

Filler material differs from specific material because it can go in any context.
Yes. It's very necessary to connect one phrase to the next.

Charlie Parker did adapt his phrases to different keys and different contexts to some extent, though.
Yes. But the very familiar, great blues phrases that he played, I guess he could play them in F and maybe B-flat also—but I don't think he played them in A or F-sharp. I'm sure he could if he tried, but that means the rhythm section has to do it too!

Red Rodney said that—strange to say—playing with Charlie Parker got a bit predictable. He tried to persuade Parker to play different songs, and in different keys.[5]

[Laughs.] That's like me, I want to do different keys, but I still want to do the tunes that I know. But I opened up the fake book today, trying to find other material to play.

Filler material is an integral part of the line. I'm just thinking of how flexible it can be, compared to a certain phrase that starts at the beginning of a bridge, or progression. I think of my phrases as something that can be used in any place, in any harmonic context. I have no two-bar phrases—I don't have one that I can call on, that will take me through an A minor–D7 into G major.

Conrad Cork said to me that a book of Konitz's cadence phrases would be very short!

Cork is right!

[We listen to Tristano's improvisation on "All The Things You Are," from *Lennie Tristano* (Atlantic)]

Fillers are motifs, in the traditional sense, that you can use as flexibly as this, and develop in different kinds of ways. I'm hearing familiar things here, but he's playing them in a new way. The groups of four eighth notes is one of the traditional ones that Coltrane and everybody's doing—"de-dah-dah-dah"—A-flat, B-flat, C, E-flat; B, C-sharp, D-sharp, F-sharp; E, F-sharp, G-sharp, B; G, A, B, D—and so on.

But Tristano's motifs would fit into more contexts than Parker's.

They're more like a filler than a specific lick—he was more flexible in his use of four eighth notes.

Calling them fillers sounds rather derogatory.

It just means that they're used as part of the development of a line—inserted at any point in a string of notes. At best they're parts of melodic phrases.

It's a matter of connecting one substantial idea with another. In terms of playing a continuous long line, it's not just one major idea, you're going through little patterns that could be called filler material.

You felt that Charlie Parker's motifs would be plugged into very specific places, whereas Tristano's are not so harmonically specific—they fit over many different harmonies, so they can be used more freely.

Yes, that's part of it. I think Lennie was, ultimately, more intuitive than Bird.

Your improvisations also are often based on motifs—so if you're playing a song with a melody that has three quarter notes ascending, you might begin your solo with those notes, then develop it by transposing the motif

to fit other chord changes, changing the rhythm to eighth notes or stretching the melody but retaining its shape, and so on. Are you conscious of that as your main improvising technique?

Yes. I'm very much aware of the developmental possibilities of the notes I choose at the moment. It's what I think of as a note-to-note procedure, rather than a phrase-by-phrase procedure. It's fundamental. It's very essential to me the more I do this.

Do you hear yourself using a phrase you've used before?

Of course! But instead of ignoring it, I try to develop it, maybe, in a different way from last time. Familiar phrases that can be used one way or another are still vital, I think. I've heard very good versions of patterns of licks by some musicians. I try to avoid that myself. But sometimes a sequence is in order.

It's not possible to really improvise when you're playing very fast.

Not for me. The idea of having to "burn," and having to swing hard, and all of those concepts, I'm too old for that—but I was really too old for that when I was twenty, I guess! I tried to play as hard as I could, but obviously I couldn't get up to where the really hard players were. And you know, that's like a contest in some way, to be able to swing as strongly as possible. One of the reasons I wasn't able to do that, is that I didn't know what I was going to play, like they do. You can play as strongly as you want, when you're not thinking about what note to select.

But then who needs to play "strong" all the time? There are many dynamics possible besides strong.

You're very insistent that people shouldn't be playing mechanically. You said that when you started out you were more mechanical, and your ideal has been to eliminate that. Does that mean you should be surprised by what you're playing?

You should be surprised! That's what I love about improvising, that it's full of surprises. Jack Zeigler, the cartoonist, said that "I find that when I'm doodling I am most interested in what surprises me, and that's what I end up using." No surprises, back to the drawing board!

But shouldn't you be hearing in your head what you're going to play—and so not surprised?

When I'm playing, the only thing I hear in my head is the note that I just played; there's no room to hear anything else. I never know what people are talking about, "playing what you hear" as you play. Although in a moment of pause in the play, something can occur—a note, a phrase—to suggest direction.

And yet as you say, you're making a logical construction.

Yes, as a result of all the thinking, and singing, and practicing that I do. And I feel confident to go out and make up a new melody—that, simply put, is my goal. I'm not looking for new rhythms, or world music expressions, which everything seems to be going in the direction of. I'm not looking to be original; just to play as sincerely as possible in the discipline I inherited. I'm still fascinated with this basic discipline of theme and variations.

"Hearing internally" is another way of saying that you're fully conscious of what you're playing, that it's not mechanical. You must at least be *able* to play what you hear. This is a really important training, to be able to hear lines in your head, and play them.

This is important as a meditation technique. You can meditate on a word, and you can meditate on a note, or a series of notes.

But practically, if you're going to be a good improviser, you've got to be able to hear or sing a phrase, and then go to the piano or horn and play it.

Right—but as a practice thing. That's very important I think.

Because another way of playing is to play what's in the fingers, in the muscular memory.

That's when it's mechanical. As Bob Brookmeyer says, there are familiar areas in every instrument that are so much fun you can't stop yourself from using them, but that's a far cry from real improvising.

♪ Interview with Bob Brookmeyer

> **BOB BROOKMEYER,** *born Kansas City in 1929, began his career as a pianist, but specialized in valve trombone and replaced Chet Baker in Gerry Mulligan's piano-less quartet. He worked with Jimmy Giuffre, appearing with him on* Jazz on a Summer's Day *playing "The Train And The River." He is one of jazz's most highly regarded composers and arrangers, notably for the Thad Jones–Mel Lewis Orchestra, and for his own orchestras.*

Lee is one of the finest improvisers I have ever had the joy of hearing and knowing. He is not exactly an extrovert, personally, but it doesn't show in his playing. He is aggressive, passionate, and swinging. His early period should not be the golden mean—listen to him now. The awful label of "cool jazz" has haunted many of us since the fifties. If you played with intelligence, sensitivity, and courage, the label often stuck to you, sometimes accompanied by "West Coast." Lee is a "hot" player now, and has been for most of his life. All emotional jazz *has* to be deeply felt and close to orgasmic. It is one of the bodily thrills that we have in the world.

Improvisation is a mutilated word, since Charlie Parker brought us a codified system of playing. No one could escape Parker, but Tristano's group certainly made a very large dent in accepted wisdom. If one has the talent and desire to speak honestly, the art of improvisation becomes a reality. There are these "vanilla fudge" areas in every instrument that give instant gratification from their historical reference, but some of us try to avoid such cheap thrills in search of some meaning in our work. Lee has his own way, and things like that are a gift from the Music God.[6] 𝄢

Singing will put you more immediately in touch with what you're hearing. It's harder to sing mechanically—at least for a nonsinger.
I think so. But hearing in your inner ear is the first step.[7] Something is popping around inside, and you start humming or singing. Chet Baker sang, or played, what he could hear, and so he sounds like himself in both cases. Singing is the main instrument, there's nowhere to hide.
And when someone else plays a phrase, you've got to be able to play that very phrase, or answer it.
Right. That's an ear-training process. When I played with Brad Mehldau, soon enough he was anticipating what I was playing. He was right there—as I was to him—and sometimes too soon.
How far ahead do you think when you're playing a solo?
Just, ideally, on the note that I'm playing. I know, on some level, where I'm headed in the tune, but it's most important for me to play each note as clearly as I can. I've heard a number of people describe how they think ahead, and kind of aim for a certain note, or a certain place. Hal Galper wrote in his book about looking forward to how you develop the phrase, and how it's going to end. I don't know how that's possible, if you're improvising. But it's different for each player, I'm sure.
What kind of state of mind are you in when you're improvising?
Just trying to be "there," basically, and be interested in what's going on around me, besides my own obligation to play. I want to hear the other players as clearly as possible. It's an almost selfish need—besides the satisfaction of hearing them play, even if it isn't first-rate. If I hear what they're doing, I never run out of things to play, because they'll always feed me something. It's really not possible to run out of something to play if you tune in to the bass drum, the sock cymbal, or the bass notes, or the piano chord. But if 100

percent of my attention is on thinking, "What's the next note?" it's hard to listen to anything else.

How do you get beyond playing things that are in the "muscular memory"—phrases that have been learned and are then unconsciously repeated?

By believing that it's possible to do it, first of all, and wanting to do it. I have complete faith in the spontaneous process. I think most people think that can be very naive, and that you do your improvising at home, and when you go out, you play prepared material, so the paying customers don't get shortchanged. It's the picture I've seen all of my life. And very talented people can do it effectively—the rest sound like hacks, to me.

I need to talk about these things, to clarify whatever's not fully clarified yet.

Obviously, playing mechanically suggests a lack of real connection to what you are doing at the moment. We learn to play through things that feel good at the time of discovery. They go into the "muscular memory" and are recalled as a matter of habit. If I know a pattern on a [chord] progression that feels good at the time of discovery, every time I come to that place I could play that pattern, knowing it works, rather than making a fresh try. Up to a point this is the choice you make with a working vocabulary—how much you want to flex those ideas.

[The saxophonist] James Moody is a very good example of this prepared playing—playing what he knows. I never really enjoyed listening to him that much, though last time I heard him, at a Charlie Parker concert in New York, I was very impressed that this seventy-five-year-old man was playing so well. But what he played is basically very set, it's like he's actually playing exercises sometimes, it's so obvious. He was playing the same things that I've heard him play over and over again. But he does it very well, and with a sense of humor in between; everything is very enjoyable to listen to. He even told a great joke that he's been telling for forty years! That is a true professional performance—not easy, but that's what it is. I'm just trying to clarify the difference between him and Charlie Parker. Charlie had a truly dynamic feeling for the music, and these great phrases that he put together ingeniously. A very special kind of expression only known to a major player.

I don't put that down [what Moody does], I just try to put it in its place. Sonny Stitt was more musical, I think. James Moody tried to get more chromatic in his playing, and he worked out phrases and things, and they always sounded worked out and stuck in, and that's not the point, to me. Sonny managed to integrate all those Charlie Parker phrases, or Lester Young or

Dexter Gordon or whoever he was emulating, and make a musical state-ment. It's some kind of an art form, but not the work of a true adventurous, chance-taking spirit.

James Moody is a hard practicer and he learns his things. And he knows how to deliver his punch when he's out there. This isn't meant to be a criti-cism of *him,* because I respect him for doing what he can do very well. I'm not saying he should be doing something else, I'm just trying to make a point that there is something else to be done, and then you make your choice whether you want to do it. I can't play the way Moody does, playing a finished product, as good as you can come up with, for the paying audi-ence.

Whereas with Charlie Parker, the phrases were similar—the same phrases would recur, but they make a different mosaic each time.

I think the indication of that is on some of the second and third takes on some of the early records. I heard the second take of one of Fats Navarro's solos, and it was pretty much the same.

There are a few versions of "I Remember You" on my *Motion* record with the second drummer, Nick Stabulas. And it sounds entirely different each take.

Is it quite a small number that play the way you do?

I think most people who play professionally want to do a good job, and pre-pare as much as possible to do that. I do in my way, but that's my way of preparation—to not be prepared. And that takes a lot of preparation!

We talk about learning every change that existed, every inversion, every lick. And then when you play you forget about what you practiced and try to really invent something for the moment, according to what the rhythm's playing, according to the acoustics, the audience, how you feel at the moment, and so on. And certainly I don't do that all the time. When I get in trouble, for acoustic reasons, or because it's the wrong band for me, or whatever, I have to rely on what I know more. And that's less satisfying, but necessary, certainly.

I wish, at times, that I could have a readily available vocabulary to use on less inspiring occasions; but it would be too easy to rely on that.

[Drummer] Shelly Manne once joked about someone that "The guy was so hip he never played the same solo once"!

You think that a lot of players are missing out on something, when they go in for prepared playing.

Yes—though they're having a different experience that I'm missing.

No jazz player would say this, but what do you say to someone who asks, "What's the advantage of being spontaneous in the performance, with all

the risks that involves. Why not plan it out in advance?"

I think there's a very obvious energy, let's say, for the players, and the listeners who are tuned in to that kind of thing, that doesn't exist in a prepared delivery. There's something maybe more tentative about it, maybe less strong or whatever, that makes it sound like someone is really reacting to the moment. I presume you know what I'm talking about. It's hard to catch what it really is, but I feel that way is very apparent to people who are doing it, and the people in the audience who can appreciate it.

I recorded with Phil Woods and Enrico Rava at the Umbria Jazz Festival in 2003. Both Phil and Enrico are very fine players. They were playing strong, and definite—which is a result of "knowing" what they are going to play.

So, here comes me—and as soon as I play the first note the whole intensity comes down from a spirited swing to a thoughtful, respectful volume and listening intensity. It's very difficult to start from scratch after all that pizzazz! It's a very welcome dynamic, but a psychological problem for me.

But as you say, if you're coming out with a prepared statement, however energetic it is, there's a definite limit to how far you can react to the moment.

I think so. And that also means that the second time you hear that person, it's not going to be too different from the first time. When you hear Phil Woods, you hear familiar phrases. And Stan Getz was kind of the same. They had a style, very musically worked out, and they found success with that and stuck with it. I think that defines "style" in a way. Doing something that catches on, and repeating it every time, as long as it is effective.

I was surprised when you said that on some classic recordings, you felt the ideas weren't coming.

That can happen at any time, still. That possibility continues to make the process real, in a way, and a never-ending problem in another way that I don't care for. I haven't solved that problem. I'm thankful I can get a good average out of it. It's a matter of slowing down the process with enough space to stay relaxed. Not getting tense and breathing in a relaxed way are the keys to the good ideas department.

As improvising instrumentalists, composing as we press the keys, we have the desire and obligation to play as logical, well-structured, great-sounding, rhythmically loose, accurate, and meaningful stream of notes as possible, that add up to a valid creation. But I commit many errors along the way, and thankfully, jazz is not a perfect art! As has been said, "An improviser needs the anxiety of imminent failure."

Have you ever heard something that you thought was really spontaneous

and improvised, and then found out that it was worked out beforehand? Or could you always really tell?[8]

Sometimes I'm not sure, actually. When it's done as ingeniously as Warne [Marsh] did it, sometimes, it sounds like he wrote it out—amazing.[9] He had access to his material in a most spontaneous way.

So you mean, when you heard him, you thought, "How could someone do that spontaneously?"

Yes, really. It's just so intricate, so well taken care of in the detail. Warne was a true musician, to the core. A rare bird!

Phrase and Rhythm

Clare Fischer sent me a transcription of a solo I played with Gerry Mulligan on "Lover Man" in the fifties, and it looked like the most complicated thing, with groups of 9's and groups of 11's and 7's and all kinds of odd things that I hadn't intended to play.[10] I was just playing a little bit behind the beat, and he was hearing it as precisely, in relation to the beat, as possible. Usually they just put a sign that says, "Lay back a little bit." That simplifies it.

It was a very literal transcription. I was very impressed by that, and a little intimidated by it, that he was so technically aware.

It sounds like a transcription that would enable a classical musician to play the solo—making explicit what a jazz player would do intuitively.

Well, I think he thought I was really trying to do those things. Because that was one of the things that Tristano was trying to convey to us—employing odd groupings to enrich the rhythms of the line. But I wasn't too precise with those ideas.

Was Clare Fischer taught by Tristano?

Not personally, I think, but through the records he was very much influenced by him.

He's a very interesting player, and a marvelous writer. I worked with him once in the sixties, at Shelly's Manne-Hole. We didn't relate too well, so we didn't play together again. He's a fantastic musician, writer, and pianist who basically does commercial work for Prince and pop people, and makes money. But when he does a musical project it's good. I have a great love for a lot of the things he's done. In the early days he was playing alto, a bit influenced by me, I'm told.

But to return to rhythmic structure—Safford Chamberlain's biography quotes a pianist who worked with Marsh in the 50s saying that "Warne tried his whole life to demolish bar lines."

He succeeded very well. He had a great feeling for starting and finishing a phrase anywhere in the bar. Definitely a development after Bird.

That was part of the fun of playing around in the structure like that—to be able to start and stop where you want, without being inhibited by the basic structure.

It means things like starting a phrase on 2, or 3½?

If this is the beat—"1, 2, 3, 4"—and you go "do de dah do de . . . ," that 5/8 rhythm can occur in different places in the bar, five eighth notes imposed over 4/4 time. That's one way of saying it. These are the kinds of rhythmic exercises that you can do to free up the bar lines.

Warne kept developing in that direction. I've gone backwards, in a way, to simplify. I have been preoccupied with making my playing—notes, rhythms, sound, etc.—as clear, to me, as possible, which is very, very demanding. Simplifying can help that process. Warne got amazingly complicated. It was right on, swinging, and it had all those ingredients.

Do you feel when you're playing a solo, you want to try and avoid the idea of "This is thirty-two bars being repeated"—you want to disguise the chorus structure as well, to avoid the impression of a repeating set of chords?

That's the name of the game, I think. To use this very obvious structure, and make it less obvious in some way—just in terms of an ongoing composition that is more or less seamless, so that you're not pointing out the A section and the B section so specifically. I think that would be one ideal. Yet someone who listens to the music should be aware of the structure.

This is part of a reply to the classical critics who object to the simple structures of the music.

Well, it's always a challenge to revisit those same simple structures, and complicate them a bit.

I'm sitting by an open window as I think about these questions, and the sun is coming in. I'm enjoying the breeze and the antiwar demonstrators [in Cologne] and everything, just waiting for some philosophical revelations.

Well, when we were talking about being cerebral and intuitive, that was philosophical.

I'm talking about life philosophy.

I just read, on my wife's recommendation, a chapter by Schopenhauer, and he talks about the different arts. The section on music is *very* interesting—very complicated, and I have to read it a second time today. I don't know if he was a musician, but he sounds like he was; it's really very profound. Wasn't his philosophy very negative?

Yes, he was a pessimist. He believed that there was a lot of agony in the

world, and that the amount of it always remained constant—it just got distributed differently. [Konitz laughs.] He really elevated music above all the arts.

You also showed me something from Heraclitus.

I love this quote: "Everything flows. . . . When I step into the river the second time, neither I nor the river are the same." I wonder if he played an instrument![11]

But I have to have some misgivings about my lack of philosophical awareness. I hear some of these people—Keith Jarrett and Brad Mehldau—talking about some heavy kind of stuff.

Well, everyone I've shown this manuscript to has recognized that you're a deep thinker yourself.

I imagine most of those people are just happy that I finally talked in public a little bit!

I was with a piano player that I work with in Germany, Frank Wunsch. We played a gig and afterwards we were talking, and he said, "You're the only musician I know that wants to talk about the music!"

But you must have mixed feelings about talking about your work.

I do. I don't like to do that before I play, I ask if we could do it after the concert. If it helps a young person to get an insight, it's good.

Talking about your playing is exposing you in a way.

But if I say that I don't know anything about what I'm doing, that's as exposing as you can get! And I do know *something* about what I'm doing. I wish that Lester Young had talked more, and Bird when we hung out on that Stan Kenton tour. We did not talk about music much—very strange.

❧ Interview with Rufus Reid

RUFUS REID *is a bassist, composer, and educator, author of* The Evolving Bassist *(1974), which has become the standard text. Born 1944 in Atlanta, Georgia, he began playing trumpet, and switched to bass while in the U.S. Air Force. He studied music in Seattle and Chicago, and worked with Sonny Stitt, James Moody, Dizzy Gillespie, and Kenny Dorham. In the 1970s he toured with Bobby Hutcherson, Harold Land, and Freddie Hubbard, and after moving to New York, worked with Thad Jones and Mel Lewis, and J. J. Johnson. His recordings with Konitz include* Figure and Spirit *and* Ideal Scene.

I worked with Lee at least once a year at the Jazz Showcase in Chicago, before I moved to New York in 1976. He's been one of my regular "clients" as a freelance musician. In 1985, Harold Danko, Al Harewood, and I went to Japan in a group with Lee, and worked on a lot of new material. But the Japanese just wanted him to play the things he'd made popular. At that time—I don't know about now—the Japanese were the second-largest producers and consumers of the music. But there was never enough work to really establish that group, and I was disappointed about that, because on that trip we were really excited about the music— it was strong, it was new music, and yet it was still "Lee."

I played with him last year, and I'm going to play with him next month, here in New York. It's very gratifying, and a challenge at the same time. I call Lee a "melody maker"—it just flows, he really understands the sounds of these songs. As a bass player you're not relegated to the "basement" with him. We get our material from one another, and that's what real jazz is—what you hear is what's happening right now. In many situations, you can almost "phone in" your part, but not with Lee.

When I work with James Moody, he isn't an "automatic pilot" pre-pared player. Maybe at one time he had been, I don't really know, though because of his wealth of experience he's got a core that you've heard before at one time or another. It depends on the surroundings, of course. If you're playing with people that really don't get out of the box, you can't get out of it either. But Lee is consciously more in the moment. He has his "Lee-isms," which is where he gets his voice, but he really keeps the clichés at bay. He's been very adamant about not playing "verbatim."[12] 🔾

The Focus on Melody

You said in your interview with David Kastin on learning to improvise [see below] that "first and foremost you have to adhere to the song for a much, much longer period of time. You have to find out the *meaning* of embellishment before going on to try to create new melodies."
Getting a good melody to swing loosely with a beautiful sound is no easy thing to do. Then, you slowly add and subtract to keep it loose and beauti-ful. It's a very gradual process. I tried to break it down into small steps, so that people could measure their progress. The novice should be trying, in some way, to create original melodies; but they have to ease into this disci-

pline, of playing a theme and variations in the traditional way, and play on a level in which they can get all the moving parts into sync. It's hard as hell to do that in reality. I'm trying to find out how you can work at that at home, to build up the belief that it really is possible to improvise. Tristano suggested knowing the song as thoroughly as possible, but he never went into those details, that I can recall. He encouraged his students to play in all keys, and so on, but never talked about this step-by-step development.

But the specific examples in that article [of mine] are much too complicated.[13]

When you learn a new song, do you start out by sticking fairly close to the melody at first, as you advise students to do, and then gradually make more variations?

The first improvising step as I understand it is stretching the rhythm, and the expression of the melody notes. So before adding anything, I play the song. If I can't play that melody as if I just made it up, I need to work on it until I can. Change the key, or the tempo, and make it sound like real music, and not just some way to get into the variations too soon. Unless the basic groundwork—melody—is strong, the variations certainly will not be convincing.

There are infinite possibilities, rhythmically, on these melodies, and that's improvising already. Not adding a note. Then I suggest adding a grace note, or something to dress up the melody little by little before making a new melody.

I came to harmony later in my life—I was just interested in melody, because of my single-note instrument. I realized the significance, harmonically, of every note, but I can't hear a chord in my head as I play, unless someone else plays the chord. So I'm certainly more concerned with moving from note to note, and interval to interval.[14]

But too often the melody is thrown away, in order to get into the serious business of pattern-playing.

Those sound like my words! [Laughs.] By now, though, I don't really love to play the melody of "All The Things." I have to find a new way to make it real.

You composed "Thingin'," on the chords of "All The Things You Are," and you play the melody of that.

Sometimes.

When did you write that piece?

Who knows! In the last ten years, I would say. It modifies the chord structure, though, and I like playing on that new chord structure more than the standard one. I've not written anything else on "All the Things," but Warne wrote a great line on it, "Dixie's Dilemma."

Most jazz improvisers improvise on the harmonies, and the melody is almost inconsequential.

A few weeks ago [in 2005] I played in a small town near Munich, in a duo with a fine pianist, Walter Lang, and I took my soprano. And because of my need to be very careful with the pitch on the soprano, I was playing very softly, and very much around the melody. It was such a nice feeling, and I felt that communication with the audience was very special as a result. Usually I start out playing embellishments on a melody that's very familiar to me, but unfortunately a lot of people don't pick up what I'm playing on.

But if someone can play the melody—they've learned it and can play it without any mistakes—what more do they need to do to internalize it?

Well, I'm talking about note-to-note responsibility. Every time I play one of these melodies, I'm trying to tune in to every note—how it feels in itself, and how it connects with the next note, whether I'm tonguing it or legato-ing it or vibrating it. It's a constant challenge, and the more meaningfully it's played, the more meaningful the second chorus of embellishments is.

And you feel that often the melody is not played very meaningfully.

That's the way it feels. It's either done mechanically—it feels like that's the way they always play it, it's what I call a "throw-away"—just to get to the variations, which also sound mechanical . . .

Or it's distorted from the start in an effort to "update" it.

Updating is valid, distortion is not, for me. I think that, no matter how old the tune is, the first step is always to play the melody, "improvising it" so to speak—improvising rhythmically, or timbrally, so it's not mechanical. All the details have to be reviewed.

My approach, when I'm talking to a player who's beginning, is that they shouldn't even think of the chord progressions—just play on the melody for a while, and then add the chord progressions.

If somebody just gives you a set of chord progressions without a melody, could you improvise on this?

I can, but it doesn't really thrill me to see all those fucking chords. It's not the same. It would tend to be up and down more than across.

You've said that "practicing solos is the way to learn, those are our études"—that is, the solos of the great players that you can now often find transcribed.

Practicing solos is an essential step in this process of developing a real conception. I have suggested that to learn a solo from a record you should listen, sing it, play it, write it down, and analyze it. The same should be done for your own solos, so you can confront what you play, study it, and enjoy the process.

¶ Interview with Conrad Cork

CONRAD CORK, *born Birmingham, England, during an air raid in 1940, is an alto saxophonist, bassist, and former Director of Jazz Studies at the Performing Arts Department, De Montfort University, Leicester. He is author of* Harmony with LEGO Bricks, *a guide to jazz improvisation that shows how standard songs are constructed from common components, and so explains how they can be learned in all keys without effort.*

In 1987, Derek Bailey persuaded Lee to play at Company Week. I think Lee must have found it odd, because Derek has this radar in his system which means that every time he feels a jazz phrase coming on, he plays something else. At the end of the week, Lee had a free night, so Derek called Gavin Bryars in Leicester, and asked, "Any chance of a gig? Lee's happy to play with a local rhythm section." Gavin replied that inasmuch as there's a local rhythm section any more, it consists of bass, drums, and alto sax, but Derek thought Lee would be cool with that. Our trio came under the name Nardis. Gavin was already a famous composer—he'd done *Medea* with Robert Wilson, and he was Professor of Music at the then Leicester Polytechnic. Earlier, of course, he'd been in the trio with Derek Bailey and Tony Oxley that helped to launch free improvisation in the UK.

And so Lee came up to Leicester. He gave a master class at the Poly, then came over to The Cooler. He had a one-minute run-through with Gavin and John Runcie [the drummer], and told John straightaway, "You're too loud—play softer." After playing the first number, "Stella By Starlight," with just bass and drums, he beckoned me onstage. I was nervous as hell. About halfway through the first set, he called out, "You— play a ballad!" I'd been very taken with late Art Pepper versions of "Over The Rainbow," where he did a bluesy a cappella introduction, and I did that. As the piece developed, Lee played the most beautiful soprano behind me—it was transcendentally gorgeous. And as the gig continued, Lee's brusqueness disappeared as he became more relaxed with us.

Playing with Lee was the ultimate challenge, and though I knew I was not really up to it, I decided not to have anything preplanned, nor to have any sheet music with me. I got away with it, sort of—my only problem was my fingers not obeying my brain so that a few times, on the tape we made, it sounds like I don't know the heads.

The organizers of the gig had a complete sellout, and because Nardis didn't take a fee, they paid Lee and had five-pound profit—the first profit they'd ever made. In the curry house afterwards, Lee said to me, "If you want some advice, cut out them Art Pepper licks!" The next day I took him to the station, and we had a long talk about learning to improvise. On the platform before the train came in, he told me "The jury is in—studying solos is the best way to learn." In *LEGO Bricks* I'd presented an alternative to the mechanical approach of deriving the improvised line from the harmony rather than the melody of the song—an alternative which Lee had always followed. People would say to me, "Would you really improvise any differently if it was 'Ornithology' rather than 'How High The Moon?' or 'Donna Lee' rather than 'Indiana'?"—which are on the same chords. I'd say, "Listen to what Lee does." If you're any good you play them differently. Lee puts harmony in its place, second to the melody. Learning the common harmonic building-bricks of songs makes the harmony so familiar you don't need to think about it.[15] 🖝

The Group Situation

As a peripatetic improviser, Konitz has played with pickup rhythm sections rather than leading a band, though he has his regular collaborators. But he gains vital inspiration and sustenance from those in the group around him. Here he discusses the process of negotiation and interaction in that situation, and in particular the rhythmic attunement with bass and drums in his favored trio format.

I had a group in the fifties with Ronnie Ball, Peter Ind, and Dick Scott or Jeff Morton. We had some gigs and recordings, George Wein managed me.[16] I worked in his club in Boston, Storyville, a couple of times a year at least. Then he got me something in California and left me there—one gig!

I had a nonet which worked every week in the late seventies. And around 1986 I had a quartet with Harold Danko, and Rufus Reid on bass, and Al Harewood, a fine drummer. We played at Nice, and I thought that was going to open the door to bringing a group in every year. But George Wein, the man in charge, never hired me again after that! It was a fine band, though I guess it didn't impress *him*. But that was really fun, I really felt like a bandleader for a while.

I have thought of myself as a sideman, although I usually stood up front of the rhythm section, and my name was bigger than the others, usually.

Thinking about bass players, do you prefer a bassist like Charlie Haden, with "the sound of the earth" that keeps you anchored, or one like Scott LaFaro who is creating melodies all the time?

It depends. I never played with Scott. I love a variety of players, from Niels-Henning Ørsted Pedersen to much freer kinds of players. Charlie Haden is beautiful to work with. He was not in the best of health when we played with Brad Mehldau; his back was in bad shape. When I listen to him playing with Ornette Coleman and then playing with me it's like night and day. When I was with Charlie and Paul Bley, very rarely did he play in four. The music didn't call for that. But when Charlie would finally open up, it was very nice to hear and feel.

Why is it like night and day?

Because Ornette was playing very fast tempos and a free kind of music—these young guys came on the scene and really made an effect, playing hard. A different music, different age. I was just thrilled when [Charlie] decided to go into four for a couple of choruses, but I don't insist on anything because he always has a nice feeling. On the records with Brad Mehldau, he's even playing in two for Brad, then Brad really burns it up and he comes into four, reluctantly almost.

I love the bass to be as melodic as possible, and I try to get the bassist not to feel obliged to play quarter notes all the time. Gary Peacock is great at that—playing time, and just playing melodically. And so is Marc Johnson.

Because you feel that everyone should be hearing the beat anyway, so it doesn't have to be stated all the time.

To keep the music interesting, you can't just keep plodding away, trying to swing. You must have good melodies and good counterpoint. I prefer going in and out of the swing.

Do you have a problem with bassists who play a lot in the upper register, competing with you?

I don't enjoy competitive music, period! I just have a problem with bassists who are trying to tell me where the quarter note is. This is tempo I'm speaking of, and the intensity with which the tempo is expressed also. They start to play time like they're saying to me, "This is where it is, you gotta play it here." And I say, "Now wait a minute, maybe it's where I'm at, you play it with me." Then it's competitive.

Is that a case of a bassist who doesn't really listen to what *you're* doing?

He might listen, but he's more concerned with my listening to him as the timekeeper, which he is in the traditional function of the rhythm section.

There's a tendency for the bassist to think that his tempo is indisputable. I could do without that stipulation.

It's a matter of negotiation.

Exactly. How do you put that negotiation into music, is the eternal question.

Though I think it's pretty well agreed, in this context, that if the bassist starts the tune, that's where we've got to play it.

Is it an ego thing?

In a way it is, yes. The bassist's job, at its best, is to listen—to interpret what is going on around him, and play as musically and strong as necessary for the given situation. There's a difference between a session with Phil Woods and one with me, for instance—between a more intense time-feeling and one that's more laid-back.

Because bassists are not generally solo instruments, this is how they get their status.

Exactly. That's why I like the bass function loosening up, and playing more melodically, and less quarter notes. Then the tempo is more implied, and I exercise my concept more freely.

But you've also talked about the virtues of a traditional rhythm section [in chapter 3].

I love a rhythm section that's relaxed. Playing with Marc Johnson and Joey Baron is a delight.

But when you talked about Brad Mehldau and Peter Bernstein playing with two other young players, what I took you to mean by a traditional rhythm section was one that did state the beat.

Very definitely, but the solo line takes the lead in determining the rhythmic impetus.

Maybe you'd say that stating the quarter note or not, as Scott La Faro did not feel obliged to, is immaterial provided the players are really listening to each other.

From the few times that I played with Niels-Henning [Ørsted Pedersen], I just had the feeling that he loved to play those quarter notes, and played them as strong as hell, and so musically that they were never offensive to me. I think that's a large part of it—how the feeling of that assertiveness is. You've got to be assertive to be a rhythm section player, by definition, but Niels-Henning listened to the rest of the guys. I'm very sad that he passed away recently.

What other bassists do you like working with?

Steve Swallow I just know as an electric bass player, though he did do some acoustic records. You have to enjoy the sound the man is making—he's a great electric bassist. I made a nice CD with him and Paul Motian.[17] I do miss the sound and the feeling of the upright bass—there's something lacking, in terms of the groundwork of a bass-violin. But he does it as good as you can do it, I think, with that instrument. And there is an advantage, sonically, to the electric bass. I can hear the notes more immediately, and clearer, and I really appreciate that very much. Plus he plays solos in the upper register sometimes that sound like a guitar. Steve pretty much plays what he's familiar with, but he fits into the spirit of what's playing, and he plays very well.

He does play it with quite a light touch.
Yes, and it's beautifully done.

I loved Paul Chambers—a great sound and deep into the time, very loose. But I asked him to do a record date, and he didn't bother to show up—Henry Grimes, fortunately, was available.

Rufus Reid is a delight, Derek Oles is special too, also Dave Holland.

You played quite a lot with Peter Ind in the fifties.
He was a student of Tristano and so I felt an affinity. He is an accomplished recording engineer and he brought his recording equipment to the Half Note, to do the album with Warne and Bill Evans. He also brought it to Pittsburgh to record a session we did at a club there. And he recorded a quartet with himself, Al Levitt, Warne, and myself at Ronnie Scott's for his label Wave, which was very nice. Peter was a fine player. We had many special musical times together.

I don't wonder that I never became a rhythm section player. I can't imagine being as assertive as some of these good drummers and bassists are. I don't have the weight in my horn that a drum and a bass and a piano have. They far outweigh me and I can feel trapped by them. So it becomes a period of adjustment.

It's your style as well. Someone like Michael Brecker can take on a rhythm section.
Yes, exactly. It takes that kind of power to do it. It takes a different sensitivity to do it with my way of playing, I think. Michael Brecker is a great saxophone player. He is very well prepared, but I heard him play an unaccompanied ballad, "Naima," at Carnegie Hall, and it was great, it got a standing ovation—I stood up too. I'd like to get that record—oh man, there's so much to listen to!

Who are your favorite drummers?
Paul Motian is fun to play with always. Great time, and very much a listener. Sometimes he would get a little hokey, and start to make a little noise. But I think that was just a need to show off for a minute. He's a character, but

really a beautiful guy, very loving. He's in his seventies now and he looks like a young man—he *is* a young man!

You have that negotiation of tempo and intensity with the drummer as well as the bassist.

Yes of course. It's even more offensive when the drummer's not right, because he can make so much noise.

Matt Wilson didn't make one sound that went under the heading of noise, to me. Hitting the snare drum in the wrong place—or the bass drum—can sound so loud and unmusical sometimes.

This is not something that's talked about enough—the touch or the tone that a drummer has. Listeners don't think of the drums as a melody instrument.

Yes. The touch or tone can get unmelodic, but Matt Wilson is just melodic from the first beat on. Paul Motian usually is also, and Joey Baron and Jeff Williams. The great players are playing melodies in their solos—Elvin, Max Roach, Roy Haynes, Shelly Manne . . .

¶ Interview with George Schuller

Drummer **GEORGE SCHULLER,** *born 1958, is the son of composer and writer Gunther Schuller, and brother of bassist Ed. He studied at New England Conservatory in Boston, working with Jaki Byard, George Garzone, Jerry Bergonzi, and Ran Blake. In 1994 he moved to New York City, where he worked with Joe Lovano, Mose Allison, Fred Hersch, and Dave Douglas, and with his own bands including Orange Then Blue and Schulldogs.*

I first played with Lee in a trio in 1992, in the Boston area. He loves the freedom of a small group with bass and drums, and for the past year or so my brother Ed and I have been playing with him. We've done two European tours, and four nights at Birdland, New York, in February [2005]. Lee is very particular about how the bass sounds—acoustic versus amplified—so there was a need to compromise, as Eddie is used to plugging into an amp. There was one amazing gig in Switzerland where there was no amp, so Eddie played acoustically and it was great.

Lee is a really good example of someone who plays in front of and behind the changes without losing the form or time—Joe Lovano is another. Lee and I would often end up performing "The Way You Look Tonight" as a duo, and he would be spot on [in keeping to the thirty-two-bar structure]. While there would be this sense of dancing around the changes, he would always stick to the form. He has this uncanny ablility to displace the beat, and in part the harmony, during these long twisting phrases—which makes it sound like he's stretching the form, a trait probably due to his association with the Tristano school.

When we first got together, Lee said, "You know, I'd like to play free." So Eddie and I literally played free—but then we figured out that Lee wasn't so comfortable with that concept. Perhaps especially when he's accompanied by drums, I think he feels that he still has to play some kind of a swinging pulse when—usually alone—he begins a tune. When we first started to play with him we would really try to go against that and float freely behind him as if we were David Izenzon and Charles Moffett [with Ornette Coleman]. At one gig in Paris where Eddie and I played "Cherokee" in an extremely fast double-time loose feel, and Lee played in half time over us, it was one of those rare epiphanies. The changes going by at double speed while Lee played in this slow-motion effect really gave the performance a wild, yet cohesive logic. However, Lee was still search-ing for the comfort zone, so we collectively went back to a steady, more traditional, but loose time feel for the rest of the tour. Maybe he was try-ing to find his own "threshold of freedom" while staying true to the form and harmony of those standard tunes he loves to play.[18] 🖈

I remember playing with Dave Holland and Ed Blackwell, at Karl Berger's Woodstock school, and I had the feeling that they were so on top of the beat, that they were pushing me past where I could really relax. So I could never settle in and be comfortable with them. I've played with Dave with a differ-ent drummer, but those particular two guys gave me that feeling. That's the way they like to play, and I had to get with them. There wasn't time for them to adjust to me.

When you say "on top of the beat," you mean pushing the beat.
Yes. That keeps it very lively, but not easy for me to play with.
So the group could speed up.
That's the tendency a rhythm section has when they're trying to swing. It's been described as a false syncopation, to get the beat way up on the top, to give that kind of friction. Ron Carter and Tony Williams and Herbie Han-cock did that a lot with Wayne Shorter, and it's very effective.
But you like to play behind the beat?
Well, just by definition, for the most part I'm putting the notes together in as spontaneous way as possible, and it's very hard to do that in sync with that beat. When I play a longer phrase, and get down to the bottom, it'll slow

down a little bit. That would be okay if I try to land back into the pocket. But sometimes I just hang on by the shirttails for a while. My intention is to play around the middle of the beat.

So an inexperienced rhythm section might slow down.

That would be their way of going with me. And then they would debate it during the intermission, and say, "Wait a minute, that's not the thing to do." I don't care about the tempo slowing down, if it's still vital in some way. But if the feeling is lost, if it's like a resignation, then that's a problem.

It's not likely to be good, though, if the tempo is slowing down.

It depends. It would generally lose some energy and spirit.

I always respected [bassist] Ray Brown's kind of solid beat. I was scheduled to play with him in Vicenza, Italy, in 2001. But I just had a feeling he wouldn't be sympathetic to my playing—I'd never played with Oscar Peterson, for instance, because I felt that he didn't like me. But still I was looking forward to finally playing with Ray. Unfortunately it didn't work out well.

He likes "hot" players.

Yes, I'm sure.

You've done a lot of duos with pianists. Is that a format you particularly enjoy?

I do enjoy playing in a duet situation. But a bass and drums trio is the best situation for me, because I don't feel like I have to share the solo space so much, and I can stretch more. It's difficult hearing the chords while in motion, sometimes.

Again, I'll try to visualize the situation on stage, with piano, bass, and drums. I'm usually standing with my back to them, which I don't like. And, since I don't use a microphone and monitor most of the time, they can't hear me face to face. Now, I start to play—without a count-off, frequently—and, one by one, they join me . . . such a nice feeling to hear another sympathetic voice—nothing can compare to this process for me.

So, I hear the bass notes, then the piano plays a chord, and I say—in some part of me—"Wow, what was that?" Not enough time to really put a label on it, so I do the best I can to match that sound. Then the drums enter—great to hear! So now I am listening to myself in relation to three other sounds. "What's the pianist doing now? Interesting, but what can I do to correspond to that nice progression . . . No, that didn't really work—and what's that chord? Ah, that was nice! What is the bass doing now, with the drums? How nice—how can I fit that sound?" And it continues in a most fascinating way, sometimes not really adding up to a "complete, well-structured composition"—but the special feeling of doing it as an ensemble, in front of listeners, makes it an extraordinary undertaking, I think.

I don't know the answer to being able, within the standard song format, to function spontaneously with others. In the so-called free format you are more compelled to hear each other and react, and in some ways it's easier. But the same end-product of a good composition is at stake.

If you're playing alone, 100 percent attention is on your creating process, hopefully—when you're in a duo, it's only 50 percent, and 50 percent on the other person, especially if it's a chordal instrument that's so complicated. And my equation goes down to 33.3 percent for a trio, and 25 percent for a quartet. But to get more than a superficial feeling for what the other player is doing, a specific tune-in to the quality of the sounds that he's playing— how do you do it, I ask myself and you? It's almost impossible in motion, and you're supposed to not only hear it, but figure out what the hell it is, and play something that fits it—that's asking an awful lot! That's one of the reasons that I prefer to play without a chordal instrument, but when I do play with it, and the guy is really responding to me, it's an experience that I love. It takes some of the pressure off you, that you could feel in having to deliver a great solo. You're just there in the moment, enjoying.

Last night [in Paris] the piano player was like a Jamey Aebersold record, he was just comping, keeping time—it had little to do with what I was doing. So a couple of times I signaled for him to lay out. I just wanted to play with the bass player because he was listening to me.

So making music in a group is a compromise between focusing on your own line, and hearing what the others are doing.

It's as much a compromise as trying to have a conversation with another person. It's a test of your ability to communicate. In a situation like last night, where the sounds were so unpleasant sometimes, you just want to not even try any more. But it's a gig, and you're obliged to make the best of it. When the guitarist was playing chords, I never had any sensation of them— I couldn't hear them, I wasn't affected by them at all. But in most situations it's possible to speak and be understood to some extent.

I guess the occasions when it doesn't feel like a compromise are when it's inspired.

Yes. That's what we all live for. And it happens more than you'd think.

Do you ever get lost in the changes?

Frequently—especially without a chordal instrument, or if the bass player's really improvising, and not just playing tonics and fifths and whatever. At those times, when I'm cool, I just stop playing, and let him play, and some place he'll give me a clue and I'll come back in. Or else I'll play some and he'll come up to me. I remember playing with a very fine guitar player Ben Monder, and Matt Wilson. I don't know if we decided on tunes ahead of time, or just went into tunes spontaneously, but when we talked about it afterwards, we discovered that very frequently we were playing two different tunes together—and it felt great! Which underlines my feeling that two good strong lines form a counterpoint. It doesn't matter about the key or the chord progression or whatever, especially if the lines are being affected each by each.

Do you prefer playing with a guitarist to a pianist?
Well it depends who it is. But the guitar sound is a little softer, somehow, kind of easier to relate to. The piano would tend to get more complicated, and if the feeling isn't right, it gets in the way. I played a few years ago at a high school in Cologne with [pianist] Frank Wunsch. [The composer] George Crumb was being celebrated at the school, and we were asked to play a couple of pieces at the concert as a duo. Frank started being very busy, and I said, "Give me some space!" He got angry and put his hands on his lap, and after sixteen bars or so I said, "Not so much space!" And they heard me out in the audience and laughed.

Frank is a fine pianist, and we've had some inspired concerts together. He's famous for the waltzes he composes. I call him "the second Johann Strauss"![19]

There are marvelous pianists out there—Brad Mehldau, Enrico Pieranunzi, Franco D'Andrea, Martial Solal, Barry Harris—and many others that I've enjoyed playing with, especially in a duo format.

Martial Solal is totally unique in his accompanying, always reacting. There's nothing more inspiring to me than to hear someone react to something I just did, and to tell me that he's interested. Maybe he doesn't love it, but he's interested. I will respond *immediately*. Whatever I had in mind, I will go in that direction immediately, because he's talking to me.

The independent kind of comping, I hate that! I can do that with Jamey Aebersold records.

This has a bearing on what you were saying about thinking ahead. If you're responding to another player, the amount of thinking ahead has to be limited.
I'm talking about my playing a phrase, and hearing a chord [from the pianist] in the middle of the phrase, or before the phrase even starts, telling me that this is the sound I have to function on. And I say, "Now wait a minute, let me play the phrase, and react to me now. We take turns. I'll be happy to try to react to your little cluster or whatever, but let me play one now. Or, if you don't like what I'm playing, or don't hear what I'm doing, just cool it for a minute." We say "stroll" when we ask the guy to lay out for a little bit. The same for me, ideally: "Nothing to say, don't play!"

❧ Interview with Harold Danko

Pianist **HAROLD DANKO** *worked with Lee Konitz in many varied formats throughout the late 1970s and 1980s. Born in 1947, he graduated from Youngstown State University and performed with the U.S. Army band, then joined Woody Herman. He worked with Chet Baker, Gerry Mulligan, and the Thad Jones–Mel Lewis Orchestra and led his own groups, recording for SteepleChase and Sunnyside labels. The quartet albums he recorded with Konitz,* Ideal Scene *and* The New York Album, *are two of the finest from the saxophonist's later career. He also recorded two duo albums with Konitz,* Wild as Springtime *and* Once upon a Line. *Harold Danko is chair of the Jazz and Contemporary Media Department at Eastman School of Music, Rochester, New York.*

I'd convinced the army that they should release me early, so I could become an apprentice to a woodwind repair man in New York City. That's where I first met Lee, in 1972. I met him again about a year later, when I was working with Chet Baker at Stryker's Pub. Chet had a Tuesday gig, Lee had a Wednesday, and my electric piano was already there, so Lee invited me to play with him. Over time we became a partnership, in a way, touring as a duo, and with pickup rhythm sections. In a duo, I saw my role as supporting and orchestrating Lee's lines, acting as a catalyst, and leaving some space that he could create something with.

Lee used to tape the gig pretty much every night. On the UK tour we did in 1984, we were starting off on a train ride for five hours or so, and Lee was listening to the tape, and quite soon he hands me the earphones and says, "What did you think of your playing last night?" I thought, "Jesus, I have to deal with this on my five-hour train ride!" But it was an honest question, and I knew it had been one of those situations where I was trying to create some heat with a pickup band. Lee explained to me, "I think you were trying to play at an inspirational level of seven, whereas what could have worked with this band was maybe two or three." That was a really wonderful way of analyzing it. The other players were probably sight-reading the music, and possibly felt intimidated by playing with Lee.

When we hooked up with Dave Green and Trevor Tomkins later, that was a nice band. In those situations I was like a musical director. One night I got the drummer to do some accents [in line with the rhythm of] the theme of "Subconscious-Lee," and Lee loved it. He'd never thought of that, because the Tristano thing was that the rhythm section kept time. I told him that his tunes are wonderful rhythmic vehicles, and to hear Trevor Tomkins and these people join in, I think created a more "contemporary" take, and allowed other compositional aspects to come out.

On those train rides, Lee would talk about how he'd never had a band, and I thought, "This is where I come in!" We evolved a lineup that included Rufus Reid or Lisle Atkinson on bass, and sometimes Marc Johnson, with Al Harewood on drums. The advantage of having a working band is a wider repertoire, and of knowing stuff so you feel, "Now we can really get loose." I always wanted to hear Lee playing jazz compositions other than standards—the tunes from the sixties by the writers who were emerging, such as Wayne Shorter. Lee loved to look at these tunes in rehearsals, but we'd get to the gig and he'd say he was more comfortable doing "Stella" in a key I didn't know! It was also my idea to arrange some of his old tunes in new ways, such as "Subconscious-Lee" and "Hi Beck."

Lee's wife Tavia was working hard on booking the gigs, but the band stopped eventually because there wasn't a real three-months-ahead schedule, like there was with Gerry Mulligan or Thad Jones. Other than the New York gigs, there was hardly anything in America. But I'm very proud of what we accomplished. *Ideal Scene* and *New York Album* capture the spirit of that period.[20] 🎵

Solo Playing

I don't do solo concerts too much, but I frequently start a set at a concert with a solo piece. With single-note instruments, we're supposed to do the whole thing by ourselves before we get together with somebody else. So I am used to that independence.

Do you feel you're a pioneer of solo saxophone playing? I can only think of Coleman Hawkins, Sonny Rollins, and Eric Dolphy before you—Braxton's *For Alto* was later, in 1968.

I don't know about "pioneer," but I am one of the many people who have tried it in public. If I were a pianist I think I'd enjoy playing solo recitals.

Playing solo must be particularly demanding.

Well it is, actually, when I think about it. But I do not think about it too much—that's the way I play most of the time when at home.

What made you decide to play a solo blues at the Charlie Parker Memorial Concert in 1965?

That was a tribute to Charlie Parker, and the blues was Bird's world. There were many musicians there, and they were coming on and playing short pieces. I had the choice of a good rhythm section, which I would probably spend my five minutes adjusting to, so I thought I'd just enjoy playing at Carnegie Hall all by myself. I remember walking out and looking up at the top balcony, and resolving to direct my sound to it. It was a very exciting experience for me.

Alone, I could stretch the parameters. I love the challenge of playing a twelve-bar blues. But since I can't identify with the original birth of the blues, it is just a twelve-bar form to play something meaningful on.[21]

The Voice

It's very important to me to sing first and then play with the feeling I get from singing. I think it's strange that musicians don't sing!

Your singing is something that's not been much revealed.

That's a pretty private thing! Every once in a while I burst out.

When I was with Claude Thornhill, I asked John LaPorta to write an arrangement for me singing "Don't Worry About That Mule."

You were *singing* with Claude Thornhill?

I tried it and it didn't work! It didn't fit anything, and I wasn't going to be the novelty singer with the band. He had two singers already, legitimate singers. I don't know what I had in mind. It was a strange occurrence—but everything that happened with that band was very strange!

So when you started out in the forties with these dance bands, you sang the occasional vocal?

Yes, I sang some blues—when I was with Jimmy Dale, I sang "Round The Clock Blues" at the Pershing Ballroom. And I also sang a Billie Eckstine number, with that *basso profundo* sound, more or less!

So you thought you might become a crooner.

Well, I liked the idea, and then I realized that I wasn't that special, and it was distracting from my playing.

When someone's learning to improvise, getting them to sing a line is a way of getting them to avoid doing licks or patterns that fall under the fingers.

Being able to sing what's in your heart is the opportunity to use your natural instrument, before translating to another instrument outside of yourself. Singing can be a nonanalytic process of just enjoying producing a musical sound. Then we choose an instrument to make our sound, because, I guess, we admit that we aren't great singers!

Who are your favorite singers?

Billie Holiday was one of the main ones, of course. I like this description by Cassandra Wilson that I found recently: "She would find the center of the note and weave a small tight circle around it, and shape it like no one else could . . . and weave patterns that give rise to colors and overtones and to a clear emotional message."

I loved Ella [Fitzgerald]. Frank Sinatra was very important to me. He gave a clear reading of the lyrics with a nice swing and a great feeling for the notes and pitch—and he always had a good band playing good arrangements. I've read many things about Frank, and hardly any of them spoke about his musical training. All I got really is that he had perfect pitch—he was a natural! I enjoy Jon Hendricks, and Ray Charles, and Sting. I love to hear great opera singers as well—Renée Fleming, Pavarotti, Domingo, Callas.

Do you have a preference for singers who are really improvising? It seems to me there are those who interpret a lyric, like Billie Holiday, which imposes constraints, and there are the real improvisers, like Betty Carter or Ella Fitzgerald.

I just love Billie Holiday for what she was able to do, in terms of improvising the very melody. But it felt like it was pretty fixed with her; she had an interpretation and did it that way. Ella was capable of singing without the words, and did it well. But I have a problem with that usually, because often the melodies the singers choose aren't as good as the ones played on an instrument. And the choice of scat syllables sometimes sounds kind of cutesy. Betty Carter had a very fine ability, but sometimes she lost me. I never knew exactly what she was doing, making vocalized sounds. Sarah Vaughan could sing like an angel—she should have had a special opera written for her. Sometimes her classical-inspired ability to vibrate, like Billy Eckstine's, was a bit much, and when she did her "shoobie-doobie"'s it was a drag for me.

Sheila Jordan is a singer who's a real improviser. She also studied with Tristano, I believe.

Sheila Jordan is a sweetheart. She's graced us with her thoughtful voice for many years. I know for sure that she and I had Lennie Tristano's blessings. She can make you cry, and then swing like a swinger. She's also dedicated to teaching new swingers to swing better!

Over the years we did some things occasionally. She recorded one tune with me and bassist Harvie Swartz, "You Don't Know What Love Is," on a record with a whole bunch of other people—she told me later that that was one of her favorite recordings of hers.[22] She's been doing some very creative singing, all through these years. She loves the music, though sometimes she gets a little bit schmaltzy for me.

You've got zero tolerance for schmaltz! You said that listening to Johnny Hodges recently, you found him schmaltzy. You even find your own playing schmaltzy at times!

Something like that, yeah! I detect it first of all in myself.

She wants to use her voice as instrument. You can do that and interpret the lyrics, but it's not easy.

I think she's trying to do both. But she is an improviser, and I admire that very much.

It's very hard for jazz singers, though. You're either trapped by the words in some way, or you scat, which has its own problems.

You're "trapped" if you don't love the message. I've really been thinking a lot about that. The lyrics have to mean something in themselves, and to you. "All The Things You Are" has some great poetry, I think, though many of the fine melodies are trapped in mediocre poetry. But Billie Holiday could sing anything with that sound, and it would still be very expressive.

Have you ever taken singing lessons?

A couple along the way. I just enjoy singing with my records of singers, or Jamey Aebersold records, it's nice to get the music warmed up that way.

You've worked with quite a few singers.

Not really. I worked with Chris Connor, Sheila Jordan, Judy Niemack, and Helen Merrill, and with the Italian singer Tiziana Ghiglioni. One of the nicest situations was when I worked with Barbara Casini. She stretches the time the way the great Brazilians can do. Talk about over the bar line—she was all over the place, and it was swinging!

What did you feel about the singers with Stan Kenton when you worked with him?

I was there when Chris Connor was the singer. She never really pulled my heartstrings. She was good though, with an Anita O'Day kind of hipness. A couple of years ago I heard her and she was very soulful. Aging can help!

One night when I was playing with Kenton at the Blue Note in Chicago, I noticed that Rosemary Clooney was sitting in front of the band, and I thought she looked just great. When I looked at her, she smiled. This happened a couple of times and I started to feel good. Then I turned and realized she was actually smiling at Richie Kamuca, who was sitting next to me! They hung out for some time.

What did you make of June Christy?

I did one tour with her. But somehow these singers never were my favorites. Anita O'Day was never really a great favorite of mine, but she was the start of that whole group of big-band jazz singers, with a feeling to swing.

❦ Interview with Sheila Jordan

Born in Detroit in 1928, **SHEILA JORDAN** *became a fan of Charlie Parker while at high school, where she got to know Tommy Flanagan, Kenny Burrell, and Barry Harris. She made her way to New York in pursuit of Parker's music, and eventually sat in with him, and married his piano player, Duke Jordan. She studied with Lennie Tristano. As a vocalist, most of her influences have been instrumentalists rather than singers. She was the first singer to release an album for Blue Note (Portrait of Sheila, 1962), and was featured on George Russell's The Outer View, on a ten-minute version of "You Are My Sunshine." By the late 1970s her uncompromising vocal style had become more recognized, and she recorded albums with pianist Steve Kuhn. After working in a duo with Kuhn's bassist, Harvie Swartz, she now works with bassist Cameron Brown. She has taught vocal classes at City College in New York since 1975.*

After I record something, I get it ready for production—and then I never want to hear it back again! The track I did with Lee is the only one I've ever recorded where I can listen back and say, "You know, that's not so bad."[23]

Bird was my idol. He and Lennie Tristano both told me, "Be yourself." I studied with Lennie for several years—Charlie Mingus took me to him, this was in 1951 or '52, and Max Roach had also told me about him. Mingus admired Tristano very much, but he [Mingus] would get mad at people because of his illness—you never knew whether he was going to love someone or hate them. It just depended on where his head was at that moment. There was just one other singer having lessons from Tristano when I was there. At my first lesson, he asked me to learn this Bird line and I said, "I already know it!" I sang it, so then he said, "How about a Lester Young solo?" I didn't know any, so I had to learn some. It was great for me to find out that what I had been doing from instinct, was the way Lennie started you out. He looked at the structure of the songs and the harmony with the pianists and horn players, but since I didn't play the piano I didn't get into that. Lennie was beautiful with me. I got along with him fine.

On Friday and Saturday nights Lennie used to have sessions in his loft. That's where I first heard Lee. I was just enthralled at the way Lee and Warne Marsh were playing. Lee was so original. He came up when Bird was on the scene, but he never sounded like Bird. He's totally Lee! I hated that expression *cool player*. I don't find Lee "cool." It makes it sound like he has no emotion, and that's bullshit. The Tristano players were right to resent that because they had their own sound and their own feeling. Lee was a very emotional and fiery player. He was hotter than hell—man, this cat's playing his heart out! And Lennie was the first free player I heard, way before Cecil Taylor.

Lennie and his group were so ahead of their time. That's why Bird loved them so much, but they weren't accepted so readily. A lot of times I wondered, "Are they not accepting them because they're white?" I don't mean the black musicians, but the white audiences. The 1960s and 1970s were the worst time for Lee, as they were for me. Now it's happening for Lee, at this age—he's been waiting a long time. We have to do the music whether the people listen to us or not. You work in these little clubs—I used them as a rehearsal spot. But if you keep doing it, eventually people hear it, I think. It's your dedication to the music.[24] 🖝

Composition and Improvisation

Although barriers have been coming down, there's still some mutual incomprehension between composers and improvisers. Many classical composers have been critical of the possibilities of improvisation, objecting, for instance, to the way that jazz musicians work on simple structures. Although many jazz players, from Jelly Roll Morton to Anthony Braxton, have used larger structures, Konitz is typical of most improvisers in rarely addressing such possibilities. Here he responds to these criticisms, and expresses his feelings about composition and Western concert music. His own original compositions are discussed in chapter 10, "The Material."

Even classical composers who appreciate jazz, Mark-Anthony Turnage for instance, are still bothered that most jazz players repeat the same simple structure.
I think they're right, it is simple. Paul Bley has been talking about that, repeatedly playing the same AABA progression. I agree. But I haven't come up with a better idea. And I still find it satisfying doing this. Mark [-Anthony Turnage] is doing very interesting things with his music, no question. But I can only assume that what he likes in jazz is a result of its limited, repetitive structure. Thirty-two bars, sixteen bars, twelve bars—classic forms that offer continuing challenges.

In improvising, there's a virtue in having a simple form: you get more freedom that way.

I'm just amazed that these simple forms can lend themselves to such complex music. But all you have to do is listen to Art Tatum, Lennie Tristano, Charlie Parker, Lester Young, John Coltrane . . .

Like you said, or didn't say, to Barry Ulanov in 1948, you need "not four choruses, but a four-chorus statement." A solo can, maybe ought to be, a through-composed, yet improvised, statement that only happens to have a certain number of choruses.

I probably didn't say it in those words, but I agree. Whatever way the process is verbalized, our intention is to end up with a composition.

The criticism from classical people is based on a misunderstanding.

I don't know that it's a misunderstanding. But what does it mean that they criticize the music intellectually? Let them go out and play one chorus on "All The Things You Are" and then they can talk about it. I would love to have heard Beethoven's variations on that song! They're right, it's a simple form compared to a Beethoven symphony, though Ludwig would have appreciated Jerome Kern, I'm pretty sure. But that's the way we function here.

Sometimes jazz players have been frustrated by this. Charlie Parker wanted lessons from avant-garde composer Edgard Varèse. He said, "I only play one line, I want to be taught to compose." But you've found constant sustenance from this material.

I have. I'm also frustrated that I can't play more than one line, and that I can't orchestrate. But I haven't taken the steps to change that, nor did Charlie Parker. Some people are able to divide their interests, and do a lot of different things in the music. Bird, and Warne and me, and many others spend most of their musical time mastering the instrument they play—it's not easy!

In Montepulciano, Italy, I saw how hard these classical people were working at doing the *same* thing over and over again, playing George Crumb's very complicated compositions—he's very special, and makes unbelievably original-looking scores. The performance was very worthwhile. But I could go in my room, with a beautiful view out of the window, up in the mountains, no straight lines in view, fields of different colors and textures slanting this way and that way, and just improvise. I thought, "Wait a minute, this seems kind of naive after listening to that complicated music of George Crumb." But in my later reflection I realized how grateful I am for the geniuses who compose this wonderful orchestral music. I somehow add that new experience to what is real for me and shouldn't compare our mutual efforts. I felt good that I'd chosen to spend my time improvising, rather than rehearsing some kind of an overture over and over again. But the rule is that since I take those liberties, I have to go as far as I can with it and really compose, and not just try to perfect what I know—an improvisation that really stands up to analysis as a good piece of music.

Classical performances should be spontaneous too.

Well, in April 2005 I played at the Glenn Gould Hall in Toronto. As I listened to a copy of the concert on CD, I was very pleased that it met the standards, pretty well, that he functioned by. Of course Glenn Gould was not a fan of improvised music. But he didn't believe in competitive playing—focusing on the audience and trying to arouse them—or repetitiveness. Every time was supposed to be different, if you can compare a "new" version of a Bach Prelude to a good, fresh variation on a standard pop tune like "Cherokee."

I believe you did study composition, with Hall Overton.

Briefly, yes. Privately, and then he invited me to audit his classes at Juilliard. I ended up going to all four years of his Literature and Material course. It was very interesting to see how he analyzed scores and talked about the music. Sometimes if he had a hard night before, he would do the same lecture for the first year, second year, third year, fourth year, so I got a good review! But that still didn't get me to orchestrate.

You thought it might get you to compose.

I was hoping that it would stimulate that. I mean, I write every day, but just lines, and little harmonies, not orchestration per se. As much as I'm fascinated listening to classical music—I just got another version of Alban Berg's *Kammerkonzert*—I know how much time it takes to sit down and write. I admire the guys that can do that, certainly. But the horn is my way of being able to communicate.

Hall Overton is known in jazz for his Monk orchestrations.

He was really fond of Monk and did some nice things with Monk's tunes. I think Monk enjoyed hanging with Hall and talking about writing. I thought it great that Hall loved the music and helped a lot of players. He used to have a loft in midtown Manhattan where we went to play. Many of the jazz sessions there have been recorded. He also enjoyed improvising—he was a pianist. But he was especially a very fine classical composer, who left us too early.

Like so many talented people who cannot make a living at their chosen activity, he had to teach to add to the week's wages, and he was a great teacher. Jim Hall and Jimmy Raney studied with Hall, and Stan Getz wanted to.

What are your feelings about so-called Third Stream, which mixed classical and jazz procedures?

The idea was fine, but most of the time Third Stream didn't really work for me. I just spent some time with Gunther Schuller [who advocated that approach], in Cologne. He did a beautiful concert of some small-group pieces that he had written over the years.

It was through the Birth of the Cool that you met him.

Yes, and I learned quickly that this was a very well schooled musician, and a brilliant guy. In the later years I heard some of his music, but I never had done any projects with him. I said once, "Listen, Gunther, if you have a few minutes maybe you could write me a little concerto." And he did this [makes gesture signifying "money"].

He was very attracted to the Tristano context, and very much connected with the so-called avant-garde players, such as Ornette Coleman, encouraging that situation. He was very close to Eric Dolphy. And Miles was asking for technical advice—Gunther was a great French horn player.

I did a piece with the Dutch Metropole Orchestra that Bill Holman wrote for me—that might be called Third Stream of the most effective kind, to me, because he was able seamlessly to move in and out of traditional big-band jazz into Bartók, or whatever.

Are there particular things you've got out of listening to classical composers?

Just contact with beautiful expression. When I heard Bartók in 1949 it thrilled me immediately, because of his logic, and the profound feeling of the music. I'm not very analytic in my listening habits. I was introduced to Bartók's music by a friend who played with Lennie; he gave me a tape of the string quartets, and they're very inspiring. Of all the classical music I've listened to over the years Bartók remains a favorite, but there are many composers that I love. I could make a long list starting with Bach up to Lutoslawski, Dutilleux, John Adams, Mark-Anthony Turnage, Thomas Adès.

You played some Bartók pieces on the album *Peacemeal*.

Marshall Brown, the trombone player, was a very clever guy who wrote some pop hits in the early years, but he was basically playing in Dixieland situations—he had a group with Pee Wee Russell. We got together and planned a recording—I suggested the possibility of doing some of these Bartók pieces that I was noodling on the piano with. And he actually went to [Bartók's son] Peter, who was living on West Fifty-second Street at the time, and asked him if he would approve of that—and there was no question about it. Marshall made some clever arrangements of the pieces, and I had transcribed one of my favorite Roy Eldridge solos on "Body And Soul," that he had done with Chu Berry in the early years, and we played that. Dick Katz wrote something nice, and Eddie Gomez and Jack DeJohnette [on bass and drums] were probably asking, "Qu'est-ce que c'est?"

I don't analyze scores too much. I bought a book on Messiaen a few years back because I've been listening a lot to him. I love some of his music very much—his orchestral and organ works are beautiful—but I saw analyses of his rhythms, and I almost closed the book! It was almost bizarrely complicated. Bartók is complicated in a way that I was interested to get into to a degree. I have his scores and I have looked at them, but I haven't really studied them too much.

I'm just happy that I can listen to that music in a nonintellectual, nonanalytic way. I really listen to most music that way. In terms of jazz solos, analysis is hearing as accurately as possible what's being played, and being able to reproduce it. I don't need to look at it and say, "This is a 4th, followed by a 3rd, by a 10th or whatever." In a regular study situation, a student can make a line to show the shape of the solo—that could be very interesting. But I don't seem to need to know any more about that.

I just enjoy, very much, being immersed in the sound and activity of a great orchestra playing brilliantly conceived material. I listen to classical music much more than to jazz. I get much more out of listening than I do visually. Looking at great pictures is a special treat, but for me not as meaningful as the great music.

Konitz the Teacher

Konitz has long had an interest in teaching improvisation, and he developed a step-by-step method for learning to improvise, based on embellishing the melody as opposed to creating new lines on the chord changes from the outset. This approach is closely connected with his melodic as opposed to harmonic conception of improvisation.

Teaching is not my main goal—I hope I can teach through my playing. But I do like teaching very much. I still do some workshops on the road—that's the extent of it and that's the way I like it. I'm not about to dedicate my life to teaching, unless I'm not able to play anymore. But when I needed to make a living, for a time I tried teaching. I was never really interested in teaching the techniques of the saxophone, instead mostly talking about, and trying, musical ideas—to develop a conception for an improviser. Many accomplished players stopped by for a meeting or two, and I tried to point them ι. what I felt was the right direction.

On the Zen principle of not really stating the secrets, I was not a great teacher, I felt. I wanted to give them all the secrets, and somehow that didn't sit right with me. But I have had some people say that they appreciated the few lessons they took. I feel that my main job is to play well, in person and on recordings. Go directly to the music you love and be inspired by it.

You joined the staff at Temple University, Philadelphia, quite briefly.

I was there not very long, some weeks, maybe a semester—sometime in the eighties. The situation was not right for me, or I for it, apparently. But I was able to communicate with some people. I think I can say that I'm not equipped for a school setting—I prefer being in charge.

Bob Wilber, the clarinettist and saxophonist, was an early student of yours.

He just came by a couple of times; he studied with Lennie also. He was very interested in what we were doing. Obviously he made the decision to stay in the past [playing in a traditional/mainstream style], but he's a marvelous player and writer. That is great music from that period, but quite stylized by now.

The British alto player Bruce Turner was a student too.

He would come over on the *Queen Mary*. I saw him a few times—he was a talented man. I tried to update him a little bit. He was really dedicated business-wise to older music, but he was interested in newer techniques. A nice man—I miss him. That was his identification, as a Dixieland/swing player, and I think he did that music pretty well.

Look at Woody Allen, that's the strangest one. He exercises the freedom that he does making his movies, then goes back to New Orleans music on the clarinet. He can do it, and he's pretty serious about it.

Konitz's step-by-step method begins with the song itself, and progresses incrementally through more sophisticated stages of embellishment, gradually displacing the original theme with an entirely new melodic structure. The emphasis is on melody throughout, as opposed to the traditional concern with harmony, in line with the discussion earlier in this chapter. A good statement of Konitz's method is found in an interview with David Kastin in *Down Beat* (December 1985), from which the following is extracted:[25]

In order to play, you need a very solid view of the most basic information: the tune and the harmony (about 10 7th chords); that's all the harmony we're dealing with in the traditional kind of tune playing. I have tried to find a more organic way of developing and using this information so that people don't overshoot the mark when in their enthusiasm they attempt to create new melodies.

The goal of having to unfold a completely new melody on the spot and appraise it as you go, the closer you look at it, can be frightening! So I think that first and foremost you have to adhere to the song for a much, much longer period of time. You have to find out the meaning of embellishment before going on to try to create new melodies. I believe that the security of the song itself can relieve much of the anxiety of jumping into the unknown.

I suggest the kinds of compositional devices that are available: a trill, a passing tone, an appoggiatura that can bridge one melody note to another. The point is, you're still playing the melody, but you're doing something to it now. And there are many levels of this process before you get anywhere near creating new melody material.

Starting out as a performer, I had never explored these ideas enough. There I was just a kid really, playing with all these people [Miles, Tristano, Mulligan]. It was as a result of that experience that I went back to analyze what made me feel off-balance sometimes, like I was overextending myself in some way. Certainly with the proper stimulus you can function for a while, and my spirituality carried me through in many situations. But then I started backtracking, and it was in my own backtracking that it occurred to me that there might be a way of possibly taking some of the mystery out of the process with more knowingness.

I also base my ideas about practice on the playing of tunes and working with embellishment. So if one is given a two-hour period of time to practice, I feel that a student can play tunes for two hours and end up knowing those tunes better and faster than if he warmed-up on scales and arpeggios for an hour-and-half and played tunes for half-an-hour. I think, though, that in a daily practice routine there should be a little section called "go for it!" Even if it's way beyond what you're dealing with, just go for it, anytime you feel like it, and then get back and finish the practice.

I try to address playing the instrument properly, knowing as many of the principles as possible and still being flexible. A player can choose what kind of embouchure is most natural to him, which feels best and helps him produce the sound he wants. But there are some right and wrong ways to do things. For example, there's a right way of touching the reed to produce what is called an "attack"; a large variety of ways from the so called "brush," a light brush of the reed, to staccato, the hardest kind of hit, and all the degrees in between that can be experienced and then brought to the music in a personal way.

Then to play a tune like "All The Things You Are," what you need aside from the basic information I've outlined is an example of someone you admire playing a version of it, and, overall, an intimate familiarity with the great soloists, and an understanding of what a great solo consists of. It's the most logical and sensible thing to do if you want to learn how to hear Charlie Parker's music, duplicate his solos. Listening that closely, you can experience every detail. It's a matter of being able to hear it, duplicate it on your instrument, write it out, experience it and draw your own conclusions.

A Short Lesson from Lee

[At Konitz's apartment in Cologne, AH sings and plays piano on "There Will Never Be Another You"]

It would be very difficult to follow or develop what you're doing at that level, starting out at that very high intensity, for ten choruses or whatever you would do.

I do usually try and start it quite simple, with some simple motif. But too often the faster passages are quite mechanical.

Well, it sounds *very* mechanical. It sounds like you've really worked out something to make an effect, and it's not going to go anyplace. If you want it to go someplace, you have to really simplify quite a bit, I think.

[AH tries again.]

The tempo you're doing it, it sounds like it's prearranged. At a slower tempo you have a better chance to really concentrate on the notes.

I would play with the right hand on its own, because you're setting up an arrangement immediately with the left hand, and that's I think going to suggest playing what you're most familiar with.

I guess I've played it too often as an arrangement.

You have to approach it like a horn player, as a single line, and then add the left hand in as nonarranged a way as possible.

If you don't play the left-hand chords, you've really got to know the harmony. Probably I'm going to get lost if I don't play them.

That would determine what level you're going to improvise at. You have to play simply enough, close enough to the melody to ensure you don't get lost.

To get intimately aware of the melody is really the first thing.

Very much so, it's all based on that. The harmony is after the fact. When I'm working regularly with someone, I deal with the harmony much later in the process—because I'm not that harmonically astute.[26] I do it the way I think about it myself, as more a horizontal phenomenon—even on piano. But the fact that you're singing is great; that's our first instrument.

I guess you'd find the singing was mechanical as well.

Yes—it sounds like you've set up a little arrangement, to perform at your bar or wherever.

It was very dangerous, the amount of anticipation of the beat you did. You were playing a chord, and singing a phrase that was on a different chord progression—it was on the verge of being wrong. Though it is effective the way João Gilberto does it.

To sing in as straightforward a way as possible first of all would be desirable. All the variations and embellishments should come after a strong straight-ahead reading of this material. Swinging, but the very literal material has to be very clearly expressed, I think.

The whole secret to me is just the daily investment in going through those routines, hopefully not mechanical ones—so you build faith in the act of inventing new melodies as you caress the keys.

7 ☙ The 1960s

Motion

The 1960s and 1970s were the most difficult decades in Konitz's career. The market for jazz was shrinking, and opportunities for playing and recording were reduced. In 1961 he left New York, where he and his wife had been living in Tristano's house, for California, but found little work there. He first lived in rural isolation in San Geronimo, north of San Francisco, then moved to Carmel Valley, fifteen miles inland from Monterey. As he told Ira Gitler, "That was purely because I wanted to live there, because I knew there would be no opportunity to work. So that was the best year out there. . . . [I] did odd jobs, like digging gardens and painting bathrooms. Then I got some teaching in San Jose." This was at a music store, and he really became interested in teaching from this time. Konitz did some playing with bassist Peter Ind, who then lived at Big Sur. He commented to Gitler, "I wanted to work outside of music, but it didn't work out," though he denies that in our discussion. To Gitler he added, "Then I talked to Lennie, who was going into the Half Note, so I came to New York."[1] This was in 1964, and Tristano asked him to join him at the Half Note, and also in Toronto with Tristano's group that included Warne Marsh. They recorded live from the club for the unlikely outlet of the Protestant religious TV program *Look Up And Live*.[2] This was the final reunion of the Tristano group—just a quintet, no guitar—and after it Konitz never played with his mentor again.

If the 1960s were lean in terms of playing opportunities, they nonetheless resulted in some of Konitz's most artistically satisfying work. In 1961 he made one of his most famous recordings, *Motion* with Elvin Jones, refuting those who felt that the saxophonist was too "cerebral" to work with such a hot player. Jones was working with Coltrane that week at the Village Gate, but played very sympathetically with Konitz, quieter but very interactively. Themes are stated only sketchily till the final choruses, and Konitz's playing, almost continuously over the length of the original recording, has rightly been described as a "merciless exposure of his creative thinking processes."[3] He was quoted on the original sleeve as saying that the trio format "gives me the most room to go in whichever direction I choose; a chordal instrument is restricting to me." *The Lee Konitz Duets* from 1967 reunited him on one track with Elvin Jones, and also featured valve trombonist Marshall Brown, tenor player Joe Henderson, vibist Karl Berger, pianist Dick Katz, guitarist Jim Hall, and others. On *Peace-meal* from 1969, Konitz interprets compositions by Bartók as well as standards. Like many American players Konitz toured Europe as a single, in 1965–66 and then in the 1970s, though not as frequently as he did later.

In this chapter, after discussing *Motion,* Konitz talks about his attitude toward leaders of the 1960s avant-garde, John Coltrane, Ornette Coleman, Cecil Taylor, and Wayne Shorter.

It seems like for a time in the early 1960s you kind of left music.
No, I just didn't have any work. I had to do something else, just odd jobs around, working in a record store selling my own records sometimes, but that was just for a brief period. I never prepared myself to do other work, so I wasn't about to retire from what I could do. I felt that I needed to work more on my playing, so that I could do a better job when I was asked to play. But there just wasn't much interest in my direction, and I wasn't hustling for work.

The 1960s was probably the hardest period in your career.
I have that impression. And I think the 1970s, too. I think starting in the 1980s, with my getting older and still trying to develop my playing, more of an interest occurred. And then, more opportunities in Europe were possible.

In the beginning, people were calling me, and I thought that was the way it was going to be. Then I stopped getting the calls, and I didn't know quite what to do. I didn't seem to do the business part very well, and nobody was representing me. So I just did whatever I could, getting a few students in, or playing a wedding, or whatever I could do to earn some money.

But you'd just made this great album *Motion,* you'd think there'd be some response to that.
There was, but just among the few who liked the trio. It didn't make the kind of impression that made people want to hire me.

On *Motion* you were partnered by Elvin Jones. On the face of it you'd seem to be very different players.

Originally I had asked Max Roach to do the date, but he was under contract, and suggested Elvin. I didn't know Elvin, and thought from what I'd heard that he was a "wild man." I didn't identify with that. But Elvin is an angel! He turned out to be just a beautiful player, a beautiful man. He was working the night before [at the Village Gate] with Coltrane and two basses or whatever, playing with that kind of intensity. And he came in for the recording session at nine o'clock in the morning, and the first tune was with brushes—it was a take. It was exactly what I wanted to hear—a beautiful time-feeling. He and Sonny [Dallas] locked in immediately, and made a great response to me.

Elvin is a real musician who loves to play with people who are trying to play, whoever they are. We had different conceptions, a difference in the kind of intensity; but swinging together in our individual ways, we both tried to make music as real as we could.

When you say he was a wild man, what do you mean?

I mean I thought of Elvin as a very dynamic, passionate player, and a guy using hard drugs—that was his reputation. But he was beautiful in the situation with me, and I appreciated that.

As I said, a lot of people were surprised that I was able to play with Elvin, because they didn't think I could play with that kind of intensity. And I've shied away from that in many respects, because it's kind of intimidating to have someone back of you, churning up a lot of energy. You've got to match that in some way. A rhythm section will frequently play harder than you're feeling, at that moment. It can stir you up to play with more energy, or run you over with theirs.

So that was special of Elvin Jones—obviously he really listens.

He immediately found the right level to play at, without compromising himself. He played as intensely as the situation called for, and with complete enthusiasm. It was a great surprise, and a pleasure.

You were nervous about it. You were expecting to be overwhelmed, possibly.

Yes, I was a bit anxious. And I'm sure Elvin was, for different reasons. But I knew [bassist] Sonny Dallas, so I thought that he would be a middleman. And it worked out that way. Sonny was very strong, very musical. I think he was one of the few guys who could play with Tristano comfortably. He played pretty much all Tristano's last gigs with him, with Nick Stabulas, frequently. He played with just about everybody.

He could hold his own in that company.

Yes—he was a former football player, and very strong, very street-wise. And he loved Shakespeare—at the drop of a hat, he could go into a lengthy recitation, with this Pittsburgh accent—it was priceless! He is a very special character, a very lovable guy. I'm glad he was there that day.

We also did some sessions with [drummer] Nick Stabulas, a fine player too. I enjoyed those sessions, I think there were two. Thirty-seven years later, they found that music—two more hours of playing with Nick and Sonny—and released a three-CD set.

Then I was released from my contract with Verve. That always seemed interesting to me. Norman Granz, who was responsible for my recording with Verve, was not a fan of mine, but he encouraged me, and even made me a weekly advance, because I was raising a family and could use that money. Maybe Norman was advised that I was trying, and took a chance, though his personal taste was for the older music. I always appreciated that. Then Creed Taylor took over at Verve, and he didn't need me in his roster anymore. I didn't investigate his reasons too much. It was a bit strange to drop me after making a good recording—try to figure!

❧ Interview with Sonny Dallas

SONNY DALLAS, *born Pittsburgh 1931, is a bassist, music therapist, and educator. After moving to New York he worked with Bob Brookmeyer, Bill Evans, Jimmy Giuffre, Jim Hall, and Phil Woods. He was Tristano's regular bass player during the last decade of the pianist's playing career. Despite recent illness, he continues to play in the New York area.*

I call him "Leo." We went in to the session together because at that time we were living in Lennie's house—it was a big, beautiful house; I think it's still there. Charlie Parker told Lennie that he was not happy about being imitated—and one of the first things Lennie laid on Leo was to have his own sound. But Lee could play like Bird. He lived upstairs from me [in Tristano's house] and I would hear him practicing Bird's solos, and it was astonishing, it was like Bird in the next room. And he could imitate Bird's sound—I don't think many people know that. He just used it as a practicing technique.

I was surprised to hear we were doing a session with Elvin Jones, because we had already done two sessions with Nick Stabulas on drums. I'd done a lot of playing with Nick, with Phil Woods and Gene Quill and everybody, but I thought that maybe Leo didn't dig Nick as much as I did. Nick was a wonderful friend of mine, as Leo is of course. I think I misinterpreted that [that Lee didn't dig Stabulas]. I played with "Philly" Joe Jones, too, and I put Nick Stabulas right on the same echelon as any of those guys—so smooth, so hip, and so cool.

I had played with Elvin before, but I don't think Lee had. Not too long ago, Lee was asked whether he was frightened going on that date with Elvin, and he said, "No, I knew Sonny Dallas was there, and he knows like five thousand songs!" Lee is like the Pope playing, with that group. He's the main man! That was his date.

I had played with Warne and Lee, on some session—they seemed to like me. Then at the Composer nightclub, a very hip piano-bar, I think it was on Fifty-sixth or Fifty-seventh Street East, I was working with [pianist] George Wallington—this was around 1959, I think. Lee and Warne were there every night one week, and they took turns in hitting on me about working with Lennie Tristano. I knew that a lot of cats said he's ruthless, and I didn't need that—he'd gone through every bass player in New York, including my favorites, Paul Chambers, Teddy Kotick . . . But they said, "He'll love you, I'm telling you!" I finally accepted the gig, and I was with him ten years! The session at the Half Note [in 1964] appeared as *Continuity*—an excellent record, man. That was a TV show, a Christian program. We played at the Half Note a lot. After the [quintet] broke up, Lennie and I played together—duets, upstairs in his studio, but not in public. He did play solo in public—in Germany he was in some piano thing. When you watch [the Berlin Jazz Piano TV program], when Lennie comes on, he just blows you away. He plays blues like nobody in the world could ever play the blues.

Lennie had not been my inspiration, it was always Bird and Pres. I didn't listen to him as much as I should have, but I sure made up for it later! We used probably every drummer in New York. They would come in and say to Lennie, "How do you want us to play?" And Lennie invariably used to say, "Just swing, man!"[4] 🎔

In 1967 you made a famous album of duets.
The duo album for Milestone was really a special event. I wanted to learn more about direct, one-to-one kind of improvising. Knowing how difficult it could be to make these meetings, I made a list of different players and called them, offering to come to them if they preferred; and many responded. It was so gratifying, I thought it should be recorded, and Orrin Keepnews [the producer] agreed.

You didn't ask Warne Marsh to appear on it?
I think Warne was living in California at the time. We scheduled the different players for half an hour each. So I played a duo with Joe Henderson. Then it was, "Next!"—kinda! Ray Nance played a "free" piece with me on tour, and I couldn't get him to stop—it was real fun. And to play a duo on tenor with Elvin was a bold decision, since I don't play tenor very much. But I really like it, and Elvin sounds great. There were also duos with Jim Hall, Marshall Brown, Dick Katz, Eddie Gomez, Karl Berger. My goodness, what a way to spend an afternoon, and we finished half an hour early! All the guys were in good form, so I enjoyed it very much, and still do.

❡ Interview with Dick Katz

*Pianist **DICK KATZ**, born in Baltimore in 1924, worked a lot with Konitz during the late 1960s and 1970s. He studied with Teddy Wilson and at Manhattan School of Music. In the 1950s he worked with Tony Scott, Kenny Dorham, Ben Webster, Oscar Pettiford, J. J. Johnson, and Kai Winding. In 1966 he began a long association with Roy Eldridge and founded Milestone Records with Orrin Keepnews. He continued freelancing and returned to playing full-time in 1971 with Konitz and Eldridge.*

We first played together back in the late fifties at Café Bohemia. Lee is a constant experimenter, and in that respect he differs from all the other Lennie Tristano disciples. Most people, once they get a style that's solidified, refine it but don't change the settings that much, but Lee is open to any kind of material. He's always been a true improviser. He reminds me of Sonny Rollins in that respect, though their styles are totally different.

The *Duets* album was Lee's idea, and I produced it with Orrin Keepnews's supervision. We prepared that pretty carefully. Lee and I play an original of mine, called "Checkerboard," in conventional AABA form, with a contemporary-sounding line. Then Lee said he'd like to do something completely free—no chords, no melody, let's just play. We realized it wouldn't be fair to have two examples of us together, so we spliced the free thing together with "Checkerboard," and it came out seamless. *Duets* was extremely well received. Dan Morgenstern gave it five stars in *Down Beat,* and said if you only buy one album this year, buy this one!

For *Peacemeal,* Lee wanted to do something with *Mikrokosmos,* the exercises that Bartók wrote for his son. At the time we had a nice group with Marshall Brown, a valve trombone player and arranger, a Boston pedagogue, who was originally a Chicago-style Dixieland musician. We used to call [Lee and Marshall] the odd couple because you couldn't find two more different people on the planet! *Oleo* was meant not to have a drummer, but I wish it had. Lee and I had a gig two nights a week at a little place called Gregory's, on the Upper East Side. They had this spinet piano, and we played in the corner, with Wilbur Little on bass. Samuel Charters—the man who wrote on the blues—recorded us.

Lee always wanted interaction. Tristano loved to interact with the horn players, but not the rhythm section. He just wanted the drummer and the bass player to keep metronomic time, no bombs, no fill-ins, no responding. He went through almost every drummer around. But then I used to play with beboppers like Kenny Dorham and Gigi Gryce, and they just wanted you to lay down the chords in the right place, and hold them up, and swing. Lee likes it open though. We would sometimes have our hearts in our mouths, because he wouldn't necessarily say what he was going to play, he'd just start playing.

He has this gift of taking a melody and abstracting it, turning it inside out and playing fragments. We didn't change the form [of the standard]. But then Lee got really enamored with free playing. Now he plays standards, but in an extremely free way. He's given up pretty much what we used to call swing. In that respect he's like a lot of the younger, cutting-edge musicians such as Brad Mehldau, where the bass and drums mostly don't keep steady time. The listener has to really concentrate to follow where they are in the song.[5] 𝒓

John Coltrane

Coltrane (1926–67) was stylistically opposed to Konitz in almost every way, and his influence on saxophonists has resulted in some of the empty virtuosity that Konitz disdains, even if Coltrane himself was not guilty of that kind of playing. But still Konitz shows an abiding interest in what the saxophonist was attempting.

Coltrane changed the direction of the music, as Bird did, and Ornette—though he was more adventurous than Bird, and willing to change his approach till the end. He also, like Miles, and all great band leaders, chose the right players to join him. He went through the traditional music pretty thoroughly, then went into modal tonalities, and ate that up. My goodness, he was really sensational with Elvin, McCoy, and Garrison. He was always developing some new kind of vocabulary. I'm thinking of his modal playing, how chromatic that became, before *Ascension*—I don't really know that later period that well. Other people—and I've done this too—used to accuse him of practicing on the bandstand. He used to take a phrase and just throw it around in all directions—a form of composing.

I had a problem with that music—so much of the same high-intensity dynamic. If the level of intensity doesn't change, the music can become monotonous—even though it was necessary for John's spiritual release. It's evangelical, if you will—for many, he was the Messiah!

Do you think Coltrane had the compositional approach you described Charlie Parker as having?

I think it was very worked out, basically. Certainly there was a large, readily available vocabulary, but a great feeling to improvise with the material at hand. He was an inspiration to many young players, for good and not so good.

I didn't really know him. Just to say hello. As I've mentioned, I wasn't hanging out a lot and I didn't get to meet a lot of guys and know them personally, regrettably. The best time for hanging out is on the road; and even then I didn't really party much.

You've said harsh things about the influence of John Coltrane in terms of learning patterns, to create a high level of excitement at rapid tempos.

Well, it's against my temperament to do it. And if I hear it done very well like when Coltrane was really *on,* it's very special, and I can enjoy that very much. But to hear other people do it in that style, or play Charlie Parker's style, I don't enjoy that much. Where is the real person? Still, I heard that after someone accused him of playing like Bird, Gene Quill held out his horn and said, "Here, you play like Bird!"

Recently I heard Branford Marsalis's group, with Joey Calderazzo, Eric Revis, and Jeff "Tain" Watts, pay tribute to Coltrane by playing their version of *A Love Supreme.*[6] I think they do a great job of paying homage to John and his group.

Coltrane influenced a lot of players. He changed Art Pepper in midcareer.

That was tragic, that influence, I think. I was just listening to a set of five albums of Art Pepper's, and one I made with him was the fifth in the package. Art was not in top form. I was feeling good, but obviously there was trouble there. On the record he made with Warne Marsh years earlier, he played beautifully. Warne really got to him, like he got to me. I never heard the records he made with Miles's rhythm section; they must have been more straight-ahead. I thought his comeback was a disappointment, from the expressionistic stuff I heard. I remember sitting in the Vanguard with Bob Mover—a saxophonist who played with Chet Baker a lot—and we just looked at each other in disbelief, at how ineffective Art was playing with Elvin Jones.

He was getting a lot of attention at that point.

He was a charismatic figure, as well as being a fine saxophone player early on. I appreciated that he tried to make a change. It's very important in the development of a player to take some chances like that. But you've got to make the change definitive. He only went part of the way; his harmonic ability was limited.

Bud Shank heard Phil Woods, and started to blow "hot." I think they were tired of being part of the cool school—they graduated maybe! I've tried to play hot when it was time to play hot. But I think maybe they sacrificed some quality along the way.

You have played "Giant Steps."

By now, people are more used to it, but at that time it was a very difficult étude. I actually played a version of that with my nine-piece band on *Yes, Yes Nonet.* Ronnie Cuber, the baritone player, had a solo, and he just flew through the changes. Then it was my turn and I stumbled through them. So I thought about it at home a little bit, and came back the next day and did another take. And I managed to get through. I just don't enjoy running changes that much.

Why is it difficult?

Because each change is two beats long, and the chords are going by really fast. It's an unusual sequence of chords, two beats per chord, in the first eight bars, in a major-dominant sequence moving a major 3rd—as opposed to the usual II-V-I sequence. I played it in 3/4 time once and just that extra beat helped a lot.

You have tried to play modal pieces, like "Candlelight Shadows" with Harold Danko. How would you approach those?

Well, basically trying to express the tonality to begin with, to establish that as clearly as possible. Then, I think, the challenge is to play chromatically on top of that basic tonality—not losing the tonic somehow, returning enough to establish it. So it starts modally, and can develop intervallicly and return eventually to resolve to the basic mode.

Are you imposing chord changes over the modal system? It's said that Cannonball Adderley played II-V-I's over the modes of *Kind of Blue,* and many jazz players seem to have played modally in this "impure" way.

Modal playing is a very challenging premise. An opportunity to really get into a groove, and stay there, without the underlying melody and harmonies of a conventional tune guiding you. I'm not a "groove" player—obviously!—and have accepted the restrictions of standard tunes for my way. But hearing Trane and a few others groove is a special experience. He and McCoy really stretched out chromatically. I don't know about "impure"— maybe for a church service!

Ornette Coleman

Ornette Coleman and Lee Konitz are the two great post-Parker stylists on alto saxophone, and both had an immense influence on the development of free jazz and free improvisation, though Konitz's is less recognized (see chap. 10). Coleman was born in Fort Worth, Texas, in 1930. In the late 1950s and early 1960s he overturned modern jazz with his freedom principle of "time no changes"—playing in a groove but dispensing with traditional song structure and chord changes. This revolution posed a challenge to the discipline that Konitz had cultivated.

When he first arrived in New York [in 1959], Lennie and I went together to the Five Spot one night to check him out. Ornette was the talk of the town— good talk and bad talk! I think Lennie appreciated in some way what Ornette was doing. I didn't get the message at first; I resented the fact that he was leaving out all these details that I spent my life being concerned with, every day! I was trying to learn the rules, and he came along and just changed that all up. I thought, "Wait a minute, is that sporting?" But there was another message that he had. And years later I finally acknowledged him for what he could do, which is a very special kind of music.

You didn't appreciate the track I played you from *Sound Museum* with Geri Allen, Charnett Moffett, and Denardo Coleman.[7]

I need to hear that again. But that's not what was happening with Billy Higgins and Charlie Haden. I had a problem identifying with Ornette's sound and powerful projection. But now I just hear a totality, and it's a very unique, identifiable, passionate sound.

That's usually his identifying quality, being intuitive. He's playing without changes, without a form. He can't very well plan a solo in that framework, I don't think.

He should be up there with your heroes, the really spontaneous players.

Yes. It took me a while [to realize that] because he was ignoring the tradition that I was obliged to. But Ornette is an original—that's what we all strive for. Ornette is a beautiful guy who turned a liability into an asset. He did it his way, as Frankie said.

[We listen to "Mary Hartman, Mary Hartman" from Ornette Coleman/ Charlie Haden *Soapsuds, Soapsuds* (Verve/Harmolodic, 1978).]

He uses a lot of vibrato on those ballads on tenor. I'm not sure now how much he uses on the alto, when he's playing "Lonely Woman" or something like that. But he sounds very comfortable with the instrument, and Charlie sounds beautiful—that's a real duo sound!

What exactly was the problem you had with Ornette's playing?
The problem was that he wasn't playing tunes, that we were all dedicating our lives to learning how to play. He bypassed traditional harmony, and his sound—the "hammering it in" feeling, the shouting bluesy tonalities— wasn't my favorite. But then over the years, you get used to these things if you hear them enough, and start to accept them as realities. He had a great rhythm section all the time, and that was pulling me in, I think. Charlie Haden and Billy Higgins or Ed Blackwell—especially Billy Higgins, for me.

Did his playing just seem incoherent at first?
Not so much incoherent, just different. I had questions about what he was doing. I thought he was avoiding his responsibility to get a well-balanced musical perspective. The ideal would be to learn each step of the history of the music, leading up to your personal version. But he followed a kind of tangential development, which is real also. He still can't play a standard— which is a specific discipline that he abandoned. He did something much more dynamic than playing "All The Things You Are."

When I went to hear him with Lennie, at the Five Spot, he asked me to sit in. And I never felt free to do that. I even made some stupid remark like, "What would we play?" We would have played free. It would probably have been very exciting, but I was not ready to confront his way.

Many years later, in 1998, Ornette invited me to play with him [and Haden and Higgins] at Umbria Jazz in Perugia. We rehearsed three days in New York, at his studio in Harlem on 125th Street—a beautiful studio. He gave me about ten tunes, all new themes of his—one of which he wrote specially for me, he said, a ballad. We went through them one by one. I was following the way Ornette was phrasing—he didn't play them like they were written. The notes were there but the rhythms weren't accurate. So we went over them a number of times. During a break I said I wasn't feeling like I fit too well, but he patted me on the shoulder and said, "Nah, you're doing fine"—and Charlie said, "You're doing fine," and Billy said, "You're doing fine"! Ornette recorded the rehearsal, and gave me a CD to take home—and I rewrote the tunes so I could play them like him.

So we came back the second day and I said, "How about if after we play the theme, I play the solo?" Because by the time we'd played his theme and he'd played his solo for five minutes, I was just sitting there feeling way out of place—and then it was my turn, and where am I coming from? So he said, "Fine, whatever," very gracious. He's a very nice guy. So I felt a little better. The third day, he came in all excited, saying he had written harmonies for the tunes. I looked at them, and there were a million harmonies, every beat a different chord! I asked Charlie [Haden] on the side, "Are you going to play these harmonies?" And he said "I don't know." So we just went ahead and improvised freely on the theme.

Well, we got to the Umbria Festival and played a nice set, and I felt pretty good actually—with all my kvetching at the rehearsals, I felt more comfortable than Ornette did! I played the whole set with him—he was very generous. Then for an encore we played "All The Things You Are" duo, a strange version you never heard before, or after!

So how did you improvise on his themes?
Just trying to play a variation, on an unfamiliar theme, with no set harmonies, which is what I'm really accustomed to. But I felt like I was getting used to them after three days of rehearsing, and felt good.

I love Ornette as a very creative and friendly man, and I thank him for his kind words about me—though I still don't understand harmolodics!

◥ Interview with Ornette Coleman

ORNETTE COLEMAN *was very happy to talk about Konitz, after an enthralling concert he gave in Newcastle, England, in 2005 with his son Denardo on drums and two bassists, Greg Cohen and Tony Falanga—a performance which showed that at age 75 Ornette is still in top form, and pushing boundaries.*

Well, I tell you a story that breaks my heart [he means—finds very touching]. I had a job in Italy a few years ago. And I always loved Lee Konitz's work, so I called him up and said, "Lee, I'm playing in Perugia [at the Umbria Festival], and I'd like for you to be my guest." He said "All right," so I go and I write all the music, and I give it to the musicians.

So when we go to Perugia, I play my set, and I call him up. I said, "Lee, why don't you come now and play, and you be the leader and I'll be the sideman." And he said "OK," and he came up, and he played and I played with him. We played "All The Things You Are"—I don't think he ever heard me play a standard! And I said, "I really enjoyed it." And you know what, [afterward] he wrote me the most beautiful letter.

I always loved his playing. He played a fantastic solo on "Disc Jockey Jump"—I can't remember who he was with, I think that's what it was, forty years or more ago.[8] I didn't have a horn then, I was just listening to saxophone players.

He thought it was going to be difficult, playing with you.
So I started playing standards.

What did you admire about his playing?
When I was a teenager, he was playing not like Charlie Parker, but like himself. His own ideas—that what I like. I always like ideas, more than styles. . . . I think music itself is an idea. It's not a style, it's not a race, it's just an idea. And everybody has ideas. That's why music is so free for people to cherish, and so open—because it's how the idea is affecting you, and how you express what it means to you, regardless of what the style is.

So that was an example for you, of someone who was independent.
Yeah, that's right. I always thought that he wasn't getting the attention that he should have. I don't know why—it's not his playing. And I just wanted to support him. And I'm happy that he responded to it in the way he did.

You had a struggle to get your music accepted.
I would say that.

Were you always confident it would be accepted?
No, I never thought about it being accepted. I was thinking about writing music that the person that liked music would enjoy. I wasn't trying to write music to make money, I was trying to write music to have some meaning to people.

But still you wanted it to get out, to be heard.
Yes, I wanted it to be heard. But I was having musicians that time telling me, "Oh, you can't play like that."

Lee said to me that he admires you very much—but he didn't understand your playing at first, because you were upsetting all the rules that he'd learned, and was that sporting? Then later he understood.
Believe me, we are very good friends, and whatever he says, that's fine![9]

Cecil Taylor

The third of the great founding figures of free jazz after Coleman and Coltrane, pianist Cecil Taylor (born 1930) is the one that Konitz, and many other listeners, finds most problematic.

Cecil has always been very friendly to me. He was in communication with Tristano at some point, so I think he knew my playing to some extent. But I've never played with him.

I was very critical of what he was doing, at the beginning—though unknown to me, he was inspired by Tristano. After hearing him one night at the Village Vanguard, playing nonstop for an hour, I had a headache and slipped out quietly. But some months later I was at a session in Liège, Belgium, and everybody had left, and I sat at the piano and started to play "tactilely." And ever since then I've enjoyed just playing by touch, rhythmically, without looking at the keyboard, most of the time, and enjoying the surprise of the sound that comes out.

Would you like to play with him?
I'd love to try.

I haven't heard him for some years now. The few times we have spoken have been very relaxed. He's a very unique character, and found a unique way to put the notes together.

Have you listened to the set on Codanza again?[10]
Well, I'm having a problem with that. When I want to listen to something, that's not it, and when I do listen to it, I take it off pretty soon.

You still sometimes feel that each CD is "an hour of bedlam," as you put it?
I really have to make an effort, because it's very free playing. Thankfully, there's not a saxophone there—it's a trio with the very fine William Parker and Tony Oxley—so I don't have that offensive sound. But it keeps churning and never seems to settle anyplace. It's fascinating, for a while, but I crave some form, and more melodic interplay, in a traditional way. Sometimes it's very exciting, and sometimes too complex for me. Is this great composition, spontaneously done? I can't stay with it for long enough to find out. I will try again tonight!

I share your view. I find it very hard to listen to, and have to be in a particular mood.
Yes, exactly. And I haven't found that mood lately.

Is that a problem with you, or with him?

That's to be debated! But he's playing what he believes in, and enjoying it. We should thank him for devoting a long life to his belief.

Wayne Shorter

One of Konitz's great musical heroes is saxophonist Wayne Shorter (born 1933), both in his classic 1960s recordings with Miles Davis's quintet, and recently with his quartet of Danilo Perez, John Patitucci, and Brian Blade.

I heard Wayne recently here at the Philharmonie in Cologne—and I got a tape in the mail today from a concert he did in Glasgow. I also have one that he did in Hungary, and his record *Alegria*.[11]

Afterwards, I went down to say Hi. I've never had a chance to really speak with Wayne. John Patitucci [Shorter's bassist] said, "Look who's here!" and Wayne got up and we hugged and it was really great. I was very pleased to hear the group and pay my respects.

He's playing superbly now—one of the great jazz comebacks, I'd say.

He is superb, and the trio is great. Danilo Perez is very interesting—it almost sounds like his group frequently, but it works. Wayne is listening, and comes in when it's time.

Wayne has a reputation for being "Mr. Weird."

Well, he was very loquacious, talking about living in Florida, and one thing and another. He said, "I'm tired of music that sounds too much like music!" I guess he meant that as a kind of a rationale for playing free, and distorted, and things like that—it's the "ugly beauty" that Monk was referring to. On *Alegria* he plays that beautiful Villa-Lobos theme and then growls and makes funny sounds. Why, I wonder? I'd rather hear him play some variations on that beautiful melody.

I love his playing when he's really playing.

Does he play variations, though, some of the time?

I've never heard him play a traditional tune, with fairly straightforward changes, that effectively. But what he does at the Plugged Nickel is a work of genius. Nobody has played a more interesting set of variations on a standard, totally free of all the obligations of the harmonies, than he did there—just playing on the form. Sometimes Ron Carter was playing the changes, but Wayne was just playing a chromatically based series of melodies. On "Stella By Starlight," he went into the melody after a number of brilliant choruses and it knocked me out. But I've never really heard him play the levels below that, like Warne did.

The economy of his playing is so great. [In Cologne] Danilo [Perez] was playing all over the place, usually, and the drums were great, but most of the time Wayne was just playing a note, or two notes. Whatever thematic things they played were very sparse. It was fascinating. And the people loved it, and stood up and asked for more.

At this concert at the Philharmonie I got there early, and stood at the entrance to see who was coming in to hear Wayne Shorter. People were pouring in—older people, younger people. I thought this was really great. I was reminded about his pop credits, and Miles, and Weather Report—he's got a big following.

Isn't this some of Wayne Shorter's best playing in many years?
Well, in terms of just standing there and waiting till he feels like playing something, I really love that. It's so traditional just to stand up and press the switch, and spit out the eighth notes. But he doesn't do that, he was listening to his band.

When you compare the Plugged Nickel to what he's doing today, it's a totally different approach. On the Plugged Nickel, there's this fantastically technical, complex playing on standards. Before [he worked with] Miles, there was more of a Coltrane influence, which isn't my favorite.

He's simplified.
He's absolutely essentialized. Once in a while, he'll play extremely fast segments. But for the most part he's playing just sounds, hardly a line at all, sometimes.

But because he's got this dynamic trio behind him, it's a kind of relief. That's why he's got these virtuosos.
Exactly. The same as Miles Davis. He always had a great rhythm section. He played his two or three choruses and sat down and listened to the rest of the people play—the long-winded tenor players and so on.

I've been working on that for a long time, trying to essentialize a tune. I still love playing on a progression rather than totally free. But I want to find out how to be loose on that progression. When I practice, I practice half notes, and whole notes, and longer note-values, almost like a subsidiary line that you would play. It gives a really nice groundwork for the tune, I think, and the chance to really dig in to each note before unfolding all of the fury and the faster rhythms.

You were saying it's also to do with intonation, and getting the pitch.
The whole thing about feeling the note, and hearing the people I'm playing with, facilitates that process. It sounds like Wayne's doing that. He'll just

hold a note, and listen to what's around him.[12] I like the anagram, LISTEN = SILENT. And when he finally plays a phrase, it's pretty spontaneous-sounding. It's fascinating what he's doing with that quartet. I'd love to be in a situation like that.

Could you ask to work with him?

That's absolutely out of the question—but thanks for the thought! If he ever asked me to join him, I'd jump in there. When Ornette asked me to play with him, I had great misgivings about it, but I was more than interested in trying.

Maybe Wayne wouldn't ask you for the same reason you wouldn't ask him.

It's the classic story about the beautiful woman not having a date, because everybody's afraid to ask her.

I was struck by how you went backstage to see him recently, and he was so friendly. There's a community of people who know each other's work, even though they may not know each other very well personally.

Yes, he knows my work from the 1940s onwards. I met him once before, and he sang one of the themes from the first record we made with Tristano.[13]

He couldn't stop talking in the dressing room that day—it was very nice to hear.

But he goes off on wild tangents, it seems.

I think he's an improviser all the way, and one of the greatest!

¶ Interview with Wayne Shorter

In his interview, **WAYNE SHORTER** *is as poetic as his playing.*

I've known Lee for a long time. His rendition of "Lover Man" [from 1953] is one of the pièces de résistance. The first time I heard him, with Warne Marsh and Lennie Tristano, I immediately knew that Lee was going another route to Charlie Parker—an original way of expressing life, the perception of life at that moment. He played the alto sax and it had its own tone—and this whole thing about the alto being hard to play in tune, just like the soprano sax, that was no factor. I thought, "Here we've got a guy who's right in there!"

They were playing at a place in New Jersey that was usually a dance hall—and didn't they play! I was young, and I sneaked in. I think Bud Powell was supposed to be there with a group, and he couldn't make it.

This was a dance place in a rough part of town, in Broom Street, Lloyd's Manor—the roughest street in Newark, New Jersey! "Cornbread" by Big Jay McNeely was a hit then, and all the honking saxes were going on, and Ruth Brown, and Bullmoose Jackson, and the guys who were singing high, like Smokey Robinson, contralto singers. That's what they usually booked in that place, but this time they booked jazz.

I have a CD of Charlie Parker talking, and he's saying he liked Lee Konitz. Leonard Bernstein had put down Stan Kenton [for being too self-consciously modern], saying something like, "You don't play music, and say 'Look how modern I am!'" And Charlie Parker said that Stan Kenton contributed a lot—and then he said that Lee Konitz is doing good stuff. He was solid in his comments.

[About Lee's comments on his playing:] My long notes could be to check intonation, but also to see what meaning that note has, in reflecting life. Sometimes one note can inspire an awakening. You can speak about life in words, but to speak about life in other forms is a challenge too. I'm just celebrating the phenomena of what life is, which is eternal.

[About playing with Lee:] Sonny Rollins said to me [imitates Rollins's slow, deep delivery], "We should do something together, before it's too late!" [Laughs.]

The word *jazz* is just a sound for the movement, ever-changing in the name of celebrating originality. Lee is one of the guys who grasps what that creative involvement is—the essence of living.[14]

8 ✒ The Instrument

In this chapter Konitz discusses his approach to the saxophone as an instrument: the influence on his style from his first instrument, the clarinet, how this style developed, the question of legato and vibrato, "correct" intonation, and how he practices and relaxes. The parallels between Konitz and Lester Young are instructive. Young also played clarinet, and his tone has also been described as shaped by clarinettists, in his case the New Orleans Creoles—like Konitz's, it has also been misdescribed as vibratoless.[1] Although Konitz's tone could be described as pure, it is never vibratoless, as albums such as *The Jobim Collection* attest.

Because of this apparent purity, Konitz's tone has often been described as classical.[2] But it is a real jazz tone, having nothing in common with the demands of classical saxophone, which require homogeneity throughout the range. André Hodeir was right to regard Konitz's sound as a model for classical players: "[He] has obtained from the alto saxophone a diaphanous sound that no soloist in the European [classical] tradition has. . . . Pierre Boulez, for whom I played some of Konitz's recordings, would like to see European saxophonists get round to adopting it. . . . To date, though, the cool sonority exists only in jazz, so there is every reason to conclude that it really is a jazz sonority."[3] In his long interview in this chapter, Gunther Schuller provides a subtle and persuasive account of Konitz's saxophone sound.

Sound and Tone

I think over the years my sound has become stronger. In trying to flex this very flexible instrument, I use different embouchures and different reed-strengths and mouthpieces, to get as many varieties of sound as possible. In a step-by-step process of elimination, I try and make every note *really* count.

When I'm told, as I have been, that people can identify me from the first note, I take that as a big compliment. I'm very pleased that since I haven't tried to become a stylist—my sound and my ideas have changed over the years—someone can still say that they recognize me from the first bar.

You had a classical training on clarinet, with a member of the Chicago Symphony Orchestra.

I only studied with him briefly, and nothing memorable happened, just routine stuff. I had a technical training from the books, mostly classical études. I started with the clarinet, and it seemed like the alto was the closest thing to it—sopranos were not popular then. I think it was an extension of my wanting to play the clarinet, somehow, and I got a kind of clarinet sound out of it at that time, I think.

I wonder, was that training decisive in how you formed your style?

Well, a lot of saxophonists start out on clarinet. The clarinet is considered the more difficult instrument, and you form all your musculature on that and then you've got to loosen it up on the saxophone. I brought a special, very classical, firm clarinet embouchure to the saxophone. That certainly had an impact on the kind of sound I produced. But I wasn't preparing to play in an orchestra—I knew, early on, that I wanted to play small-band music and improvise around the melodies.

What do you think about soloists on classical saxophone?

Well, some players are very impressive. I don't like the classical saxophone sound per se; it's hard to get past that. But sometimes it's so brilliantly executed, and the literature is getting better.

Why do they have that sound?

I think it has something to do with the possibility of fitting in an ensemble. A personal sound is not that desirable.

Is the classical sax sound a tight embouchure?

I think so—usually a soft reed and a firm embouchure.

They could have a uniform sound that was a bit more appealing.

Well, I agree. But unless a player puts a personal music into the saxophone, it can sound very uninteresting. The instrument is begging to be "warmed up."

Some people say I have a more classical tone, and I think my sound would blend with woodwinds and strings.

You played tenor on a couple of recordings in the 1950s, and more recently.

I have one that I just had fixed up last year, with the intention of playing it more. But I don't really have occasion to do so. I play the soprano sometimes. The tenor is one of my favorite instruments, strangely enough. I like it because it's closer to my vocal range. But when I've played it for a brief time, I haven't really loved the sound I was making much. It would mean playing it steadily for a while. The few times that I recorded, I just took it out of the closet without thinking whether I was prepared or not, and just went for pot luck—and I do enjoy listening to those records, especially the duo with Elvin [on *Duets*].

You also bought a flute at one point.

I couldn't make much of that. At some point I thought I could qualify to play one of the television shows or theater gigs to support my family, but I realized quickly that there were guys who could really play the flute and my efforts were lame. I didn't love it that much, so I just stuck it in the closet.

Do you have a "tenor sax" sound on alto?

Well, I envision the tenor when I play in the low register.

People say that the soprano is very hard to play, and hard to keep in tune.

I would guess that the sopranino, being the highest instrument, would be the hardest. I've never even tried that one. But I love the soprano for its trumpetlike brilliance.

I said before that the sound can't really be separated from the notes, though I could get a good sound and not play an interesting phrase. That sounds a bit contradictory. You can produce a decent sound with a poor phrase—sometimes Paul Desmond's phrases were not terribly exciting, but he always had that nice sound, and Stan Getz also was capable of making that beautiful sound no matter what he played.

But more often the problems are connected?

I had a problem with Dexter Gordon's kind of Billy Eckstine/opera sound, and with his line also—I thought that his notes were definitely the result of that kind of operatic sound that he got. At first it was more of a Lester Young kind of sound, but then it became, not like Coleman Hawkins exactly, but Don Byas, a bit more lush. Sonny Rollins got that, but more effectively because of a better selection of notes.

When I described your mature tone as richer and more expressive, but also starker and bleaker, you laughed, saying, "Starker and Bleaker sounds like a detective agency."

I was always trying to play as strong as I possibly could, and sometimes I'd hear this kind of raw sound coming out, and I'd enjoy that dimension of tone production. But I don't design stark and bleak phrases, to have that effect. As I said earlier, I'm not thinking of expressing sadness, I'm just thinking of playing a melodic succession of notes.

¶ Interview with Larry Kart

Writer and journalist **LARRY KART** *is, like Konitz, a native of Chicago.*
He wrote the liner notes to the Mosaic issue of Tristano Atlantic record-
ings, and his book Jazz in Search of Itself *was recently published by Yale*
University Press. I began by asking him about his comment, from a review
in Down Beat *in 1970, that Konitz had by that time eliminated the*
"patches of rhythmic awkwardness" in his playing, and had developed a
mature style that included more overtly expressive qualities.

In 1970 I identified with the attempt Lee seemed to be making to "warm
up" his playing, to get a little closer to what appeared to be the mainstream tradition. But almost from the first, Lee was a fully formed
figure—and arguably he's playing as well now as he ever has. The first
time I heard him live was 1962, when Lennie Tristano came to
Chicago—a very rare appearance on Tristano's part. What I called the
"rhythmic awkwardness" of Lee's earlier playing, I now just think of as
"strange" or "odd," but I wouldn't trade it for the world! His sound in the
early sixties began to be a little rounder, with a little more vibrato, richer,
less "piping" if you will—I wouldn't put a value judgment on that
though. He never got as warm as Ben Webster or Phil Woods—though
maybe Phil Woods isn't warm, just greasy!

Rhythmically, I think there's an underlying "on/off" pulsation to Lee's
lines—even when he's playing rubato, there's a very subtle sense of pulse
or swing. He can break down that "on/off" pulsation into as many micro-
subdivisions of the beat as he needs to get a very subtle curved or angu-
lar feeling. Charlie Parker might have thought in five or seven, or whatever—and the results might sound equally subtle rhythmically or even
more so—but somehow I feel that Lee's rhythmic subtleties are always
built on that on/off basis. It's a Lester Young thing, for sure, and something that Tristano emphasized—building layers of rhythmic complexity
on top of an internalized, heartbeat pulse.

Early on, almost all the rhythmic detail in Lee's playing was outside
the sound—note-to-note. Then it was as though each note was made of
porcelain, and had a hard, smooth "surface." But since then, his sound
has become more porous and grainy—more permeable and open to
spontaneous variation by him in these areas. It's as though he can do
more things inside the note. These are subtle timbral changes—there'll
be a change in the density of the note, which may or may not have to do
with vibrato—and these changes have a rhythmic component. Lester

Young did that all the time, changing the timbre of notes within a phrase, sometimes with false fingering—more extreme cases would be Ben Webster or Johnny Hodges. The components of music—timbre, harmony, rhythm, and melody—are able to turn into one another. Think of Debussy—in *Jeux* or *La Mer,* timbral and rhythmic events shade into each other imperceptibly.

Lee is the most amazing "singer," [in that] his approach is primarily melodic, compared say to Bill Evans, whose lines often seem to be determined by whatever harmonic pattern he's using. Lee's harmonic ear is incredible, but I think that's basically so he can go where he wants to melodically. That was one of the key elements of Tristano's thinking. I've heard Lee play very close to the melody with remarkable depth, but also play the most extreme paraphrase, where if you hadn't been told what the song was, you'd be baffled.

It's crucial to how the music comes across that it's intensely improvised. There's nothing egotistical about Lee. The personality and style of the music is a by-product of its in-the-moment musical inventiveness and activity. With Bird, the music that he did so much to create—bebop—very quickly became a style, and that arguably became restrictive to him. I would say that at his most inspired, there was never anyone more inspired and spontaneous than Bird, and yet the highest inspiration in his case seemed to be roughly coincident with a high level of agitation. Only on a few occasions does Bird at his most inspired also seem relaxed or at ease. With Lee and Warne Marsh, that's not the case—for them inspiration and relaxation often seem to go together. Lee's my favorite soloist of all—there's no end to the beauty he can create.[4] 🎝

Embouchure

At this point, those who aren't horn players will need some basic information about playing the saxophone. With woodwind instruments, aside from flute, piccolo, and recorder, the sound is generated by a reed and not with the lips alone. The embouchure—the shaping of the lips to the mouthpiece of the instrument—seals the area around the reed and the mouthpiece, to prevent air from escaping and to support the reed, allowing it to vibrate, while constricting it to prevent it from vibrating too much. When the mouthpiece is placed too far into the mouth, too much vibration results, with no control and a harsher sound. But if the mouthpiece isn't placed far enough into the mouth, the reed won't vibrate, and no sound results. With single-reed woodwinds like clarinet and saxophone, either a single-lip or double-lip embouchure can be used. The single-lip embouchure is the most common in jazz, and the reed rests upon the inside of the bottom lip, or on the bottom lip, which is placed on top of the bottom teeth. The top teeth are then used to bite down on the mouthpiece, and the top lips are wrapped around them in order to create a seal. With the double-lip embouchure, the top lip is placed under or around the top teeth. Here, Konitz describes how he uses the double-lip embouchure in certain contexts.

The whole physical aspect of blowing on the mouthpiece and reed is everpresent. I'm always trying different amounts of the mouthpiece in the mouth, different tensions in the jaw, using the top teeth on the mouthpiece, or not using them. I don't know whether it's my getting older, or having some dental work, that makes me so in need of changing that physical aspect around. It's very good in the sense that it keeps things moving, not fixed, but it's frustrating sometimes. I had this habit of blowing my cheeks out, and my neck, when I blow, and I would look into the mirror to try and correct that. More recently, I found a position of the mouthpiece in my mouth that helps—also flattening my cheeks inward.

Is that a habit you've had over the years?

Pretty much. I figured look at Dizzy, and Zoot Sims—they used to blow out their cheeks, so it's okay. But it feels better, and the sound is more controlled, when the musculature isn't stretching out needlessly.

You have a more classical sound on your string quartet recordings.

Ohad Talmor, who's been arranging my pieces, asked, "How did you get that sound? I never heard you make a nicer sound." I explained that I was using an embouchure without the teeth on the top of the mouthpiece, which opens up the throat and all the musculature, and so on—playing softer to fit in with the string quartet, instead of trying to barrel through a loud drummer.

It's called a "double-lip" embouchure, a French embouchure. They introduced it for classical saxophone. Usually you rest the top teeth on the mouthpiece. This time the teeth are in the lip, and I very much enjoy the fact that releasing the top teeth from the mouthpiece opens the throat a little more. It lowers the pitch, which is something I constantly have to be particular about, but generally makes it easier to stay in tune. It loosens up the whole articulation, and produces a very nice relaxed sound. I wanted to be sure that I was in tune with the strings. That's a closer possibility with that embouchure.

Can you get vibrato with that embouchure?
Yes. It depends on what kind of melody I'm playing.

I think classical players tend to use that "double-lip" embouchure more. There's an old TV film made with Warne and me, and Billy Taylor. Warne is playing a beautiful solo, and the mouthpiece is moving from side to side in his mouth, from phrase to phrase. It must be that kind of embouchure—I know he was experimenting with that.[5] It was a very loose articulation, which he was a master of, and he vibrated!

I can't really use [that kind of embouchure] at a good tempo with a rhythm section. I use it on a ballad mostly. I love to practice softly, with a loose embouchure. I like the idea of flexing the musculature on the mouthpiece. I started using the double-lip embouchure a long time ago. I remember discussing it with Jimmy Giuffre. Johnny Hodges was one of my first heroes—he had big lips, as I remember, and I'm pretty sure he used it.

What make of instrument do you play? And what reeds and mouthpieces?
At the moment I play a Selmer Mark VI in the States and a Selmer Balanced Action—my first horn I got in 1945—in Europe.

Is that to avoid carrying them from one continent to the other?
I like both of them, and it eliminates carrying them. It's getting harder to schlep all this shit around, I can tell you!

I have used Vandoren mouthpieces, and Vandoren reeds for many years. Now I use a 2.5 and a 3.5 reed, and with a big band, a 4. I never used a soft reed before. For a few years, I used plastic reeds, and I loved them. They were very strong, and consistent, in comparison to cane reeds. I could even play different mouthpieces on the job—I didn't have to wet the reed. But I went back to cane—the sound is much more resonant.

It's hard for me to describe those differences technically. The softer reed enables me to play in the low register more effortlessly, and the sound seems to expand. It's a full sound all over. It's more difficult for the high register—I tend to bite up and close the opening. One day, a bunch of reeds feel great, the next day they don't feel good. Tiredness, or humidity, or the acoustics of the room, play a role.

Have you ever played a plastic saxophone?
Yeah, they sent me one, one time, and I was surprised it sounded so good. But I sent it back; it wasn't as good as the one I was playing. I would think they're quite breakable. I think Charlie Parker's cheap little plastic saxophone was sold at an auction for five figures. He sounded great at the Massey Hall concert on that horn.

Vibrato and Legato

It's often said that Tristano required an uninflected, vibratoless tone from his students on saxophone. The entry on Tristano in *Jazz: The Essential Companion*, for instance, says that he wanted saxophonists to use a "flat, uninflected tone, so that their lines would depend on the quality of their construction." And in his discussion of the Half Note recording from 1959, Peter Pettinger refers to Warne Marsh as "the more committed to a uniform tone on the line, thus faithfully upholding the Tristano philosophy," compared to "the tonally inflected and harder-edged Konitz."[6] In his discussion, Konitz corrects this misconception. What he did learn from Tristano's teaching was legato phrasing—that is, playing several phrases with the same breath. There is still inflection and articulation, but it is subtler and cooler than that of bebop players such as Sonny Stitt, Phil Woods, and Jackie McLean—Konitz's attack on each note is much less emphatic. Here, Konitz explains how he's now trying to mix up and combine these different styles, while the interviews with Gunther Schuller and Dave Liebman clarify the question of articulation and legato.

"Uninflected" is not the word—Tristano very definitely wanted inflection. But he encouraged a more legato line. I think the people who say that [he didn't want vibrato] don't listen closely enough to the ends of the phrases. Because Lester Young used a vibrato most of the time—and always at the end of the phrase. I use vibrato quite a bit of the time, it was a bit schmaltzy in the earlier days. I was listening to some of my early records with Stan Kenton, and *oy vey!* it was very corny.

"Vibrato" strictly means the pitch going up and down ever so slightly, at various speeds.[7] But I think that by vibrato people often mean any kind of variety in the tone. It's not very well understood by listeners.

Not judging by some of the comments. I remember Lennie was listening to Charlie Parker's chorus on "Yardbird Suite," on the original take, and he said, "It's a perfect solo except that he goes 'da-da-daaa', and that note vibrates too fast at the end of the phrase."

It's milking an effect?

It just sounds a little bit out of control, a little nervous, or schmaltzy, or whatever—it's an expressive device, vibrato. It depends on the intensity of the phrase that's being played. A really emotional vibrato, a kind of cultivated vibrato like Bird could get with the strings, that was almost classical, but the hippest! It's very controlled, beautifully rendered, at the end of a phrase—nobody does it as well, I think. Warne Marsh had what I call a natural vibrato. It never sounds exaggerated, but expressed the intensity of the phrase beautifully.

I was listening to Greg Osby the other day and he doesn't really use one very much. Wayne Shorter hardly ever uses a vibrato. Miles didn't much, after he left his Harry James influence.[8]

I guess Tristano was objecting to Texas tenors where vibrato was laid on with a trowel.

Well, that whole exaggeration and the sound and the emotionality was objectionable to him and me. His feeling, and mine, was to use a pulsation on a note that was felt intensely. One vibration, or more, to give the note some emphasis. I love the idea of an emotional vibrato, but the classical turning-on of the vibrato, like on a violin, I don't like that too much on the saxophone. It can be very mechanical, in the classical sense, just part of the discipline. The vibrato is usually pretty consistent, and it's part of the whole technique of playing a phrase. Very rarely do you hear a classical saxophonist playing without vibrato.

I remember my first lessons in Chicago, working on vibrato, just to loosen up the jaw.

In the interview with David Kastin, you described the range of attack on the reed, from a light brush, to staccato, the hardest kind of attack.

You start the note either with a push on the breath, or by touching the reed and closing it up to the mouthpiece with your tongue, producing a non-legato phrasing. Just blowing the air from one note to the other, without using the tongue, is legato phrasing. Some people touch the reed right at the tip, but that never appealed to me because it seemed like you could break it if you hit it hard. So I touch it on the underside. This is something that I work on every day.

Sonny Stitt, Sonny Rollins, and some of those guys had a great ability to separate all the notes even at a fast tempo, with a definite accent for each note, and it gave a very strong feeling. You can really move and swing very strongly. I'm kind of adding this technique to my palette now. But Tristano suggested legato with very strong inflections, which kind of made up for the accent of the tongue; he suggested breath accents or whatever, and of course the use of the tongue also at times, but mostly that flowing legato feeling was encouraged.

❦ Interview with Gunther Schuller

GUNTHER SCHULLER, *born 1925 in Queens, New York, is a com-*
poser, conductor, writer, and French horn player. In the early 1940s he
played horn with the Cincinnati Symphony Orchestra, then with Metro-
politan Opera in New York from 1945 to 1959. Having coined the term
Third Stream *to describe music fusing jazz and classical elements, he*
wrote many pieces in this style, performed and recorded by Eric Dolphy,
Ornette Coleman, Jim Hall, Bill Evans, John Lewis, and MJQ. He formed
the Lenox School of Jazz, and 1967–77 was President of the New England
Conservatory. He founded two music publishing companies and a record-
ing company. He is the author of Early Jazz, The Swing Era, *and other*
books. He is presently writing an autobiography in several volumes,
which he regards also as a history of American music in the last century;
his fans earnestly hope that this will be followed by the third volume of his
history of jazz.

I believe I first met Lee at the time of the Birth of the Cool—I was on the
third of the recording dates [in September 1950]. But I'd heard him on
recordings with the Thornhill Orchestra, which I loved—it was so different from any jazz orchestra, with the tuba and French horns. Lee's playing in those days particularly was very fluid—when he played sixteenth
notes or running figures, I always thought of an otter going through
water. There's a kind of sleekness, just as there is with Charlie Parker
compared with earlier saxophone players. Charlie Parker is so hot—Lee
is a little cooled off by comparison. But there was still this warmth of tone
in every pearly note that he played—and he still does that. Of course I
heard him live, because I heard the Thornhill Orchestra live. And on a
recording, even if it was only eight bars—look, in those days all the
recordings were just three minutes long!

I heard him play at the Royal Roost, when Miles Davis and he first
started what became the Birth of the Cool—of course it wasn't called anything at first, and it was a huge flop! First it was issued on 78s, and
nobody heard it, nobody liked it. You didn't dance to this stuff—"What
the hell is this?" It was just so foreign to the hot, loud, brash jazz that had
particularly been played all through the war. That lingered on with the
big bands, until bebop cooled things off. Miles reduced the Thornhill
Orchestra to only nine players—so that was even less boisterous and hec-
tic. And it was very modern—Johnny Carisi's piece ["Israel"] was a real

breakthrough, and Gil Evans's "Moon Dreams" was one of the ultimate masterpieces in jazz, a complete transformation, almost in the sense of a classical composition, of a tune by Glenn Miller's pianist, Chummy McGregor.

Lee and I joke about it a lot, but at the end of "Moondreams," Gil had written a unison between the trumpet and the saxophone on a high F-sharp [on saxophone, not concert pitch]. And the F-sharp on alto saxophones in those days happened to be a pretty bad note—you really had to move that around with your embouchure. On the recording, you can hear that Lee is very sharp, and of course it was at the very end of the record date and there was no overtime, so we couldn't do it over. In the same place, Miles plays a rough note, and it stays out of tune. This is the coda—the piece is over and there's a minute and a half of the most amazing classical, complicated music. While I was playing my horn, I had to conduct with my right hand in order for us to get through.

What first struck you about Lee's tone?

Lee's tone is original, but it does come out of Charlie Parker—that's the heritage. It also comes out of tenor players like Chu Berry, who was also smooth—and I don't mean either slick or really smooth, because as smooth as Lee's lines sound, there is a fantastic, individual, distinctive articulation on every one of his notes. So you have this wonderful combination of absolute clarity—every note is like a pearl—subsumed in a grand line. How he developed that, no one knows; perhaps even he doesn't. There were other players that came out of bebop, Paul Desmond for example—all these are the children of bebop. The fantastic fluency, and the idea of playing music not in 4/4 anymore, but almost always in double time, 8/8, that comes from bebop. It's a wonderful thing about jazz, that no one tells anyone how to play. It's the music of individualism and freedom.

What do you think of Pierre Boulez's comment that Konitz's tone could fit into a classical context?

That's absolutely right. One of many associations I had with Lee was in the midfifties, when John Lewis and I started a workshop orchestra. It never performed in public, we just rehearsed once a week. We were all composers, and we all composed and transcribed things—I took one of the greatest Bach Preludes and Fugues, the B-flat minor one in the Second Book. Of course it's a polyphonic piece. I played the horn, J. J. [Johnson] played the trombone—and to this day, I get goose pimples when I think of Lee playing his eight bars, with this incredible clarity of articulation. It's as if he attacked every note, yet he wasn't, he was slurring. But the linearity of the way he played it—I didn't tell him how to play it, he just instinctively sight-read it like that.

Tristano suggested that saxophonists play a legato line, without articulating each note—but you're saying he got a kind of emphasis or effect on each note?

Well, "effect" and "emphasis" are too strong—it's just a subtle but very clear articulation. It's like a little bell sound. You hear what we call the "ictus"—when a note is produced, whether it's attacked or slurred. He did slur. I don't know how he did it, the way he went from one note to the next, whether he did that with the keys of the saxophone, or with some little tiny breath articulation on each note, you can't tell.[9] There's nothing that interrupts the flow of sound. If you imagine a necklace of seventy-five pearls, each one absolutely equal, that's the way his runs were—or his slower passages, it isn't just in fast passages. He's the only one that did that to that extent. I'm telling you something that maybe no one else has ever said. This is just what I know about him. Most writers don't get into tiny details like that.

It's incredibly hard to describe the tone of an instrument, but you've certainly given a great description.

What Lee did is something in between a real slur [legato] and real articulation. There are thousands of saxophonists who just can't do that. They just have a different way of putting air into the horn. Part of it, I'm quite sure, can come from the way that you push down the keys on the instrument. The quicker and more precisely you do that, the more you'll get a stronger articulation. Part of it also is—I'm getting very technical here—the finger pushing down the key is coordinated with the way your breath is also articulating that note.

By "articulating" you mean "separating"?

No. I mean "articulate" in the slur.

"Distinguish"?

Yes, in a way, isolate, or present in a distinctive, individual way. I keep referring to this analogy of the pearl necklace.

People leave out the word "full"—you can have a slightly softer, less projecting sound, and yet it's beautifully full. That's what really great sopranos have—they may have a lighter voice than some dramatic, crazy woman, but the fullness of the voice is what speaks, what produces the emotion.

Lee's tone filled out a little bit, like our bodies do—it just ripened more. But he always had that basic quality.

Going back to Boulez's comment, a jazz fan might say that Konitz has a pure, classical tone.

They could say that, but they'd be so completely wrong. There is no classical player I've ever heard—and I'm as much a classical musician as a jazz musician—who can slur like Lee Konitz does. No, that has nothing to do with classical music. That comes out of Charlie Parker.

One thing that might justify people in saying it is that Lee played a run of notes more evenly than a lot of jazz was before, in the Swing Era. When we classical musicians write a bunch of eighth notes, we play it even—in jazz, you have some kind of "tripletization."[10] Well, Lee didn't do that—nor did Miles Davis by the way—but it still swings. But to make that swing—that's another high art, and it's so complicated we'll be here for nine hours!

What makes it *not* classical is the articulation I've been talking about—it's like the notes "pop" out in a tiny, tiny way, and that you *never* hear in classical music. But I love that word *pure*. By "pure" I mean—as a wind player myself, and this is the greatest compliment one can make— that the entire area of the note is fully filled. It's what we call a centered tone. I used to teach hundreds of horn players and trumpet players, and the way they put the air into an instrument, the air is mostly around the edge of the sound, which is the exact opposite—you get a kind of nasal sound that way. I don't know whether Lee considers himself one of the cool players, like Gerry Mulligan. I think he probably does, but he has this particular kind of warm, pure sound.

When I spoke to Phil Woods, and unimaginatively mentioned that he was regarded as a hot player and Lee as cool, he really didn't like that.

No, because the best players are in a way everything from hot to cool.

I know Lee is a great practicer, but this must have been the result of many hours of practice.

They all practice. I knew Eric Dolphy very well, and he practiced seventeen hours a day. A classical player practices for five, six, seven, eight years the great concertos and études, until they have virtually perfected that entire repertory. But a jazz musician, of course, is not working on a repertory, he's working on his own creations. And as he is practicing, he is also creating. But in order to assemble that awesome ability to get up instantaneously and be able to play something beautiful, intelligent, striking, you have to have practiced for hours and hours over years. Coleman Hawkins, John Coltrane—I knew those people, and they practiced!

You're making the point about Lee Konitz, that he's one of the highest examples of the craft.

In every way you want to talk about his playing—from a technical, or creative, or idea point of view—there's an absolute sovereignty.

Would you say of some other players that technically they weren't quite up there, but the ideas are fantastic—Ornette Coleman for instance?

I have to beg to differ with that, because Ornette is such a unique case. He has his own high perfection, but it's almost in another world—he got it out of a combination of the Texas blues band and Charlie Parker. Also his instrument is a plastic saxophone—there's a lot of things there. But I would say yes, there is a kind of all-round perfection, from the technical to the ideational, that some players just never achieve.

The Charlie Parker influence—this is a really difficult issue. When I reminded Lee that you'd said he fused the conceptions of Parker and Tristano, he questioned that.

All I said is that he came out of Parker. I certainly don't mean that he imitated Parker, or plagiarized Parker, or sounds like Parker. Look, Parker changed the saxophone. Before Parker there was Johnny Hodges—this ultimately lyric, almost sexual way of playing the alto saxophone. There were a lot of tenor players like that. Charlie Parker did something entirely different out of his unique talent, which he just created out of his own imagination. One of the reasons I say Lee comes out of Parker is the feeling of the doubling up of time. The speed with which Charlie Parker thought or heard his notes was incomprehensible then. Now there are other players that can do it. They worked their ass off to get to that point. But Parker invented that—just a blaze of notes. In some of those runs there are eighty-five notes, just one after the other, at maximum speed! That was brand new on the face of the earth—no one had ever played that fast, and thought that fast, and played changes that fast. And Lee, in his teens, heard that, and being a sensitive musician with terrific ears, there's no way he could not have been influenced. But that's all I'm saying. There must be "57 Varieties" of Charlie Parker's epigones! That's the great thing about jazz—they learn from one master, and they go their own way.

Lee's clarity of articulation is different from Parker's. With [Bird], every note is hard, but in a beautiful way, it doesn't hit you in your face, it just has a kind of strength to it, each note. Lee's personality required that he would do that a little more on the elegant or softer side.

Look, I want to interrupt myself here, and say that one of the great things about Lee is that he has the highest artistic and personal integrity, and at the same time, a remarkable outspokenness. Lee will never tell a lie. You get the absolute, direct, full answer. I've heard him say things about some of his great colleagues where he dared to point out a slight flaw in some really great musician who's in the pantheon. He can do that because he has that kind of honesty, that kind of brilliance of analysis.

But the thing is, Lee may not himself fully realize to what extent he comes out of Parker.

He was studying with Tristano before he heard Parker, though.

Well, even so . . . Now, talking about Tristano—he plays essentially a percussion instrument. The articulation you get on any piano—I don't care how smooth you try to play—is not duplicable on any other instrument. It's a little "ping" you get with every note. That also might be a cause of the articulation on Lee's saxophone. On the piano, every note has an attack and then a decay. Lee has the attack, and he doesn't do the decay part.

What you're saying sounds completely right. When you think of saxophonists before Parker, there was a sea change.

It's like Lester Young and Coleman Hawkins. Lester is listening to a white C-melody sax player [Frank Trumbauer]. The tenor saxophone is supposed to be this strong, masculine, very expressive, almost erotic instrument, and here comes Lester with this extraordinarily smooth playing. I would hazard a guess that Lee also heard a lot of Lester Young.

Lester Young is his number one, really.

Still, the articulation that Lee has does not come out of Lester Young. It has to come out of Parker, but personalized by him. All talented people learn from their predecessors—and when they're really great, they subsume that influence and it comes out in a totally personal way.

I think you're right that he may not realize the extent of the influence, and I agree with you also about Lee's frankness—he has no hidden agenda in these conversations. But he obviously wanted to stand apart from Parker.

That's true. But there's no contradiction with what I said.

It could be also that he's just heard and read so many comments that he's an alternative to Parker.

That's a good point.

There's another point, though. When Lee talks about Lester Young, or Lennie Tristano also, he has virtually no criticism. With Charlie Parker, he says that he couldn't adopt Parker's "compositional" method of improvisation, based on motifs. He regards Tristano and himself as intuitive improvisers, and Parker as less intuitive.

That's a valid point. Even in the early years, you never had the feeling that Lee's playing had that same turn again and again—which you can say of Parker. But we have to bear in mind that Parker was so sick and full of drugs, that at least half of him is not his best. I knew Charlie Parker very well and talked with him often. He wanted to study with me for a while, not long before he died, and he was so sick and tired of playing the blues, and the same changes. At the end of his life he wanted nothing more than to study Bartók's music, and Stravinsky and Schoenberg.

By comparison, certainly by the time he went with Stan Kenton, Lee hung out with Bill Russo and these modern composers, and that opened up his mind and his playing.

One idea that he emphasizes is that he improvises on the melody, not the harmonies—which makes him belong to a fairly small category of players.

Yes, that's the main thing that comes out of Lester Young. Because if anyone ever did that, and preached it, saying, "It must be that way!" it was Lester. He was obsessive about that.

How do you account for the lack of recognition of Lee?

It's very hard to assess that. But if I were to struggle for an answer, it would be that there's a subtlety in [Lee's] playing. It's not so overt, it's not in your face. Whatever drama there is in his playing is of such a cultivated kind that it isn't what people expect—especially now, since our culture has been so decimated. And it's also the high intelligence of his playing. It's just too refined—not in the sense of wimpy or bland, it's just not made for the mass of people. Intellect or intelligence is rarely mentioned in connection with music making—but it turns out that the greatest musical products, whether in classical or jazz, are a combination of a great mind and a great feeling. When they are equivalent, you have great art. And subtlety and intelligence are just what is least appreciated!

I tell you frankly, I think Miles Davis is so amazingly overrated and overcelebrated, and Lee hardly at all, even though they've worked closely together in some very significant work. John Coltrane is overcelebrated, Eric Dolphy is forgotten. I can't explain this really—it's just idiotic.

But do you think there is also sometimes an emotional inhibition in his playing—which Lee himself has suggested? Inhibition could mean lack of confidence, or it could mean not being able to express your feelings.

Well he said that to me too, now that you mention it. I never knew whether that came from how someone played, or more, how so many other people were praised, or in his mind overpraised. That can get you down!

What do you feel about his playing now, in his late seventies?
Certainly things have become abstract and unpredictable. One used to be able to—more or less—predict how a solo of his would go. I don't mean in any particular moment, but just the general feel of the thing. You'd have a unified composition. Now, having heard him with my sons, I've found that sometimes I'm completely surprised by things he does. Either in terms of dynamics—suddenly playing very loud or very soft—or doing some very fluent thing, and then suddenly come nothing but very long notes. It's so diverse now. I even asked Lee, "Is that what you're doing now [in terms of your playing style], most of the time?" And he says, "I don't know—I just do what I feel!"[11] 🎵

Intonation

In jazz, playing on the edge of classically correct intonation can be an expressive device. It has been a common complaint, especially by those from a classical background, that Konitz plays sharp. For instance, in his biography of Bill Evans, Peter Pettinger criticized him for this.[12] Konitz wrestles with the problem in this discussion.

Whatever brilliance I have achieved in my sound was partly due to being up at the top of the pitch, I think. That's just the way I hear it. And sometimes I could easily go over the line. After all this time, I still insist on getting way up on the edge, and sometimes over. I have to be very careful—that's been my Achilles heel in a way, but I keep working at it. The worst thing I could think of is to play flat—though strangely, a flat pitch will produce a broader sound. Playing sharp is more acceptable to me, but being "in tune" is the most enjoyable way.

I think each player of a non-fixed-pitch instrument has a concept of where it sounds best. If you play with a piano player, ideally you have to be at the very same pitch as every note on the piano that you're relating to, which is just about impossible, but that's the goal. Then you have to get in tune with the bass fiddle, which is for my instrument sometimes two octaves below me, with a whole different wooden structure. And very frequently I have no concept of getting a blend with that instrument, unless he's sustaining a note, *arco*. If he's just playing quarter notes, I don't know exactly whether I'm in tune with him or not, sometimes. Frequently I'm a little sharp to the rest of the band—as I say, that's how I get a little bit of an edge on my sound. With the drummer's cymbals sucking up the overtones of each instrument, and the volume, the weight of his instrument, I find that I can penetrate more with a higher-pitched sound.

It's a very practical flaw. But it is a flaw, and I try to solve it by having my attention very much on what the others are playing, rather than having to prove myself. So I have a better chance to really listen to them and get in tune with them. That was a very difficult one, it took a long time to realize that fully. In the beginning I was just having an impression of what the other guys were doing, and wasn't that concerned with the details.

So you don't have perfect pitch?

No, I have imperfect pitch! Sometimes when things are right, I can hear pretty accurately. But waking up in the morning and hitting a concert A or whatever, I have to think about that for a minute.

You mean you can hit a note and not be quite sure that it's concert A?

Absolutely unsure—after all these years. That's amazing. Perfect pitch is a photographic memory for pitch; some have it with words, some have it with notes. Certainly I'd like to have it! I actually worked on it for a while, and it was easier to identify a note. I simply used a tuning fork A and concentrated on the sound as long as possible, then struck the fork again and again, increasing my recall. Though without actually thinking of it specifically, I'm pretty close most of the time.[13]

I've had that unsure kind of a feeling quite a bit of the time when I've played with other people. And sometimes when I'm playing alone, from one register to another, I'm not really sure if it's a continuous intonation from bottom to top—the high register in relation to the low register if I'm going all the way up, octaves or intervals or whatever. When I talked to Jackie McLean about his pitch, his immediate reaction was, "Too bad [for you if you don't like it]!" He said that's the way he hears it, people either dig it or not. But if it disturbs the people you're playing with, then it's a real problem.

He's *very* sharp sometimes.

Extremely. I remember a session at the Café Montmartre in Copenhagen with Ben Webster, Dexter Gordon, and Jackie McLean. Afterwards I shook Jackie's hand, thinking how nice it was to play with him, and then it occurred to me I was also thanking him for playing sharper than me!

Someone described it as "acidulous," and it's part of his style.

A good word, "acidulous." Jackie had a solid sound that can get very edgy, very bitter.

I've appreciated his playing. But not when it's that high out of tune, it's very disturbing to me. The last time I heard him was at the Iridium. He came in the week after me, and he really sounded good—in tune, and getting a good sound. He was playing with his son, Rene, and a strong rhythm section. I really enjoyed it. I loved his description of himself, that he feels like a workhorse—a mule, maybe, pulling the rhythm section along. A great guy, and fine saxophonist!

He's a very assertive player who could dominate a rhythm section.
Yes. But then he sounds like someone who knows what he's about to play. I don't think he just stands up there and waits for something to happen. I hear very specific licks a lot of the time.

You seem to be in two minds about how important it is not to play sharp.
Well, I really think that it's part of how that person hears a series of notes. Many of the modern players try to allow for flexible pitch. They get quarter-tone effects and things like that. So they can justify playing on top of the pitch in that way, maybe. But I've come to think of it as an antisocial musical disease, not fully identifying with your musical neighbor. I can project my sound and still be in tune, if I can relax enough. Relaxed intensity is what I'm talking about, and trying to achieve it more of the time.

So your ideal really is to be in tune.
Yes, definitely. But since I can't always control it, I prefer to be there [sharp] than underneath the pitch.

To correct the problem, you'd need to take some very concentrated time sustaining notes before moving into high action—it's hard to do, but that would be necessary. I was listening to Wayne Shorter yesterday, and frequently he'll start out by holding a long note. And that's simply, I think, to see how he's relating to the other pitches around him. Very hip!

I mean when he's starting a solo, or during the course of it, to double check, maybe. Because as the tempo gets faster, the musculature tends to get tighter, and that would press up the pitch.

So during a performance you might be getting sharper.
Oh sure. I've worked a lot with Kenny Wheeler, and if anything he has a tendency to play at the bottom of the pitch. So I really have to be very careful, because we can sound pretty sour together. On the *Angel Song* record on ECM I was having that problem. My God, where were the angels!

Relaxation

How important is breath control? Do you think about that when you're going to take a breath?
Not when I'm really playing. Then, it's as natural as it is when talking. That's what I've tried to realize all along. With the breathing exercises in yoga, for

example, you really focus all your attention, and get the full deep breaths, and get the diaphragm working to support the sound, and so on.

Many times I just finger the horn, and blow air into it, just enough so I can hear pitches. I'm reminded that breath is there all the time, even when it's covered up with the sound of the note.

Our sound has to do with our whole anatomy. What comes out when I put a breath through is controlled by the musculature. I was pretty tight and tense in the early years—I was flying all over the place, with a tight sound I thought, more of this classical kind of sound. One of the reasons for smoking pot was to loosen up. I'm much, much looser now, without having to smoke.

We are the sound! When Charlie Parker borrowed my horn for a set at Birdland, to my complete astonishment, it no longer sounded familiar to me. It's a most flexible instrument.

It must be as important as it is for a singer to be relaxed and not to force things, and I guess a lot of saxophonists, maybe even more than singers, don't really attend to that.

Well, I think a lot of them are trying to sound so intense, to the point of overblowing the horn. It's hard to relax like that.

If you want to give an impression of raw, nervy music, you might think that involves not being very relaxed when you're playing. I'm thinking of players like the late Japanese altoist Kaoru Abe, or the free-jazz tenor saxist Charles Gayle.

I haven't done this, but I can imagine that there has to be a degree of relaxation to control that growling sound that Ben Webster got—or Joe Lovano in the high register, getting partials and things like that. There has to be a degree of looseness to facilitate that kind of technical playing. They're coordinated to the extent that they can spit out those notes at high intensity. If you're not relaxed to some degree, it's going to get so tight that the notes won't really come out effectively.

Presumably, physically the saxophone takes quite a bit of effort.

Yes, absolutely! But I swim a few times a week, when a pool is available, and walk; don't smoke, don't drink, no drugs!

So do you feel there's a difference in your tone when you're a little tense during a performance?

Yes, definitely. Pitch is the first thing that goes; there's a tendency to push up the high notes, so that in contrast the lower register sounds flat when I come down there. So that's one of the things I really concentrate on a lot when I'm practicing.

Certainly one's tone changes with the degree of tension involved—the throat tightening, the mouth and facial muscles tense, the breathing shallow, and so on. It has to change the sound that comes out. Just listen to the same player when he's relaxed—a very obvious difference.

When you're tired, that's the same problem.
I think so. It might have the opposite effect—but again, it's not the best sound production.

¶ Interview with David Liebman

Born in Brooklyn, New York, in 1946, tenor and soprano saxophonist **DAVID LIEBMAN** *studied with Charles Lloyd and Lennie Tristano, and studied American history at New York University. He recorded and toured with Elvin Jones and Miles Davis in the early 1970s. Strongly influenced by John Coltrane, he has become one of the major stylists on soprano saxophone. He is a leading jazz educator and educational writer.*

I would be careful about differing with Gunther Schuller because he's so astute, but I just don't see that Lee came out of Bird that much. Of course Bird affected everybody—but Lee's sound or articulation was just a completely different animal. I have to say the more important influence was from Lester Young—the sound, and the horizontal, melodic aspect of his playing. Lee's comments [in this book] about Bird are very astute—that he put together things, spontaneously, that he already had down. There are some definite similarities between Konitz and Rollins [on the one hand], and Parker and Coltrane. You know a lot of the older guys before Bird had their solos planned and played the same solo night after night—if not note for note and nuance for nuance.

On the subject of articulation, Gunther Schuller is talking about what we call "legato-staccato": you have a dot *and* a slur over the note. Lee has that beautiful, light yet definite attack when he articulates combined with "slurring," which in this case means legato—but with a slight interruption. You don't hear [true] legato in jazz because eighth notes need to be articulated to make it swing—you need some kind of hitting the note and coming off it. In jazz you're not going to get those extremes of legato and staccato that you get in classical music.

Warne played tenor like an alto, while Lee plays alto like a tenor, with a really dark, bottomy sound. Those heads they played together are so hard—like "Marshmallow." These guys worked! Lee's articulation is unique, certainly on alto. It all comes out of his phrasing. And Lee could lay behind the time in a class like Hank Mobley or Pres!

Lee's influence was not as widespread [as Bird's] for a variety of political and cultural reasons. And he didn't have the emotional impact of Charlie Parker—you just can't negate that. You're comparing a guy who you basically have to listen hard to, with a guy who was just filling the house with sound—Phil Woods told me when you heard Bird, the sound was gigantic. The main thing is that Lee and Lennie could come up with another way to look at the same language, at the same moment as Bird and Diz and Bud. This is amazing. It's like Charles Ives and Schoenberg. Of course the most important event were those recordings where they played so-called free. Now that's really an innovation at that time.

I took lessons with Lennie Tristano around 1964–65, for one year—I was just seventeen or eighteen. I saw him with Warne and Lee, and Sonny Dallas and Nick Stabulas at the Half Note. In those days in New York there wasn't anybody teaching jazz, apart from Lennie. One thing he did for me was to make me aware of the seriousness of studying jazz—I had no idea what was involved. I wasn't really ready for it. I was a complete Coltrane fanatic at the time, and Lennie couldn't stand him.

I agree that Warne and Lennie didn't interact with the band. Lennie impaired the rhythm section! I think you're losing a source of immediate inspiration if you do that. It means everything's on you as the improviser all the time. But almost all of the bebop players felt that way. Nobody wanted "interference"; they [just] wanted to be supported. That changed in the sixties, with Miles, Paul Bley, Bill Evans. . . . In a certain way Lee is interactive—he allows things to happen, but he is not necessarily going to overtly react to it. With the older guys, when they interact it's like "You do, I do." Lee is on his own path, but it is an open-sounding style. It seems to allow for more space, as he does play spaciously and employs uneven phrases that suggest that things can happen behind him. [Compare] Miles in the sixties, [who had a] rhythm section that could be contrary to what the soloist is doing, or interrupting them, or initiating—it's an independency.

Motion is one of my all-time favorites, of course. When I talked to Lee thirty years ago, I asked, "How did you get Elvin to play so quietly?" The rumor was that Elvin was placed far away, or in another room—which of course is impossible! He said, "No, he just knew what to do." It's just great, great playing on both their parts—and Sonny Dallas does the job that's needed. It's great to hear Lee with a drummer that's as loose rhythmically as he is. Mainly it's the way Lee places his phrases—how he turns the time around, and it comes out right. He just has a way of starting and ending phrases on unusual or unaccustomed places in the bar—things you could never plan! You can hear how improvised the whole record was; it's just tune after tune, "Let's do this," and "Let's do that." With Lee, Elvin is playing in a much tighter fashion. I wouldn't say more orthodox or bebop, but not as sprawling as he played at the same time with Coltrane on *My Favorite Things*. He does quite a bit of that triplet feel he did with Coltrane, but it's contained—maybe somewhat similar to the record with Sonny Rollins at the Vanguard [in 1957].

Lee is a classicist—he has continued to refine his art. He basically has stayed within the realm of where he started. He's got this amazing yin-and-yang thing—the most amazing free playing, and playing standards—with nothing in between, like fusion, or modal music.[14] 🐦

Practicing Routine

Just like eating my breakfast or whatever, playing is part of the daily activity—and I am doing it more than ever as I get older. I play for half an hour, and another half an hour later, or an hour, whatever. I really improvise, pretty much. In the course of playing, I might come into a sequence that I like, and run it through different keys and rhythms, and try to apply it to a set of chords—or just play freely and try to use that kind of motif. I haven't read music for years. I don't enjoy doing that too much.

So what is the relation between what you play when you're practicing, and what you play when you're performing?

Well, it's a kind of frame of mind. Things that I would run over frequently become part of my vocabulary, and that stuff will come out, but I never know where, exactly. And when it does, I try to be as flexible as possible with it—I want to stop any kind of routine. Isn't it similar to learning grammar so you can put a correct sentence, and paragraph, and story together?

I make a distinction between practicing—that is, practicing my playing ability—and playing. I try to play as much as possible, on a tune or just freely. When I don't feel like playing a tune, I warm up with an exercise, or a free exposition. When I go out to play, with the stimulus of a rhythm section, and an audience, I am usually able to "play" immediately—I'm warmed up. So you can be warm and cool at the same time!

How many hours roughly do you practice?

It's not that many hours just playing the saxophone, but the whole music thing with the piano, singing and writing and all that, it's a number of hours. I don't play for eight hours. I think I could profit from it, but I don't seem to have the energy for that—I didn't when I was younger either.

Do you play "arranger's piano"?

No, I play "improviser's piano"! Just by myself, or with a student—I wouldn't play keyboards in a group, unless it was completely free form. I think it's essential for saxophone players to use a keyboard. It's the only way to really experience the sound and quality of a chord. And understanding the way to accompany a soloist is very necessary, I think.

❧ Interview with Frank Wunsch

Pianist **FRANK WUNSCH,** *born in 1945 in Bochum, Germany, studied music in Dortmund and Cologne. He first performed with Konitz in 1986, and in the following years played with him across Europe, recording six CDs. He has also worked with Benny Bailey, Albert Mangelsdorff, and Steve Lacy. He lives in Cologne, where he teaches at the Musikhochschule.*

Two qualities that strike me in particular about Lee Konitz are his uncompromising nature and his modesty. In many conversations, this great musician, who does not always make it easy for himself and his fellows, has again and again described himself as "a student of music." I remembered this as I visited Lee in his Cologne flat the other day. He asked me to play some lines on "Rhythm" changes on his piano, which he had just written, partly in an unusual rhythm and key. I enjoyed doing that because it is always like a glimpse into the master's workshop. As we played together, we started freely, which led into "Rhythm" changes. We fed each other lines, and it was, so I thought, a successful improvisation full of ideas. Lee agreed with me, but his reaction was typical: he took the metronome, set it at a slow tempo, and we played "Rhythm" through twelve keys, still inspired, but always very controlled. I find it remarkable that Lee, who as an improviser takes every risk, and is able to cope with every challenge, should, at the age of almost eighty, work on his technical skills every day and continue exploring the foundations of his art.[15] ☛

9 🎜 The 1970s

Commercially, Konitz continued to have a difficult time during the 1970s. The late sixties and early seventies were the era of jazz-rock and free jazz, and Konitz wasn't inclined toward either. He was having to advertise for pupils in the pages of *Down Beat* magazine. In 1968 he made a concession to electric jazz by fitting a Conn Multi-Vider on his alto, allowing him to play notes two octaves apart simultaneously—it is featured on *Peacemeal* from 1969. During the 1970s, following a partnership with pianist Dick Katz, he formed an association with another pianist, Harold Danko, and in this chapter Konitz discusses the pianists he worked with or admired from this time—including Paul Bley, Chick Corea, Keith Jarrett, and Martial Solal. Konitz first recorded with Paul Bley in 1977, and the following year they worked in a quartet that included Jimmy Giuffre. *Jazz à Juan,* a classic album from 1974, featured Martial Solal, and their partnership continues to flourish.

Konitz's career picked up again in the late 1970s and early 1980s, when he led his nonet. His partnership with Warne Marsh continued. In 1977 they played a week at the Jazz Showcase, Chicago, then a couple of nights at the Keystone Korner, San Francisco. *London Concert* from 1976, on Wave, documents an outstanding performance at the Shaw Theatre in London, with Peter Ind on bass and Al Levitt on drums. Warne Marsh died in 1987.

Fusion was not something you really got involved in.
No objections, but no one invited me to join that kind of setup. Occasionally I was thinking, when Wayne Shorter left Weather Report, I'd like to have a crack at that to see how it went, but it didn't work out that way. I didn't listen to Weather Report much. I heard some very nice things, but I

don't seem to pick up those records when I feel like listening to something. Wayne didn't seem to have a big enough part of that somehow—he's a very humble guy. Joe [Zawinul] was a fan of Tristano's music, and when we meet occasionally he remembers that time.

What do you think of electric keyboards, and rock rhythms?

Well I've enjoyed [electric keyboards] very much. I've heard Chick Corea play them beautifully, and many others, and I love to play my electric piano.

Rock is a beat that can be danced to, basically. It's very tight; sometimes it feels like you could use it like a metronome—just the opposite of what I love about a rhythm section. It's restricting, totally mechanical and boring. And I'm not even mentioning the melodies and lyrics and phony voices, and the cutesy names for their groups. I feel the vulgarity of music designed by business interests to reach the lowest common denominator, and I can't believe how unreal all these people are in their behavior and their looks. No one sounds like themselves. The English sound like Jimmy Witherspoon or Willie Nelson—give me a fuckin' break!

[We listen to Konitz's recording of "Weaver Of Dreams" from 1975, on *Oleo* (Sonet) with Dick Katz and Wilbur Little.]

If anyone says you don't play with vibrato, they should listen to that theme statement!

Yes, it's all over the place—sometimes effective, sometimes defective.

"Weaver Of Dreams" is not a song I've played a great deal, but I like it. It's pretty much like "There Will Never Be Another You," except for the 4th or 5th bar of the last eight. I've just had it pointed out, and somehow never quite realized it, that the bridge on "Invitation" is the same kind of construction as the bridge on "Cherokee," except that it's II-V-I minor.

Do you notice that kind of thing very often? Is it something you think about consciously?

Well, I usually recognize that. For some reason I didn't recognize that one for a while.

I guess there's nothing like "All The Things You Are."

No. Or "Have You Met Miss Jones?" with that bridge which "Giant Steps" is derived from. It's tough negotiating the bridge, but it's interesting.

I was going to say, I was having trouble about the sound of the bass on "Weaver Of Dreams." I love the sound of the bass fiddle, when it's played well, and as close to acoustic as possible.

Some people want a more natural sound of the wood, but here Wilbur Little has quite an electric sound.

Wilbur usually got a nice, acoustic type of sound, but it bothers me here. It's the way the engineer treated it, I guess. Going through a line in some way—

I never know exactly what they're doing when they put a mic on their amp, or relay it directly into the board. I don't know which technique was used here, but it didn't sound clear, sometimes. Wilbur was usually a pretty clear player.

Dick Katz can be very sympathetic, and we had some nice counterpoint. Other times he seems totally involved in the sound he's making, and we talked about this at heated length. But he's a fine musician, and friend.

Later I had a partnership with Harold Danko. Harold's a very nice player, and we worked in different situations, duos or quartets. We made some records that I like very much.

Paul Bley

Paul Bley, born in Montréal in 1932, moved to New York in 1950, and worked briefly with Charlie Parker, Lester Young, and Charles Mingus. He invited Coleman and Don Cherry to sit in when he was working at the Hillcrest Club in Los Angeles in 1958, and they showed him the way out of what he called the "bebop wilderness"—he then became a key figure in the Ornette Coleman revolution in jazz. His first wife was composer Carla Bley, and during the early 1960s he worked in a pioneering free jazz trio with Jimmy Giuffre and Steve Swallow, then with Sonny Rollins. He was involved in the Jazz Composers Guild, with Cecil Taylor, Roswell Rudd, Archie Shepp, Sun Ra, and others. A highly influential figure in jazz, in the last two decades he has been one of Konitz's most frequent partners.

Paul Bley loves standards. These are great tunes, and since I'm a standard-lover too, that's what we ended up playing. Paul talks in his autobiography *Stopping Time* about the limitations of the AABA form, so now he plays them polytonally. Within the thirty-two-bar structure, he really frees up the tonality. We laugh out loud sometimes, he plays some things that sound so surprising. He's very free within that. It's when he goes out of the key and goes elsewhere that he becomes really creative; when he plays very consonantly, very tonally, it's less interesting to me. On "Sweet And Lovely" or "All The Things You Are" Paul is all over the place, playing in a million different keys, so it's pretty spontaneous.

Paul is a one of a kind guy, and it's always a pleasure, and a challenge, to play with him. Often he plays brilliantly. But as with people that you love, there are certain tendencies that are not lovable. Sometimes I feel like he doesn't really like what he's hearing and will play antagonistically. I feel like he's not really playing with me, at those times; he's playing against me, and it makes it difficult because he plays very strongly.

Why does he do that?

Well, sometimes he just gets impatient with accompanying, I think, and wants to just plow in and play. And I try to encourage him. Playing at the Blue Note a few years ago, about the third night at the club, before the first set I asked him and Steve Swallow if we could de-emphasize the solos and play more as a group. Sometimes it worked great, but frequently Paul would just comp in a very standard way, and I hate when piano players, or anybody, accompanies me as though they're not really listening to me, and reacting to what I'm playing. Maybe he was reacting in his way and I didn't hear it, so I didn't want to keep saying anything. But overall, for the nine days that we played, it was really very creative, and I enjoyed it—and so did the listeners, I think.

Recently I played with Paul and Matt Wilson and a fine bassist, John Hebert, in the Azores, way out in the Atlantic Ocean. We got onstage and the bass played a couple of tune-up notes, and Paul answered with the notes, and I played a couple to check my pitch, and we kept playing notes back and forth for one and a half hours—it was great fun. Greg Osby's quartet played the night before, and he said the sound man was messing with his sound. We didn't use any amplification, as usual, and Greg said you could hear "pp's" [pianissimos] in the balcony.

❧ Interview with Paul Bley

PAUL BLEY *talks about Lee Konitz.*

In 1950 I came to New York from Montréal to go to Juilliard, and my roommate was the drummer Al Levitt. Al and I became fast friends, and he at the time was the host drummer for Lennie at Lennie's studio, at the private Saturday night sessions which Lee, and Warne, and Peter Ind and he attended. So without having to join the Tristano school, I had entrée.

Did you have lessons with Tristano?

Oh no no no, lessons are a very dangerous thing—they take away much more than they bring.

But you had discussions with Tristano?

At the time, no—I was just trying to get him off Chinese food because of the MSG. It eventually killed him. I was trying to bring him to Europe.

They were clamoring for Lennie in Europe, but he decided that since he had many women that were only too happy to bring him Chinese food and keep him company, Europe was a bad idea.

He wasn't a great gourmand then.

Chinese food was the quickest way of getting through the problem of dinner.

Talking to Lee, Tristano's influence is pretty positive.

Oh absolutely. I mean he had a few flaws, like wanting the rhythm section to be mechanical, but certainly from the harmonic point of view, he was a genius.

I'm not sure if that was his fault or their fault—on the recordings he did with good drummers, like Roy Haynes, they play great. The secret of playing with a drummer is finding a great drummer! Nick Stabulas was a good drummer. But rhythm section interplay was not Lennie's forte. It came way after Lennie, with the Bill Evans equal-voiced trio with Scotty LaFaro. It was the soloist with rhythm section accompaniment, at the time.

And he never really changed that.

No he did not.

If you could stand up to him, as Lee could, Tristano would be a great teacher, but if you couldn't, as perhaps Warne Marsh and maybe others couldn't, there were drawbacks.

Warne was a great player, and I think Warne stood up to him. [Tristano] was a very dominant personality, and a very brilliant thinker. Anyone who could influence a whole school of players, in New York City where there's no shortage of strong players, obviously contributed to the form. The problem with most improvisers is that they take something out of the form, and don't put anything back. In Lennie's case, he put everything back, and took hardly anything out. He was historically a very important figure, considering how few white people there were changing the landscape—he was one of the greats.

He is very neglected.

Not by me.

The crisis came when Lee realized that even though he was winning the polls opposite Charlie Parker—one year Charlie Parker came in first in *Down Beat,* the next year Lee came in first; in other words he was right up there—he realized that he wanted to be playing with a swinging rhythm section. They had a rhythm section crisis—now this is all my own personal opinion. There was a crisis that Lee addressed by motivating his own rhythm sections by his alto sax playing, as opposed to ignoring the rhythm sections, which was seemingly what Lennie was doing. So he addressed the idea of "swinging," which is a terrible expression relating to a rhythm section—Lee overcame that nonparticipation by the rhythm section in the period post-Lennie.

Lee retained his originality, but at the same point became a vital member of the rhythm section. To me that was a metamorphosis much to the credit of jazz music, period.

Because the pure Lennie–Sal Mosca school didn't bloom beyond a half dozen or a dozen players, whereas Lee went all over the world, and played and recorded with musicians from every country. And there was no division between Lee's playing and theirs from a rhythmic point of view.

Do you think his approach to rhythm changed in that at first it was very complex and polyrhythmic, like Warne Marsh developed, and then it got freer?

This is about the extra-long line, and Lee just broke the line and began working with drummers. You see drummers are a wonderful source of cross-pollination to a soloist, and the great soloists have all related to drummers. So I think Lee overcame what was not a major problem of Tristano's way of playing but it certainly put him even further up the scale in terms of being able to endure. And he's playing great, even last night!

Do you think he's playing with too many people who are not his equal?

[Laughs.] That's like a policeman asking a guy, "Do you sleep with too many women?"

Well I heard him recently with a guitar player like something out of Django Reinhardt, and it was very interesting in a way how bad they were, and how insensitive and unsuitable.

He can't be threatened. You can't put a bad rhythm section next to Lester Young and threaten Lester Young, or Bird. These people can carry a whole band, never mind just a rhythm section. These are giants, they take them on their back and walk down the street with them!

Yes, but for the sake of the listeners, it would be better . . .

Fuck the listeners! The listeners are privileged audience participants, with no relationship to anything except the fact that they're there for moral support.

Lee mentions your interest in breaking up the standard AABA progression.

There was an article in *Down Beat* in something like '54 in which I mentioned that jazz had reached a crisis, and that the AABA form had too many As, and not enough C, D, E, F, G. So I began working with groups where we would play totally free, and that led to a kind of a dead end, because "totally free" didn't necessarily allow you to continue. A totally free piece is a totally free piece, end of concert.

Ornette came along and suggested A, B, C, D, E, F, G, H, I, J, K, in which repetition was anathema. And that was the missing link—that you didn't have to relate to any early sketch of what was going to happen when. So you had pieces that went from A to Z. It wasn't totally free because totally free was A forever, metamorphosing. It was a form that took hold, because you could finally return to the written music and the audience had something to hold on to. It gave your publishing company a little bit of a break because you weren't sending all the royalties to Cole Porter.

"Intuition" was the milestone early recording that said you don't need the popular song form. That broke the dam. Once the dam was broken by Lennie and Lee and Warne, then you could have people like Ornette and Don Cherry and all that free jazz school.

If music is conversation, repetition is anathema to that idea . . . anathema to that idea . . . anathema to that idea—see I said it three times, that was two times too many! That's the problem with all of early jazz, you were playing on the same thirty-two bars, of which less eight bars it was the same thing over and over again.

Except that what people like Lee, and Charlie Parker, tried to do, was to disguise the repeating thirty-two-bar form in a "through-composed statement."

That's right. The idea was that you didn't have to play the thirty-two bars in the same sequence rhythmically, and it should be different every chorus. Repetition is the enemy. I'm sure that Lennie and Lee and those guys broke up the rhythm and the harmony and so forth, and they were students of jazz so it didn't turn out to be some classical mixture. It turned out to be real jazz with a revolutionary approach to it.

What was your response to those two free sides when they eventually came out?

I was sorry I wasn't at the date!

The only way to break free of the Charlie Parker triadic school of jazz was to write pieces that took the line beyond what the triads implied. So the writing is very important. Since we now have the Tristano language—and the atonalist language—as part of us, we no longer have to give reference to these things. They're built into our speech. We can use any one of those techniques, depending on the amount of contrast we want to throw to the audience. The audience only stays awake so long as we keep changing.

The thing about a good improviser is that when he's playing a written piece and it now becomes time for the solo, he will continue the piece as if the solo was written as well as the piece, so it's seamless. And so pieces become very influential. The writing in the Tristano school was very important, to get the players off the Charlie Parker bandwagon.

Lennie was a great player, but history judges people's importance by how many converts they make to their way of thinking and playing. Lee was able to make that adjustment without sacrificing his originality. And that makes Lee one of the geniuses of our time. He's been playing with ideas. The word *idea* is not prevalent in improvising as much as it should be. It's one thing to be a conversationalist, it's another to say something, and it's a third to say something that contains an idea.

The most important thing about Lee is what he doesn't do. The fact that he doesn't sound like a Blue Note bebopper, and the fact that it's possible to have a whole career without sounding like a Blue Note bebopper, already is refreshing to young jazz musicians.

What do you think about his ideas about the blues—that he can't or shouldn't play them?

He stole that idea from me—I have a tune called "I'm Too Rich To Play The Blues."

But he thinks he's too *white* to play the blues.

[Laughs.] It may be the same thing.

No, he plays great blues.

You're a lover of standards, as Lee is. What do you make of his commitment to playing a small number of songs, relatively?

Well, I can answer the question from my point of view. If you're going to change the standard every chorus from the preceding chorus—if you're going to change the order of the chords, if you're going to insert passing chords, the idea being that you don't want to play the same chorus twice—then the standard is not a limitation.

There are so few great players in the world. I had the privilege of playing with Lester Young when I was at Juilliard—we both worked for the Shaw Agency, and they sent me on the road to Cleveland with him. I have photos of it, in which I have a crew cut like a marine. We were on a small stage in Cleveland, at one of those clubs, and Pres had the bell of his horn right by my ear. I couldn't believe that nobody else on the planet could play that beautifully, with such a great sound. It was just Pres.

Lee's in the same situation. There's just one Lee Konitz. Anybody who gets to hear him in person has an experience that they're going to carry with them the rest of their lives. That's the difference between playing notes and making music—when you make music, you change the person's life that's listening to you.[1] ☛

Martial Solal

The French-Algerian pianist was born in Algiers in 1927, and moved to Paris in 1950, performing and recording with Django Reinhardt, Don Byas, Lucky Thompson, and recording the remarkable *Quartet* with Sidney Bechet and Kenny Clarke in 1957. In 1968 he first recorded with Lee Konitz, and performed with him in 1974 and 1980–81, and regularly thereafter. He has also led and recorded with his own big band.

Martial loves to improvise. Left to his own devices, though, he'll kind of play pretty much what he knows, brilliant stuff that he's worked out. Drummer Daniel Humair, who's played with him for many years, knows all his fancy embellishments. He told me that one night he said to him, "Could you stop the bullshit and just play?"—he knew him well enough to say that! And the next night Martial tried to just play without all the ornamentation. Then he went back to the more fancy kind of playing!

A couple of years ago they released a duo record we made at a concert in Hamburg in 1983, and that was fun—he's very orchestral, and very rhythmic, very stimulating. Last week [2003] I played a duo with Martial in Paris and it was really nice—we even played in Nice, and that was nice!

Listening to this duo in Paris, he is totally unique. A *very* obvious response to every nuance—he hears every *nuance*. And this guy is a little bit hard of hearing in one ear! He has a very strong rhythmic impetus to these clusters of sounds—it's so exciting, I just started to cry. I can hear that I'm being inspired by it.[2] I will join him at a date in Turino in September [2005]—can't wait!

Yet you said a lot of his soloing involves material he's worked out.
He has a very extensive vocabulary that he refers to, and he loves to improvise. All he needs is to play with people who inspire him to improvise more.

I heard Martial practice a couple of hours before our concert in Paris recently [2003]—some really difficult chop things—and then when we played, it was as spontaneous as hell. I mean, I hear familiar things that he plays, like we all must do, but he was more than eager to respond. As is Paul Bley in many ways.

[We listen to Konitz and Solal playing "The Song Is You" from that Paris concert.]

That went on for an hour—free playing, and tunes, a Duke Ellington medley, mixed up in a way you never heard before. I'm picking up from everything he's doing, I think. That's determining my next selection. It's just so obvious that's he's hearing what I'm doing, that it pulls me in. With all his facility, he still lays back and lets me take the lead at times.

Do you think sometimes he's parodying you?

Well, in a way, yes. But he's got a very active sense of humor going most of the time. He's always playing little cutesy paraphrases. He's not improvising all those sixty-fourth-note runs, I don't think. There's a French flamboyance to his more glib articulations, and there's so much filigree here, in the negative sense of the word—but his musicality wins out.

He can't really let the groove be too obvious for very long.

No. That's the way he writes too. I heard a new set of arrangements he wrote, and it really started to bother me, because it was "stop and start, stop and start" all the time. It's too fragmented for my taste. But his playing still sets up a groove. I've never just sat and counted the beats, but when I'm keeping time I've never felt "one" changing in his solo playing. As complex as it is, that's remarkable. People who know piano-playing certainly are aware of him.

I'm sure Martial knows Earl Hines's music—more especially Art Tatum, though. That kind of glib playing is very much out of him—the cascading runs, and so on.

When Tatum was accompanying, he didn't always respond to other players—it was almost like he was soloing himself.

Yes, exactly. But Martial is with every thing that I do. When I was playing free, he caught the little transitions. I don't know if he has perfect pitch. But he plays enough notes, and one of them is going to be the note that you played! And he plays pretty thick chord structures.

◥ Interview with Martial Solal

MARTIAL SOLAL *comments on his work with Konitz.*

I don't know if Lee remembers this, but it was at the Club St. Germain, the famous jazz club in Paris, that I first played with him. In the fifties, there was a visit by the Kenton orchestra, and Lee came to a *boeuf*—a jam session—with us. I was house pianist at the club, and so I was able to participate in some incredible sessions. One began to hear talk in Paris of this new school, called cool jazz, which became the object of passionate discussions. There were those who adored it, and those who didn't understand it. I loved it!

Lee was the first player I worked with in a duo. Since then, I've expanded my experience in this genre—I think I've participated in more than twenty duo situations, with piano, harmonica, trumpet, drums, trombone, violin, saxophone, clarinet, and bass. The duo is certainly more difficult, for the pianist and for the other musician, but it's also more exciting, and it leaves more space for the invention of new formulas. The experience with Lee is probably the one that has endured the longest—and it's not finished. Although our approach to jazz is a little different—not least because of the instruments we play—I believe that we're complementary. Above all, in this duo there's a great quality of reciprocal listening. We are always at the service of the music, and the result is equivalent to a sonata for piano and saxophone that could have been composed.

I have fantastic memories of the quartet recording *Jazz à Juan,* live at Antibes, that I did with Lee. The year 1974 represents the beginning of a new era for jazz. After several difficult years, jazz became popular again, and concerts multiplied. And that concert was a total success. Recently I heard an extract on the radio and I was astonished at the freshness of that music, thirty years later.[3] 🖙

Keith Jarrett

The lyrical, romantic style of Keith Jarrett, born 1945, is probably the most influential in contemporary jazz piano after Bill Evans's. Following a period with Miles Davis, he formed very successful American and European groups in the 1970s, featuring saxophonists Dewey Redman and Jan Garbarek respectively. He is a fervent apostle of the value of improvisation, and his work with Gary Peacock and Jack DeJohnette is some of Konitz's favorite music.

Keith is a great piano player. He has a great rhythm section, Gary Peacock and Jack DeJohnette. I think Brad Mehldau is more creative, but Keith is looser in some way. I don't know Keith's out-playing that much, except his record *Inside Out,* which I enjoyed very much—and a newer one that's great stuff, *Always Let Me Go.*

Once I did a television show with Chet Baker, and Charlie Haden and Beaver Harris, in the new Half Note club in New York. It was a jazz series on a small TV station. Keith showed up, and asked to sit in with us. That was, I think, the only time I've ever played with him. We were playing standards, and I was very impressed.[4]

I had a "Keith Jarrett" routine with Harold Danko. We went into the sounds of moaning, and gestures. We did that one time in Denmark, when Keith and his wife were in the audience. I asked Harold, "Should we?" and we did. I looked over, and Keith was kind of laughing. I could live without the vocal and body action, but the music is the end result I'm interested in. If the player is drunk or high, and the music is good, so be it!

I haven't talked to him much about improvising, really. I just know that he has an affinity for Lennie's music. On one of his albums, *Tribute,* he mentions me as one of the people that he's paying tribute to. I was very pleased with that. I didn't know his playing very much till he played standards, really. I heard one of his solo performances from Paris, and I was very impressed with that. He's a great musician—he's really an improviser.

He is a problematic player though. As Enrico Pieranunzi says, he sometimes seems to put great weight on some idea that's really very banal. There seems to be some lack of a critical faculty.

Well, the few standards records that I have with Jack DeJohnette and Gary Peacock, I have very few criticisms of them. I think musically he makes great choices. I agree he plays very uncritically and unedited in some way—but if you hear a banality come out, and can mess with it a bit, that's not a bad thing. We all coast into "banalville" occasionally.

He obviously thinks he's a great player!

Well, you've got to think that. He's not a great singer, so I wish he would not distract from the great playing with the histrionics. But Keith is a special musician, and being special can bring lots of problems adjusting to us "nonspecials." Whatever he has to do to make it happen is incidental to us, the lovers of greatness.

Chick Corea and Scientology

Pianist and composer Chick Corea, born 1941, is one of the post–Bill Evans players that Konitz most admires. Like Keith Jarrett, he became known through an early association with Miles Davis, and his group

Return To Forever was one of the most successful jazz ensembles of the 1970s. It was through Corea that Konitz became involved in Scientology.

I got to know Chick around 1973. He's a great musician and a nice guy. I saw that Chick was really functioning well in his life, and when he recommended Scientology as his inspiration, I was more than curious. I saw it as a way of facing some problems. I was looking for some help to understand myself and others better, and it was good while it lasted. When I was part of the Scientology group we played at some of the churches. That was in the seventies and eighties.

Chick asked me once when I was in Hollywood to record a tune for a record he was making—a lovely tune called "Duende," he told me he had written it for me that night. We recorded it at his studio as a duo. I also recorded his piece "Hairy Canary" with Harold Danko, and with my nonet we played a couple more of his pieces, "Times Lie" and "Matrix." The nonet was playing at the Village Vanguard, and Chick came in. He loves to jam, so I invited him to play on his pieces—the band was inspired!

At some point in the 1970s I lived in London for six or eight months, in Belgravia [a central district]. I passed by a Scientology place, and found out that I could get some of the services for less money than in the States. So I decided to check that out, and go back to the States a little more adjusted and a little more aware. I did—and I was! It was a school, and you take regular courses. I never graduated from high school and that context was a great opportunity of continuing my brief formal education also. You can also do what they call auditing, which is similar to an analytic session. I was involved in Scientology for a few years, but it was very expensive, so eventually I pulled out. I'm not an "organization" person.

How did you come to be living in London?

I was playing at Ronnie Scott's, and I met someone who wanted me to make a private record for him. He was someone who obviously had some money. He asked how much I'd want to record "Lover Man" and a few tunes that he knew about from my records when he went to school. I said, "I don't know," and he mentioned that he had some real estate dealings. I said that I wanted to stay in London for a while, and if he could help get me an apartment I'd appreciate that. And he got me a beautiful apartment that Vincent Price used to live in, in Belgravia, and paid the rent on it for about six months. He was really like a modern-day patron. And I made that recording—I have a copy of it someplace, David Lee was the piano player, Peter Ind and Al Levitt were the rhythm section. It was a private recording and wasn't issued—some nice playing.

10 ✌ The Material
Standards, Blues, and Free

Konitz is closely identified with what became known from the late 1940s or early 1950s as the standards repertoire—the Great American Songbook of classic show-tunes and film themes written mostly between the 1920s and 1950s. It became accepted that a working jazz musician should have a good knowledge of many of these tunes. The category is an expanding one because bebop and subsequent players wrote original compositions on the standard harmonic structures. The term *standard* has a use in jazz and also in wider popular culture, which began in the LP era with Ella Fitzgerald's *Songbook* albums from 1956 onward, and Frank Sinatra's contemporary releases. The songs favored by jazz musicians have strong melodies and flowing harmonic structures, which provide a fruitful basis for improvisation, and a common language that allows those who haven't met before to play together—as Konitz stresses. They can be reinterpreted in many ways without losing their identity. On several occasions, for instance in the liner notes to *The Real Lee Konitz* on Atlantic, Konitz has explained how the canon of American popular song provides an almost limitless resource for the improviser.

Konitz's attitude to the blues is more ambivalent; he doubts whether it is part of his heritage as a white jazz musician. The discussion here covers the difficult question of the status of jazz as both an authentic American art, and an authentic African-American art. Despite his protestations, however, it's clear that Konitz really is a great blues player, as witness his classic 1965 tribute "Blues for Bird." Free improvisation is another area that Konitz continues to explore. It's not always appreciated that he pioneered it on the groundbreaking recordings "Intuition" and "Digression" from 1949 with Tristano and Warne Marsh, discussed in this chapter. Konitz concludes with some cautionary comments about saxophonist Anthony Braxton's attempts to interpret Tristano from an avant-garde or free jazz perspective.

What is your feeling about the songs that you play, in their original setting—in musicals, mostly?

I love the musical movies! On stage, I didn't see too many of them—I saw *Guy and Dolls*. But the movies were spectacular—the ones with Fred Astaire, with a lot of dancing and singing. And then there were these great tunes. I didn't know too much about them at the time—that was before I was playing.

I would have heard the tune "Laura" in the film, and then when I got around to playing it, I identified it with the movie. So many of those great songs were written specifically for Fred Astaire—he was a great motivation to write a nice song.

Part of the reason you favor standards, you've said, is because they're a kind of common language.

I play them because I like them. And I realized I could connect with other people without having to go through elaborate rehearsals of new music. When you arrive at three in the afternoon and have a concert at eight, that's pretty difficult to do. One night I walked into a club in Rome, and the piano player had his Real Book out on the piano, and I started to get worried.[1] That bothers me when they don't really know the tunes. But for the most part they do. That's not the ideal in terms of having a set group. I'm so impressed when I hear a Dave Holland band, or Brad Mehldau's trio, but I haven't really needed to do that in my life, it appears.

Standard songs are good songs *and* they're very familiar. And because of that I feel I'm starting from a higher level in a sense. Having gone through "All The Things You Are" thousands and thousands of times, I still have the feeling that I'm playing the first set of variations that I ever played on it. I admire musicians trying to write tunes. I've tried to write original tunes, and I do write every day, but they never seem to compare to the great show tunes written for Fred Astaire and others.

You have played and recorded quite a few originals by other players, though, such as Kenny Wheeler's "Everyone's Song But My Own," and Frank Wunsch's "September Waltz."

Both very nice tunes. But I think the conception of those tunes by Wayne, Monk, and Horace Silver is from the Afro-American tradition. I can identify up to a point, but I don't have the kind of funk that guys who play those tunes have—Trane, Rollins, and so on. I come closer to what I can interpret and express with the old show tunes.

Maybe this is a dumb question, but how did you learn a standard? I know you grew up with them. Some people say, "Go back to the original sheet music and get the melodic line correct, don't rely on other people's interpretations." Did you have the idea of being faithful to the composer's intention?

There are no dumb questions. Answers—maybe!

I usually had the piano sheets—there were no Real Books then, no Jamey Aebersold play-along recordings. That was the exact information—you wouldn't get precisely that from Frank Sinatra or Ella Fitzgerald. They were the closest to it, probably, singing the given melody, but they usually added embellishments. I think the song as written—the composer's intention—should be the starting point.

So from the beginning of your career, you always looked at the sheet music?

Yes, I think so—then listen to what others did to it for stimulation.

On the album of Jobim songs you made with Peggy Stern, had you heard all of them performed by other people?

Yes, pretty much. There might have been one or two that we learned for the date. But they are such lovely tunes, you felt that you knew them somehow from the start.

Hearing a recording of someone singing or playing it helps a lot conceptually. Learning a tune of any kind requires visualization, internalization, externalization—being away from your instrument, ideally, singing, whistling and/or tapping rhythmically. With all these steps you get to become really familiar with the material, and at some point you feel you know it well enough to start embellishing, and finally composing an entirely different melody on the basic song. A fascinating process!

What is it about the classic songs that you love improvising on, that makes them classic?

Mostly the fact that these are great melodies with interesting chord structures and sometimes even good lyrics. They're the established songs—the jury is in. That's a very important part of it for me, and I think for Sonny Rollins, Charlie Parker, Lennie, and Warne, and people who play the same repertoire year after year. The more familiar the basic material becomes, the more possibilities open up. So I've not always been searching for new material.

The fact that they're familiar to the audience is important too.

Yes, that's a part of it—though by now, they're not so familiar. I don't know what the younger people know about these show tunes, unless they're students of the music. And if I don't play the melody, who's going to recognize the chord structure? Because I might very well play one of these familiar progressions just starting with the improvisation on the first chorus.

I guess when a song has a very strong melody—as on the Jobim songs—it dominates, and you can't escape from it.

Well, sometimes. And it's fun to just loosen it up a little bit for the second chorus, rather than throwing [the melody] away completely.

At the opposite extreme, you've got pieces like many of Monk's, which are structures of motifs. For the improviser, isn't it easier if you're given motifs that you can build on?

I don't know, it depends really. Some melodies suggest variations—those are the ones I keep playing over and over again. And some absolutely don't, to me—those are the ones I've stayed away from.

The ones that don't suggest variations, are there some of those that you like?

Yes, like "Sophisticated Lady." Somehow, everybody runs those little changes in there. The melody and the bridges to that, and "Prelude To A Kiss," are so beautiful. I recorded "Prelude To A Kiss" with Kenny Werner, very free of basic harmonies, and that enabled me to get away from the melody.

Do you feel you don't want to improvise on it because you can't improve on it, or is that not the point?

I think it's more not having spent a lot of time going through those songs. If I played them every day, like I do "Cherokee" and whatever, it would be different. But I do have trouble with Duke Ellington songs, improvising on those. Somehow, they seem complete in their melodies, and it's enough for me to play slight variations.

You and Tristano wrote new melodies, over standards, that are serpentine and complicated.

They really send you off with a bang! It's inspiring to start your solo at that level. To play one of those written lines that Tristano and I did, and Charlie Parker before us, can lift the variations on the first chorus to a higher level of intensity. And you're supposed to come out up here, continuing hopefully to raise that level and develop it in some way, and that's very demanding. If you start with [the original] melody, you have more choruses to develop in, if you can't handle the greater intensity—and sometimes I can't, I must confess.

I think also because I've been playing these songs for so long, I don't really play the melody that much. We might improvise ten choruses of "Body And Soul," and Johnny Green gets the royalties; we don't get any for our variations.

To pick up our discussion earlier [in chapter 6], Stefano Battaglia, the pianist you worked with in Italy, told me that you know a song as a set of intervals, like a singer does, rather than as a set of chords.

A song is a set of intervals. I don't sit and analyze each interval, but they certainly can be analyzed. I realized recently that "White Christmas" starts out with chromatic eighth notes, and I was listening to one of Beethoven's symphonies, the Pastoral, that had a very "White Christmassy" kind of motif. Maybe that's where Irving Berlin got it from.

Since I realized it had that chromatic beginning, [the song] seemed more hip, somehow. And who of my generation doesn't love Bing Crosby's version? I love Mel Tormé's "Chestnuts Roasting On An Open Fire" ["The Christmas Song"] more, though.

Do you like chromaticism?

It's indispensable. I mean that's all we've got in this Western system—no quarter-tones, etc. So, wail with the twelve tones!

Charlie Parker uses very elementary chromaticism, within the key. Wayne Shorter, though, is totally away from the basic harmony, in his Plugged Nickel playing especially—fantastic!

Have you ever analyzed any of the songs you love, like "All The Things You Are"? What makes it so special to improvise on?

The frequent changes of key throughout is one of the big attractions. And since I've changed the last part of the tune, from the bridge on out, to a tritone away, when I come into the last twelve bars it's no longer F minor-B flat minor, it's now B minor-E minor, etc. It becomes a much more interesting progression to play on. Someone told me that Jerome Kern got that from Bach—I haven't found the piece yet. Also there are very poetic lyrics.

I believe that tune has a chord on every one of the twelve tones.[2] And there are a lot of changes in it, that don't repeat.

I never realized that, thanks for telling me. That's what makes it very special, too.

You can presumably play these standards in any key—but do you have favorite keys for particular songs, or favorite keys in general?

I like all twelve keys, and try to play more in the less familiar ones. The keys of F-sharp and C-sharp and B are very interesting—they just need a little more slowing down of the tempo maybe, to feel comfortable. But as a result of that new series of notes and keyboard positions, new melodies can occur.

Do you ever call out a song in an unusual key and find that the other players protest?

Sometimes yes. I did a concert once with [Italian pianist] Franco D'Andrea, and we were supposed to do Gershwin tunes, and I asked him about doing twelve songs in twelve different keys, and he did it great. But sometimes I mention a key and they say "OK," and don't really know it.

I have a very small body of materials. In an interview in *Down Beat* I said that I could just spend the rest of my time playing "All The Things You Are," and I mean that. It's a little embarrassing, because I should be learning and playing new tunes, and I do. But I end up doing the same tunes most of the time—Joe Henderson did too, I think—and they usually sound different. That's the intriguing part of the process to me.

Some jazz players say the great songs are not being composed any more. David Raksin said the American contribution is not necessarily jazz, it's those great tunes for movies and the theater which those songwriters wrote during that early period. That's very true. I don't hear tunes that are that fascinating, melodically or harmonically, these days. Maybe the lyrical part is missing, so we don't hear Wayne Shorter's tunes sung, like the great show tunes were.

◤ Interview with Peggy Stern

> **PEGGY STERN,** *born in Philadelphia in 1946, worked with Lee Konitz during the 1990s. She studied classical piano at Eastman School of Music and New England Conservatory. Moving to San Francisco, she performed with salsa and R&B bands, and back in New York, worked with Konitz, Red Holloway, and Matt Wilson. She has recorded as leader with Ben Allison, Drew Gress, Bernard Purdie, and Harvie Swartz.*

We met at Stan Getz's memorial service in New York City, I think in 1991. Lee had heard my program with Marion McPartland on air, and he said, "I liked your playing and your compositions, do you want to play some?" He's had a series of partnership with pianists—Dick Katz, Harold Danko, and then myself. Often we were a duo, and sometimes a trio or quartet. I have a particular love of Latin music, and it was through me that Lee got more interested in that. He loves Jobim, but he didn't go there because Stan Getz had already done it. *The Jobim Collection* that we did is a sweet album. It's a pity it's so hard to get.

We parted several years ago, but recently an opportunity came up to play again, and he said I should be able to play "Cherokee" in every key. This is a tune I've stayed away from my whole life, because everybody plays it really fast, and I don't think fast—I think very much like Lee does, and that's how we got along! I'm certainly "in the moment" like Lee is, and looking for new melody. Lee says the melody comes first, and he's right, but he absolutely knows his harmony. He can play *anything*, but the kind of harmony that he's used to is the basic II-V-I harmony of that jazz era, and the kind of writing that I do is much more impressionistic. He had problems stringing his way through my harmonies on the album *Lunasea*. It was new to him, and I think he did that some more after me, but now I think he's reverted back to what he's most comfortable doing, playing standards. Now he's more interested in using just bass and drums, where he's not restricted by the chords the pianist is playing.

I think his most important legacy is real improvisation, and it's so much influenced my musical life. Before I met him, I was always embell-ishing the original melody—that's how I improvise. I always have that in my head—but he verbalized a lot of things that I was already doing with-out thinking. It's a very small number of people that verbalize improvisa-tion his way. Stringing together things that you've practiced before—that's what's taught in the colleges, mostly.[3] 🖝

The Blues

Safford Chamberlain in *An Unsung Cat* refers to "that overall, un-bluesy tone or feeling of Tristano's music," and I'd question that.
I don't remember Tristano saying anything to me about a "bluesy tone." It didn't feel natural for me and I didn't want to reproduce that kind of feeling. I express my blues in my own way, which doesn't include blue notes. Some-times they slip in, of course.

Tristano's tribute to Charlie Parker, "Requiem," that was the blues, but not in that blue note concept—though he played some authentic blue notes. He didn't usually play on the blues progression, but he loved Bird, and Charlie was the most sophisticated blues player that ever lived. When he died, obviously Lennie paid tribute to him in his own language—beauti-fully, I think.

As you did later with "Blues For Bird." But you didn't play many blues as such, with Tristano.
No, hardly ever. I didn't like the idea of making a standard sound bluesy, unless it was Charlie Parker or a great player who made it sound real. Bird really felt it. The rest did it automatically, and sounded artificial in some way—and even Bird did after the ideas lost their appeal to him, and became clichés.[4]

I do play the blues every day, but not "bluesy" blues. I just play it as a form, with or without the standard harmonic construction—with substitute chords added, or with the whole harmonic thing improvised. It's a great short story form. It's still a challenge to me to play that form in a simple way, on three chords basically, and not sound corny.

On one of the Blue Note records with Brad Mehldau and Charlie Haden, *Another Shade of Blue,* we play a blues. And in my sleeve notes, I said something about this, that I had a problem playing blue notes. And after I wrote those notes, I listened to it, and I'm playing blue notes! I can't get away from it. But I'm not exaggerating that feeling, I hope. I hope that they [blue notes] fit into a musical phrase, and make some sense, but they're not part of my heritage. I called them "Jew notes" when Stan Getz played them, or when I do: "oy doy doy doy doy doy doy doy doy!" [Konitz sings rising phrase.] Holy Moses!

You played them on some of your early recordings with Tristano, like "317 E. 32nd Street." But you think that throwing in blue notes is an easy way of being expressive.

Well I think it is certainly part of the black experience. The church and the blues are some of the roots of the black expression, so it's meaningful to them, but not for me—and certainly it's an easy expressive ploy.

If you're not a blues player, you're in quite a small category of jazz players—with Coleman Hawkins maybe, and Bill Evans.

Well, Coleman Hawkins played the blues, though he played them very personally. Bill Evans played a lot of blue notes, a lot of bluesy phrases—I think he identified very much with the blues, maybe to get away from the intellectual, cerebral stigma that was imposed on him. But I have always felt a part of a small category of players, for good and bad. I wanted to be part of the flow, part of the gang; but always ended up sticking out, as it were.

Since so many people think the blues is essential to jazz, doesn't your attitude put you at odds with the jazz tradition?

To that extent, maybe so. I've got klezmer in my heritage, which I don't identify with at all; I'm not trying to make a statement about Jewishness. If anything, I just feel an American heritage, the great show tunes especially, and a love for the great classical music—Ives, Copland, Bernstein. I feel very close to that kind of great music. I don't have a special interest in pop music, ethnic music, etc.

People talk about "the melting pot"—that the American heritage is the heritage of all the people that have mixed together in the United States. But your strongest identity is simply as an American?

Yes. I'm beginning to question that now a little bit [with the Iraq war]! But as Virgil Thomson said, "The way to write [or play] American music is simple. All you have to do is to be an American and then write [or play] any kind of music you wish." I identify greatly with the black music, certainly—this has been my life. I thank God for Louis and Lester and those guys.

Let me take a moment to try and clarify my position on this jazz community. Since we [the Tristano players] were all Caucasians, there was a thought about how we fit into this "black" musical world. As we all appreciate, the great players, the real innovators, have been from the African-American heritage—I hate the "black" and "white" concepts. So these great musicians are where we white guys get our inspiration, and I can only thank them for their music.

Isn't jazz really a mixture of black and white influences?
The leading figures have been black—and to that extent I identify with them, very much so. Hopefully this is a music from all people dedicated to it, inspired by the great black players.

Original Compositions

Konitz has composed pieces on original chord-progressions, as well as many original themes over standards. The latter was a familiar technique with the Tristano school, as it was with bebop. "Subconscious-Lee," based on the chords of Cole Porter's "What Is This Thing Called Love?," was the first of many titles to incorporate Lee's first name, and it is now almost his theme tune; he thus became what has been called a "living adverb." Other original lines by Konitz include those dedicated to two of his children, Rebecca and Karen ("Kary"): "Hi Beck," based on "Pennies from Heaven," and "Kary's Trance," based on "Play, Fiddle, Play."

I'm writing every day. All my books are filled up with little phrases—here's a blues in G, here's something else that I wrote before and revised, basically lines, not arrangements. My friend Ohad Talmor in New York, a very talented young saxophonist and writer, arranged music for a nine-piece band that we recorded in the spring of '05. I send him these eight-, twelve-, and thirty-two-bar lines, and he has written some very nice arrangements on them.

Ohad was responsible for that French Impressionist string quartet music, which he adapted usually from piano scores by Debussy, Fauré, and Satie.[5] These adaptations were not jazzy—my role was to play some written themes, and then to improvise over the classical writing. My concern was not to get hokey or out of character. We played live at the Knitting Factory, and next day a friend of mine said, "The music was beautiful but I wish you would have improvised." I thought, "Great, I really accomplished what I was trying to do!" because I was improvising!

On the record with Joey Baron and Greg Cohen—*Some New Stuff*—which John Zorn produced for the DIW label, I brought in a bunch of things that I had written.[6] They adapted them so quickly, I was really impressed. One was based on a standard, "Pennies from Heaven" in minor, but the rest of them were original progressions.[7] I still have ambitions for getting more involved in writing for ensembles. And I still like to write variations on familiar progressions.

Composition "June 05" on original changes, appearing on *Portology* (Omnitone, 2007).

There's also "Chick Came Around," on original changes. So you do also create your own "standards." But why haven't you done new harmonies so much? Is it because you don't play a keyboard instrument?

That's a large part of it—my interest is more horizontal than vertical. But I do play some piano.

When I played with Phil Woods at Umbria in July 2003 we did four CDs in three days for the Philology label. One of the days we played my themes, and one we played his. The third CD we added Enrico Rava, and played his material with Italian rhythm sections including the pianist Stefano Bollani. One afternoon Phil and I played some duos, even a funny one singing. Paolo Piangiarelli is the founder of that label. He used to tell me his three favorite musicians were Phil, Chet, and Lee. I said, "Thank you, but how come your label isn't Chetology or Leeology?" On the next record I did, at the bottom of the cover it said, "Leeology #1." Thanks a lot, Paolo!

¶ Interview with Evan Parker

Tenor and soprano saxophonist **EVAN PARKER**, *born in Bristol, West of England, in 1944, is one of the leading exponents of free jazz and free improvisation. He moved to London in 1965 and began an important association with guitarist Derek Bailey, coleading the Music Improvisation Company 1969–72 and cofounding the Incus record label in 1970. He subsequently played in numerous ensembles, including the Globe Unity Orchestra, with Peter Brötzmann, Alexander Von Schlippenbach, and Charlie Watts. Since 1980 he has played in a trio with Barry Guy and Paul Lytton, and in 1990 he assembled his Electro-Acoustic Ensemble, a group exploring live electronics in the digital age.*

When the Angel, in London's Soho/Covent Garden borderlands, was still a pub to meet up in, I found myself there in conversation with the legendary record collector Jacky Docherty on the subject of Lee. As is usually the case, I was probably talking about *Motion* and the great synergy between Lee and Elvin, when Jacky asserted that in his humble opinion the finest solo on record was from a much earlier period—from a Prestige record under Lee's own name, I forget which—but he then proceeded to whistle the whole thing for me. Knowing how much work Lee has done on transcribing and analysing solos I wished he could have been there.

More recently I have been thinking a lot about "Subconscious-Lee." It is said to have been written as a response to an exercise set by Tristano when Lee was studying with him. It's interesting how Lee's assignment, completed in a week, can contain enough ideas to keep me busy for years. It flows so beautifully and is intensely chromatic, but retains its relationship to "What Is This Thing Called Love?" [which it is based on], while taking nothing from "Hot House" [based on the same song].

I like *Lone-Lee* very much too and in effect parts of that are "free" but I don't think that means much—it's more important that it's Lee than that it's Free. He has an extraordinary musical mind which continues to create beautiful lines beautifulee![8] 🖝

Free Improvisation

After the more conventional numbers on the May 1949 Capitol date, Tristano's group—minus drummer Denzil Best—recorded four tracks without fixed chord progressions, meter, or specified tempo. Two were subsequently scrubbed from the acetates, but thanks to the advocacy of DJ "Symphony Sid" Torin, who obtained copies and played them regularly, the two remaining sides were released by Capitol in 1950 and 1954.[9] Journalist Barry Ulanov, a strong Tristano supporter, wrote, "The experiment was to create a spontaneous music, out of skill and intuition, which should be at once atonal, contrapuntal and improvised on a jazz base."[10] Konitz has commented that "we recorded the first totally free music in 1949 . . . we would just start playing with no plan at all. We knew each other well enough to be able to do that, and it was a lot of fun. . . . It's very difficult to really make a fine art out of, but as a procedure, it's one of the very, very important ones, I think, in playing together." Later he added, "It had its effect: Ornette Coleman heard it." However, he has also complained that "No one . . . hardly ever mentions [that date]. And you know damn well that these cats have heard that record somewhere along the line. [Free jazz of the 1960s] doesn't just come from no place."[11]

Musicians earlier in the forties and even before—such as Sidney Bechet and Roy Eldridge—may have discussed and even practiced free improvisation.[12] But some writers argue that the classical background of Tristano's "white" free jazz—his practice of playing Bach Inventions and exploring counterpoint—is as important as its origins in jazz. Ekkehard Jost in his classic *Free Jazz* writes that "'Intuition' is based exclusively on group improvisation, but it is oriented not so much on jazz practices as it is on contrapuntal techniques of European Baroque music."[13]

Tristano and Konitz questioned the free jazz movement of the 1960s, but it's important to distinguish the movement associated in its more politicized forms with Black Power, from free jazz as a general term equivalent to "free improvisation." *Free jazz* now describes a historical moment and style, while *free improvisation,* in Europe at least, denotes any contemporary improvised music that avoids grooves and chord changes, usually adopting a quieter, reflective approach—assuming that it is impossible to play loud and also be reflective. Jimmy Giuffre's work with Paul Bley and Steve Swallow in the early 1960s raises problems of categorization similar to those arising from Tristano's sides.

Even when critics recognized the importance of these recordings, they stressed that they weren't the start of a new style for Tristano, as free improvisation was for later musicians such as Derek Bailey who began in more mainstream jazz. But John Litweiler is wrong to say that "none of [the] musicians [involved in the 1949 Capitol sessions] felt more than the rarest impulse to attempt again such innovative ideas."[14] Aside from his assumption that the Tristano players' later work was not innovative, Litweiler doesn't consider possible artistic reasons for abandoning the free approach. Warne Marsh commented that "we stopped playing free music, [because] the more we played, the more difficult it seemed to be."[15] Konitz himself, however, did continue to play and record free improvisation. *The Lee Konitz Duets* (1967) and *The Sound of Surprise* (1999) feature it, as does *Four Keys* with Martial Solal, John Scofield, and Niels-Henning Ørsted Pedersen from 1979, which follows the 1949 instrumentation but omits tenor sax. And recently Konitz released the freely improvised *Gong with Wind* with drummer Matt Wilson, which he discusses here.

In our rehearsing together in the Tristano group, once in a while we got into a nice situation after playing those intricate lines and—I don't remember exactly how this happened—Tristano said, "Let's just improvise freely." We were all very pleased about doing that kind of playing, which was full of surprises.

We went into the studio [in May 1949] intending to play things that we had rehearsed quite a lot, like "Marionette," "Sax Of A Kind," and so on. When we finished recording those tunes, Tristano suggested we try doing one of the free improvisations that we had tried occasionally. We asked Barry Ulanov to give us a signal when three minutes was approaching— these were ten-inch acetates, remember—but we usually stopped some seconds before he gave the signal. I think I spotted him getting ready to give the sign! I think that's the first recording of totally free playing. As has been stated, the only thing that was planned was the order of entry—Tristano suggested that I come in after he started, and then Billy Bauer, and so on. On the recording, the drummer, Denzil Best, lays out. When we did it with a drummer, like Al Levitt or whoever was playing with us, he just improvised, without creating a time-feel. Maybe sometimes it went into time, for a minute or two.

The journalist Barry Ulanov was a strong supporter of these experiments.
He was a very interesting man. He and Tristano were very tight, and he liked what we were doing.

Why did Tristano pursue that direction?
He was really more interested in getting the music to swing, and in that context, when it was really going strong for us, the music started to get free of the progression for a spell, and then Lennie usually would pull it back into the tune. So it happened more like that, rather than a totally free exposition. We played like that sometimes in concerts, and in the clubs even, but gradually we stopped doing totally free pieces. Just playing straight-ahead was always very challenging and satisfying, when it worked.

It was the sign of things to come. But where did the idea come from?
From marijuana maybe! Just feeling good after a rehearsal one afternoon, playing tunes that we knew, and Lennie saying, "Let's just play something."

There was nothing like it in jazz before; it was completely original. Though I suppose when you do an introduction, or a cadenza, that's an ad lib tempo.
But this is taking counterpoint into consideration, and group improvisation.

When you played free in clubs, what was the reaction?
The reaction was usually one of surprise and interest, I hope, but no standing ovations. But in the original Birdland, or wherever we played, it didn't seem like nightclub music. We also tried playing Bach Inventions sometimes, but Warne or I weren't able to get through them without making mistakes. Finally Lennie said, "Use the music," but once you learn something and look at the music, you don't see it and you don't hear it any more. So we just left it out.

We were basically concerned to play with a nice swing feeling, and the free playing started to sound too classical, and in the club context, it didn't fit. When we had occasion to do it in a concert, it seemed more in order.

One day I was hanging out with Lennie in his studio, and he was expecting a visit from Leonard Bernstein, Aaron Copland, and Marc Blitzstein—they wanted to hear the free recording we did. I remember Lennie in the control room playing the record—just a three-minute piece, don't forget—

and they listened intently. Afterwards, Aaron asked if he could see the score, and I explained that it was a group improvisation. They were very impressed!

It wasn't a major part of your work. Do you think of it as an experiment?
No, I just thought it was something that was fun to do, and in retrospect I regret that we didn't develop it more.

Miles Davis used the recordings to criticize Ornette Coleman. "What's so avant-garde?" he said, "Lennie Tristano and Lee Konitz were creating ideas fifteen years ago that were stranger than any of these new things. But when they did it, it made sense."[16]
I don't think these sides sound strange at all. Classical maybe—but still with jazz lines and inflections. I just heard a few tunes from one of Ornette's early records, and that sounds strange to me, sometimes.

"Duet For Saxophone and Guitar" with Billy Bauer from 1951 features free improvisation, and has been neglected.
For that date Billy wrote some themes, and as I recall some chords, and there were also free sections.

You think this music is fun to do but not always fun to listen to?
I love to do it, but I think you somehow have to have a set of new standards to judge compositional worth. There was a session of mine that had a lot of free playing from Clark Terry and Gerry Mulligan and people that didn't generally play free.[17] I listened to it many, many times, trying to figure out, "Is this really good music? Does this really add up to good counterpoint—two or more strong melodies going together?" And for the most part I was very satisfied.

This is not only an enjoyable way to compose, separately or together, on our various instruments; but, depending on the people involved, a very meaningful way. The short three-minute pieces we did with Tristano in 1949 for Capitol still sound like well-structured compositions to me. And the many free situations I've been a part of, or have heard others play in, over the years, prove the validity of such musical procedures.

❧ Interview with John Tchicai

JOHN TCHICAI, *born in Copenhagen in 1936, is a leading free jazz saxophonist. Moving to the United States, he recorded in 1963 with the New York Contemporary Five with Archie Shepp and Don Cherry, co-led the New York Art Quartet with Roswell Rudd, and in 1965 appeared on John Coltrane's* Ascension. *Since the seventies, he has been heard mainly on tenor and soprano saxes, and has recorded frequently for the SteepleChase, Freedom, and Enja labels. Based mainly in Denmark in the 1970s and 1980s, since 1991 he has divided his time between France and California.*

Lee Konitz's importance as a keeper of the flame of free improvisation should not be underestimated. The records where he improvises freely are part of his inheritance and vocabulary and should definitely be taken into focus when talking about Lee's work. This is where my development starts from. Ever since the well-known free improvisations he did in 1949 with Lennie Tristano's group—Tristano is credited with the author's rights for these collective improvisations, which in a way is wrong—he has been a source of inspiration to younger "free" players including myself. Though in his career he has based his repertoire on show tunes and standards, he is constantly inventing new variations on these and is simultaneously performing and recording free improvisations. For many of the "free" players of the sixties the focus was on Konitz, as well as Marsh, Tristano, Ornette Coleman, Cecil Taylor, Bill Dixon, and Thelonious Monk. From these improvisers and composers much could be learned about the inevitable transition from the earlier styles of jazz—away from show tunes and standards toward a more individually composed repertoire, not necessarily based on the harmonic structures of the earlier music but with collective improvisations or other ways of organizing the new possibilities.

Of pure necessity musicians are often forced to take the offers which they get no matter where on earth it is, and this is part of why Lee left Tristano—he didn't earn anything to support himself and his family. But Lee has managed to stay true to himself and has not compromised his ideals about his music and life. I believe that it is possible to know a player's personality through his tone, and even if I didn't know Konitz personally I would claim that what he projects tells us about a wholehearted sincere human being in the service of the muses.[18] ☛

In 1987 you played in Derek Bailey's Company week. How did that come about?
I had played with Derek years earlier, playing standards, when he was doing that—with Gavin Bryars on bass and Tony Oxley on drums. It was a band put together when I was touring in Britain. I had no contact with him during the free period, but certainly he heard what we did with Tristano, or later stuff, and he asked me to join in.

Some of it was great fun. I remember playing a version of "Lover Man" with Derek. I haven't heard it in years, but it was very unusual, not much to do with "Lover Man"! There were many other players in that week who were real improvisers—Barre Phillips, Tony Oxley, Han Bennink, and so on.

What do you think of Evan Parker's playing?

Evan is a fantastic player—he can play endlessly on one breath [using a technique called "circular breathing"]. I don't know how much the actual music he plays gets to me, but as with Cecil, it's a totally unique expression that I can admire very much, in a way. I'm so hooked on what I've inherited from the great improvisers who played what I call beautiful melodies, including Ornette, that it's difficult to evaluate what some of the experimental players are doing. But it's certainly interesting, and very difficult to do.

You're known as someone who enjoys unusual playing situations.

I like the novelty, but sometimes it's less than great music. It's very liberating, and even though, as I'm doing it, I might know that this isn't really working, I'm still caught up in motion, and trying. And often it's exhilarating, just trying.

Jamey Aebersold sent me the new Kenny Werner CD to play along with. It's the first one where the rhythm section is just playing free, and you improvise freely over it. Kenny Werner has transcribed some of his own piano parts—they look very complicated. There are no themes, they're all accompaniment, and very special. I wrote back and said it's a great idea, for young people to be able to play with all these great rhythm sections—and old people too, I might add!

Do you feel someone should be able to play in a more traditional style such as bebop before they play free?

Actually, free playing precedes playing on tunes. That's how we start the process of invention. But in terms of being a thoroughly educated musician, yes, they should know how to swing, to play traditional music as creatively as possible. Free playing is a very valid discipline I respect highly and practice every day. I just don't go for overblowing, and all of the emotional frenzies that reduce the quality of the music to me. For visual purposes or for whatever reason, there's exaggeration in almost all the music I hear, either by being too loud, or too *espressivo*. "Notes are no longer the thing," someone was quoted as saying. Okay, I'm not interested in that. I'm still interested in beautiful notes, logically put together in as spontaneous a way as possible—or in as well composed a way as possible.

Do you feel that some people in that area are also not hearing what they're playing?

I just feel sorry that they have to listen to themselves practicing!

Wearing the emotion on the sleeve, as the avant-gardists did especially in the early days with the squawking and squealing, was offensive to me. Maybe it was necessary for some psycho-dramatic reasons, but it wasn't musical enough for me.

I guess there wasn't much free jazz that was reflective. Maybe Jimmy Giuffre with Paul Bley and Steve Swallow in the early 1960s.

Yes, very much so—three reflective guys! Tristano's was reflective, and that was the first example. But that wasn't "jazz"—it sounded almost like classical music.

Gong with Wind, a duo album on SteepleChase with drummer Matt Wilson from 2002, is a recent example of Konitz's free playing. In reference to the Hollywood classic *Gone with the Wind* and its theme, the saxophonist supplies the wind and the drummer the "gong." Wilson is highly responsive, nudging and prompting without trying to play like a rhythm section where the bassist hasn't turned up. The result is some of Konitz's freest yet most intensely melodic playing.

I suggested the project to Nils Winther of SteepleChase, who I've recorded for over the years. Matt and I agreed to play with no plan. We went in the studio in New Jersey and played for about one and a half hours. Matt used different percussion instruments including a gong—hence the titles. What a nice experience! Matt is a beautiful rhythmic guy. He's all ears—and some mouth too!

There are no thirty-two-bar choruses in it.

Somewhere along the line I was playing on "The Song Is You," but I think freely. We were stretching the form. I could be coming in on any part of the song, and playing any part of it—a bridge or something like that. Playing along like that, anything that's in your computer will pop out, and you just deal with it. It's absolutely as free as you could get, still playing on tunes in some way, or motifs.

Was each track based on a standard?

Oh no. We just started out and went where it was going.

But you might refer to a standard for a period.

Yes, I'd play a couple of notes and it sounds like a melody, and I'd play around with that for a while. And then I hear Matt do a rhythm pattern, and I take that pattern and do something else with it. There's a trust you must have that this process is meaningful in some way.

It's the kind of free playing that many people are not familiar with, because they think of it as very abstract, and dissonant, with multiphonics. But this album is very melodic.

That's why I've also been appreciating this new Wayne Shorter group—it really sounds very lyrical, rather than just high intensity and density. And very pure musical sounds from everybody.

❧ Interview with Matt Wilson

MATT WILSON, *born in 1964, is a drummer whom Konitz has worked with frequently in recent years. He attended Wichita State University, and in 1987 moved to Boston, where he worked with the Either/Orchestra and John Medeski. Moving to New York, he worked with Dewey Redman, Dave Liebman, and Sheila Jordan. He leads his own groups, including Arts and Crafts.*

Lee is very interactive, and has become more so even in the period that I've known him. Sometimes overtly—like he'll go with the pitch of the tom-tom and use that, or play parallel with me. At other times he's interactive in the big picture. Lee doesn't like it loud, but he wants it strong. He doesn't want to be barrelled over, but he does want it to be definite. That's why he likes Paul Motian, and Billy Hart, and Bill Stewart. Paul Motian has this great sense of playfulness, but he's clear.

I have to agree that he doesn't have any licks. There's very few things that I think "He's doing that again." It's very inspiring to think how many times Lee Konitz has played "All The Things You Are," and he always finds something new to play on it. A record I really like is *Zounds,* with Ron McClure, Bill Stewart, and Kenny Werner. I like that era, and Kenny had a nice rapport. Also Lee's work with Don Friedman and Attila Zoller. I think he's playing more lyrically now. He has a very interesting time-feel, and it's stronger now—because it moves around, it's great fun to play with. And he's more interested in playing faster tempos than he used to be.

It's brave for a bassist to work with Lee, because he modulates in his tunes all the time. I mean he changes keys within choruses, but in logical places. He treats all the instruments as being equal. It's always fun working with him. There's no ego thing—none. I love him, he's a true improviser.[19] ☛

How Not to Interpret Tristano

Konitz pulls few punches concerning music he really dislikes. In *The Wire* in 1999 he made very direct criticisms of Anthony Braxton's solo on "April" from *Eight (+3) Tristano Compositions 1989*.[20] These criticisms were unusual coming from a fellow musician, and there was some reaction to his onslaught on the Internet bulletin boards. But Konitz's attack reflected his passionate concern with mastering the instrument to play beautiful lines. Here is our discussion from that interview, plus Konitz's later reflections.

Well, it's the worst solo I've ever heard in my life, I think. I don't know what his real intention is in doing this. There are many wrong notes in the line of Tristano's, and the tempo is *impossible*—we never played the tune at that tempo. So obviously he was trying to impress with some kind of a technical flurry. Anthony doesn't relate to the rhythm section at all, they might as well be out to lunch. For some reason he pays great lip-service [to the Tristano school]. Every time I'd meet him he would sing my solos to me and I would never recognize them. I thought to myself, "I wonder if he plays them on the horn too?" because there's not too much indication of his love for just playing a good melody, in time, with a good sound. I think this is a travesty. I think it's an insult to the memory of Tristano.

You've made some pretty strong criticisms!

Well I'm having to think about that because Anthony has always said he respects my playing and especially Warne [Marsh]'s and Lennie's, and I don't relish the thought of exposing those feelings towards him, because I admire his chutzpah in some way. And certainly we were all interested in playing free as we could, on either a tune or no tune, but to play on a tune and do that has nothing to do with anything to me. So maybe I'm still living in the early part of the century . . .

It seems to me you're giving expression to a feeling about Braxton's playing that a lot of people might have, but they might be reluctant to say this.

I love very lyrical playing, it can be as intense as it needs to be in terms of reality, not in terms of trying to impress, which most of the intensity I hear seems to be. The distinction was made [by Tristano] between playing with emotion and playing with feeling. It sounds contrived to me, trying to play emotionally instead of playing with your real feeling.

Is Braxton really trying to impress?

I don't know what he's doing, actually. He's trying to go in a different direction, and I have to give him credit for trying that.

You think that he's not really hearing what he's playing?
There's no connection. All you have to do is ask him to sing that. Although he sang supposedly my lines I didn't recognize them.[21] I can't quite figure that out. Anthony is a deep thinker and he has some justification, I'm sure . . . but I don't love it.

Is it the sound as well that you have a problem with?
I can't stand his sound, I think it's awful. Paul Desmond was his hero, but I don't know what the hell he was hearing. If you love somebody you try to emulate them, you don't just destroy the whole concept.

Do you have much time for Braxton's playing of his own compositions?
I haven't heard much of his music because I don't usually enjoy what I hear. But I'm sure there's some out there that I should hear. The most interesting thing I've ever heard him do was a duet with Max Roach, where there was no longer any consideration for melodies and sound, and traditional rhythmic impetus.[22]

Later, Konitz commented on what had made him so outspoken about Braxton's interpretation of Tristano.

I feel that music should be open to any kind of interpretation, but also to any kind of reaction. When I hear Anthony honking and squealing, I say, "Get outta here!" because I don't want to hear it.

Look, his performance affected me so negatively because, somehow, he was in my neighborhood, and sounding like a wild man. Now, we are free to give our versions of a tribute to someone we admire—and I accept his gesture. But I don't like the premise of what he did. To play on an ingenious line based on "I'll Remember April" and just squeak unmercifully is a sacrilege to me. I *know* that Anthony *cannot* play a beautiful line, in the pocket, with a great sound, even if his life depended on it. That's an ability I have spent some sixty-five years of my long life trying to perfect—it will never be perfect! But I have great respect for what else Anthony can do—it's just this one thing that caught me at the wrong moment.

You're not afraid of expressing strong opinions about fellow musicians.
I don't like to criticize musicians publicly; but in private, or with friends, I have to say something about what people are doing. Charlie Parker never put anybody down in public. Neither does Sonny Rollins; he probably got that from him [Parker], I think.

If you never criticize anyone, how do people know when you're really praising someone?
I agree. One should be respectfully honest.

Have you ever said something in print, and the person has said, "I'm not playing with you again!"

No, not really. I don't think I've been that critical of people. I flipped out on Anthony Braxton because he was in an area that I know, and playing the same instrument as I am—it touched a sore spot. I have to think twice about what I say, after the fact, but I just blurt it out, sometimes.

I said exactly what I felt. Diplomatically, it's not a friendly thing to say. But I thought he's deceiving himself in some way with this aspect of the music. Whatever else he does is open to our ears to judge, but if he presumes to play a music that I've spent my whole life trying to develop, I have to make a statement about that.

Sam Rivers said about Braxton, "Some musicians do certain things as an irritant—there are some artists who want to either force you to listen or turn it off. You can't use it as part of the furniture, as background music. It's in your face."[23]

You have to make something happen when you're on the platform—you can look good, or play good, or tell good jokes. He made his choice, and it can be an irritant to some of us. I wish I could meet him and talk about it with him, as two students of the music.

❧ Interview with Gary Foster

Alto saxophonist **GARY FOSTER,** *born in 1936 in Kansas City, was much inspired by the Tristano school. Moving to Los Angeles in 1961, he worked with Warne Marsh and later Lee Konitz. He also worked with pianist Clare Fischer and guitarist Laurindo Almeida, and was a member of the Akiyoshi-Tabackin big band. With Konitz, he recorded a tribute to Warne Marsh in 1995,* Body and Soul *(Camerata).*

The 1955 recording Lee made with Warne was seminal for me; it really turned me around. I *never* heard Warne Marsh repeat himself, and I don't hear Lee doing it either. Earlier, Lee seemed to play more notes, and now he's very reflective, and selective of notes—but they're all gems. He said to me that he doesn't really get much pleasure out of playing really fast—but he can fly with the best of them. One famous solo of Lee's is "Lover Man" with the Gerry Mulligan quartet—when Keith Jarrett recorded *Tribute,* he dedicated "Lover Man" to Lee.

When I moved to California I met Clare Fischer, who became one of my mentors, and he professed a very powerful influence from Lee, rather than Lennie Tristano. Lee says that he has never quite understood that, but I believe Bill Evans said the same. Warne moved back here in 1966 and we began to play together, and made some recordings. Lee came out a few times to play at Donte's and I met him then. In 1992, Rein De Graaf brought Lee and me over to Holland—and in 1995 Lee and I did a tribute CD to Warne for a Japanese label.

[Regarding Lee's comments about Anthony Braxton]: Many years ago, Warne and I were playing at a club here. When Anthony was in L.A., he'd come by, and one night he came in with his horn. I don't think Warne knew how he played, so he asked, "Would you like to sit in?" and Anthony played several standards with us. And at no point in his playing did he ever refer to the chord-progression or the form of the song—when he stopped playing, it was frequently in the middle of a chorus. I never saw Warne's eyes as wide open—they were usually at half-mast—because he couldn't believe it. I believe Anthony does *not* know "Cherokee," or any of those tunes. His is another world—his music has to be evaluated on a different set of criteria. If he had said, "Hey guys, let's just play something free," I'll be right there, I love that—so does Lee, and so did Warne—but I wouldn't play that way on "Just Friends" or "Cherokee."[24]

11 🎵 The 1980s to the Present

Since the 1980s, Konitz has become recognized as one of the elder statesmen of the music. In 1992 he was awarded the Jazzpar Prize of the Danish Jazz Society, and in 1998 the Order of Arts and Letters from the French government. The Jazzpar Prize included thirty-five thousand dollars, a concert tour, and a recording. When the director of the Danish Jazz Society called him at home in Manhattan with the news, it was two days after his wife of thirty-two years had died. Coming when he was very down, it meant a lot: "It was a sort of justification of my entire life view," he said. The saxophonist is proud to have won the *Down Beat* critics' poll for alto sax three years running, 2003–5.

With Harold Danko on piano, Rufus Reid on bass, and Al Harewood on drums, Konitz made two of his most important later albums, *Ideal Scene* (1986) and *The New York Album* (1987). During that decade also, Konitz recorded duos with pianists Michel Petrucciani, Peggy Stern, Martial Solal, Enrico Pieranunzi, and Harold Danko. Konitz has long been a fan of Brazilian music, shown on the 1989 album of samba-based pieces with a group of Brazilian musicians, *Lee Konitz in Rio*. He has a particular love for the music of Antonio Carlos Jobim, and in the 1990s led a Brazilian quartet with Peggy Stern, recording a duo album with her, *The Jobim Collection*. Konitz maintains his interest in free improvisation, and in 1987 Konitz appeared at Derek Bailey's Company week in London, and worked with Keiji Haino and Kazuo Imai in Japan in 1996.

He follows current developments and works with younger players, recording *Alone Together* and *Another Shade of Blue* on Blue Note with Charlie Haden and Brad Mehldau, and *Parallels* with Mark Turner. He frequently works with drummer Matt Wilson, and guitarists Bill Frisell and Ben Monder, and in a trio with George and Ed Schuller. Recently he has been involved in trios with longtime partners Paul Bley and Steve Swallow. "I want to make the point that things are happening currently," he insists. "As I go into my 79th year, I'm active and I just want young people to know that's possible." As we go to press in October 2006, two albums have just been released on Omnitone to critical acclaim, *Inventions* and *Lee Konitz New Nonet*. The *Nonet* played in Chicago and before the gig it was announced that the mayor of Chicago, Richard Daley, had declared September 3 "Lee Konitz Day."

Konitz lives in Cologne in Germany much of the year, where he enjoys sitting in cafés, taking a keen interest in the passing scene. He hates noise and has a particular loathing of the mobile-phone culture—being with him in a public place can be embarrassing as his mockery of "mobile-phone boors" sometimes gets him into trouble. But he is very positive about one piece of contemporary technology—his iPod, currently loaded with 5,782 tunes, and equipped with a pair of Bose noise-reduction headphones so he can listen in peace while on tour.

His apartment is full of the memorabilia of a life in jazz. On the electric keyboard are pictures of Charlie Parker, Miles Davis, and Béla Bartók. By the upright piano, his alto and soprano saxophones are on their stands. In his apartment in New York he has an excellent Steinway grand. Konitz has a large CD collection and many books, fiction and music titles, both jazz and classical. He practices assiduously, and shoppers passing near the Rudolfplatz can hear his saxophone from his second-floor window, though few seem to stop and listen. In his late seventies, Konitz is now busier than ever, and still developing artistically. As friend and fellow musician Karl Berger puts it, he's "still trying."

You have a particular love of Brazilian music and Latin jazz.
Cuban music is pretty hot and very rhythmical and very danceable, but Brazilian music has that nice gentle beat that's very seductive, and a great rhythmic conception—and of course the Portuguese language is beautiful for the singing. Plus all the beautiful melodies that Jobim and his colleagues came up with—I love Jobim! The samba is real "shake your ass" dance music. I prefer the bossa nova—I love gentle things.

Anyone who thinks you don't use vibrato should listen to that Jobim album.
Oh man, I'm schmaltzaroony with vibrato on that one! When I listen back, sometimes I don't like it too much, but that's the way I felt it at that moment. They're beautiful melodies and obviously that was my sentimental way of delivering them.

It's unfortunate that it's on a small label without a lot of distribution—Philology—because it could have been a hit!

Philology have sold less than one thousand of my albums in total, and that was about the best-selling one. I also played this beautiful song of Jobim's, "Luisa," on an album with Steve Swallow and Paul Motian.[1] And I practically just played the melody—I didn't feel like doing much to that at all. A lot of Jobim's tunes are kind of based on jazz standards. They have very familiar and comfortable chord progressions.

Peggy Stern and I were partners for a while, and this was a musical development. We did two albums for Philology; the other one was originals of hers and mine, and pretty interesting I think. She's a fine musician. Peggy plays synthesizer as well as piano.

Have you ever played with Hammond organ?

I did on a recent album I made for SteepleChase with George Colligan.[2] There was an organ in the room and he knew how to play it. The first piece we did was kind of Jimmy Smith, so for the second one I said, "How about a little Olivier Messiaen?" And George went out completely, in a version of "Lover Man" you never heard before or since.

How was it to work with Michel Petrucciani?

I admired him very much. The record we made was done the first time we played together. I was fascinated with this little guy sitting at a nine-foot Bösendorfer in the Bösendorfer showroom in Paris. And then we did some tours, and I thought, "Jesus, I'm getting popular in France, people are really turning out."[3] And then I looked at this little guy, and I thought, "Oh yeah." But he never included me in any of his situations over the years when he became successful. And I was very surprised to hear, in an interview, him mentioning me as one of his influences. He lived a short but full life, and played a lot of music. A very special human being.

You did a couple of things with Franz Koglmann, the Austrian trumpeter and composer.

Yes, in fact that's how I met my wife, at a concert we played here in Cologne. I first of all thought of him as the only one-lipped trumpet player that I ever saw. He held his trumpet downwards, and it looked like it was really glued into his top lip. But of course he was playing with both. He got a pretty unique sound; he's a very musical guy. But I didn't love the music that much at the time—some interesting instrumentation and sounds, I must say.

In *Down Beat* August 2003, I won the alto division of the critic's poll—I also won in 2004 and 2005. After all of these years it was a total surprise to me—Phil Woods was always winning, or Kenny Garrett, or Greg Osby. I feel very pleased that I was given an okay by the critics. But why all of a sud-

den? They must like my playing now better than they did before, these critics! Again I say, "It ain't over till it's over!"

❡ Interview with Enrico Pieranunzi

ENRICO PIERANUNZI, *born in Rome in 1949, is one of the leading contemporary jazz pianists, working with such as Chet Baker, Art Farmer,
Johnny Griffin, Charlie Haden, and Jim Hall. He has recorded as leader
and as solo pianist for Soul Note, EGEA, CamJazz, and others. He has
given master classes at Siena and elsewhere in Europe and the United
States, and until recently taught piano in Italian public conservatories.*

Whereas Chet was very interested in tunes, Konitz is really interested in
improvisation. We did many concerts in the middle eighties in which we
completely improvised without any reference to tunes. Working with
him was a great school for me, and it became natural for me to alternate
tunes with freely improvised stuff.

The paradox is that the Berklee approach, which is very routine, is
very old-fashioned compared with Tristano's. There was a lot of Bartók,
a lot of Hindemith, a very wide conception of twentieth-century music,
in Tristano. The main thing, as becomes clear from his compositions, is
that he considered all the notes equally. There was not a priority, as in,
"These are good notes to be used on this chord, these are second-class
notes." This is what I found in Konitz too. He has a range and combination of notes that sounds different and which is virtually endless, and this
is very particular.

On one session I did, Charlie Haden said, "We don't need that blues
we recorded at the beginning."[4] But it was a great performance. So I was
struck by that too—I felt it was the same feeling I found in Lee Konitz.
They accept the blues but they don't really identify themselves with that
form, that expression. This is true also for Bill Evans.

Stan Getz was a giant, but compared to Konitz his playing was a bit
self-gratifying. Konitz forces you to interact, somehow—just because of
his phrasing or his approach. He puts you in a different, unpredictable
territory. It's really a kind of tabula rasa. This is very special. I remember
one time, just before going onstage, he said to us, me and the bassist and
the drummer, "Okay guys, you ready to really improvise?" We were kind
of shaken by that. We felt very free, even to play the wrong notes, to go
everywhere. He's a great guy and a friend.[5] ❡

Konitz's greater lyrical tendency in recent years goes with his sensitivity to noise, in music or elsewhere. Listening to Herbie Hancock's *Sextant* (Columbia), however, he commented on one response he had to contemporary pop music.

That reminds me of a project that happened downstairs from where I live in Cologne. They erected a stage and there was a CD booth pretty close to our window, playing one techno record for ten hours, over and over again. And at some point, after being annoyed, I opened up the window and started to play along with it, and it was a lot of fun. And eventually I went downstairs and said, "Which record are you playing?" and bought it!

The Next Generation

I'm very optimistic about the future of jazz. Dave Holland's group is very interesting. There's Brad Mehldau and his trio, and I've enjoyed Steve Coleman and Greg Osby, Branford Marsalis, Kenny Garrett sometimes, Steve Wilson, Mark Turner, and Stefon Harris, the vibraphone player. Chris Potter is getting to be a really outstanding player. I try to keep up to date— that's an inspiration for me.

What material do you think the young jazz players of today should be using, since Tin Pan Alley songs no longer have the meaning for them that they have for you?

That's a good question. They seem to be writing their own material; that's a good solution. If they can come up with a song as good as "All The Things," then they're in business. Don't forget this is a concern for good melodies.

I feel confident that I'll always have something to play. All I have to do is live for another twenty years or so, so I can continue doing it!

Brad Mehldau, born 1970, has become recognized in the last decade as one of the outstanding contemporary jazz pianists, with a succession of highly regarded solo and trio albums.

What I like is that he listens, first thing.

I was due to play and record at the Jazz Bakery in Los Angeles with Charlie Haden. I thought, "This should be nice," with his beautiful sound and great time-feeling. And a Japanese company wanted to record us—great! Also I thought I can finally play with someone I'm faster than. I had been working on becoming the slowest saxophone player around—I'm being serious![6] Anyway, Charlie called me a week before and said that Brad could use a gig. I had never played with Brad, and didn't really know how special he was. So here I was playing with another virtuoso, and I was a bit disturbed—it's impossible for me to play faster than a piano player! But by the second set, Brad was listening and changing his playing, and I appreciated that very much. Blue Note found out that the trio was playing, and we ended up making three CDs in two days there.

When you say he gradually changed his style to fit in with you, did he simplify it?

When he played his solo he played the way he plays. But I think it was in keeping with Charlie and me. Charlie was mostly playing two to the bar, sometimes one to the bar, so it wasn't really digging-in kind of playing, most of the time. And after I'd finished my solo and Brad started to play, and increased the intensity and the number of notes and everything, Charlie was still playing two to the bar, and one to the bar, and then finally he would get to playing four. But his notes were beautiful, and that left a lot of space, which I enjoyed very much. Charlie was having back problems. He had to leave Paul Bley and me in the middle of a European tour to go and have his back fixed.

Brad as an accompanist is just so fast, almost too fast in a way, in terms of mimicking something I would play—almost anticipating to such a point that I started to become a little self-conscious. Was I that obvious in what I was playing that he could hear it so fast? Sometimes it got annoying, like saying, "Challenge me a little more, 'cause I got that covered."

You felt he was being a little too clever.

He was telling me that he was listening to me, and whether he agreed with it or not, he played with me. But it wasn't an expansion of it, necessarily. Martial [Solal] expands it into a symphony.

Brad has got a great trio with Larry Grenadier and Jorge Rossy, playing real trio music effortlessly in odd meters like 7/4 and 5/4, with original arrangements. Stanley Crouch, the New York writer, was sitting with me and my wife one night at the Vanguard, when Brad was playing. He was remarking about the European influence and kind of criticizing Brad, and he got up and said, "Think I'll go home and listen to one of *your* records." I thought, "What the hell is he talking about?" But I saw Stanley just recently and he said, "That boy can play!" He had heard him finally.

Brad is an interesting writer too, judging by the liner notes on a couple of his CDs. I'm expecting more literature from him.

There's a lot of classical influences there.

There is. His new recording with Renée Fleming, doing his compositions, is beautiful. But he can swing, in a very traditional way, nonstop.

You also worked with Geri Allen recently.

I thought it would be so nice to do something with her, and I was very pleased when she invited me [in Italy in 2004]. She insisted on playing my tunes, so I sent her some. When we met near Milan, we got together in the afternoon of the concert, and she was really playing the tunes well. Sometimes it sounds like she was very determined to play many, many notes, and it got a little confusing to me. But I said next time, if it's possible, I'd like to play some of her tunes.

Tenor saxophonist **Mark Turner,** born 1965, has commented enthusiastically on his debt to the Tristano school: "It was so improvised. Their note placement was always so excellent. . . . Here was another vocabulary [to bop] altogether. When I was at Berklee, nobody, professors or students, talked about this music. I ran into it—luckily. Now it's part of me."[7] Here Konitz returns the compliment.

Mark Turner is one of the few men of color who have acknowledged Warne Marsh so effectively. He's a real serious full-time student, who's studying all the guys that can play, and combining them in very effective ways sometimes. I think his Warne part might come out when he's playing with me. But I've also heard a record he made with a very nice saxophone player who lives in Switzerland, named Nat Su. He's from Cameroon, a really sweet guy and a fine player. They played all of those lines we played with Lennie very effectively together, and a lot of that feeling came out in both of them—Nat for me, and Mark for Warne. A nice compliment, and a reminder to move on!

I think Mark is a very serious contender. He's a very quiet man, similar to Warne. Not much small talk, I suspect. I was just listening to one of his records, and he wrote interesting things and really improvised very well.

One of the things he's said he got from Warne Marsh was playing in the altissimo register.

He's really mastered that part of the instrument. That's quite rare among tenor players; they usually just squeal out a high note. But he's really playing lines up there, as Warne could do—and Mark uses that register much more than Warne did.

Does he do the same kind of rhythmically complex things that Warne Marsh did?

He's actually working in that direction—it's very complex music.

We did a concert a few years ago; that was the time I was introduced to him. We talked about doing an unaccompanied duo. I asked him what he wanted to play, and he said, "How about [Tristano's composition] '317 E. 32nd Street'?" I said, "My goodness!" We didn't rehearse it, and just went out and played it pretty well together, and improvised counterpoint through the whole tune—it was really a great experience. Then he agreed to do four tunes on my record a couple of years ago for Chesky Records [*Parallels*]. I also played a nice set with him in Greece in October [2002].

Nat Su is another "cool player" from that kind of tradition. But he's not really had the exposure.

I don't know how much opportunity he has to play. I think he's teaching and studying, mostly. But he's a fine guy and player. I heard him recently, playing better than ever.

I heard a young guy named Mark Shim, who's got an extraordinary sound, and he hasn't really distorted it. He's really playing these fantastic, chromatic kind of lines with this unique sound. Greg Osby even refers to him as "the little guy"—it seems incongruous somehow, that he gets such a big sound. I heard him on *New Directions* [Blue Note]. I wasn't that interested in those sixties Blue Note compositions at the time, but hearing them now with these kind of chromatic solos and different arrangements, they're fun to listen to. I guess that's another example of cultural lag. I'm glad I got around to it, finally.

You said that you admire Chris Potter.

I think Chris is the "no one told me it's difficult" guy—fantastic facility on alto, tenor, and soprano. I just heard that he played a club in New York with his new tentet that he wrote the arrangements for. He has the ability, I think, to be a great, creative player, but there's a danger that he's grandstanding sometimes.

Greg Osby is a marvellous saxophone player. Whatever Steve Coleman and that group put together, with whatever intellectual basis, it was very unique. Sometimes it's not what I call singable, "heart" music. I heard Greg in the Azores, and then I heard him with Jim Hall in New York, in a new room there, Dizzy's Coca-Cola Room, and it was lovely. In deference to Jim, he wasn't really pushing it, he was playing more laid-back, for him, but very oddly intervallic melodies. After Jim's very diatonic stuff, it was very effective.

He really does play almost without vibrato.

I have that impression, yes. But he's full of ideas, constantly trying things.

¶ Interview with Greg Osby

Alto saxophonist **GREG OSBY** *was born in 1960 in St Louis. He attended Howard University and the Berklee College of Music. Moving to New York, he worked with Andrew Hill, Herbie Hancock, and Jack DeJohnette. During the mid-1980s he was a member of the M-Base Collective with Steve Coleman, Cassandra Wilson, Gary Thomas, and others, and since then has recorded frequently for the Blue Note label, including with Andrew Hill and Jim Hall.*

Yes, Lee's music is cerebral—as is Duke Ellington's, and John Coltrane's, and Charles Mingus's, and Bill Evans's. That's not a criticism—if somebody calls me cerebral, well thank you very much! It's a misconception that you can't be cerebral and passionate.

I saw a concert with him and Paul Bley, six months ago [in 2004]—we were on the same festival in Portugal. The concert was amazing—Lee was reaching, he was probing. He's devoid of patterns, clichés, prescribed content. We hung out, and he was very interested in how I was coming to certain conclusions in music. This appealed to me. Here is Lee Konitz, interested in what I'm doing—and that keeps him progressive and current.

He recognizes that standards are little more than an environment for improvisation. He transcends that environment. He's honoring the composer by making references and recapitulations, but after a while it becomes a Lee Konitz composition. True improvisers like him, and Sonny Rollins, and Charlie Parker, go so far beyond that twelve-bar or thirty-two-bar framework. I was always aware of him as one of the master players. I deliberately stayed away from their music as a student, until I had a strong foothold in what I wanted to do myself. At the level of counterpoint and interplay, the Tristano stuff with Warne Marsh is so wonderful—a great marriage of Western European sensibilities with swing and improvisation. I really appreciate that Lee didn't allow himself to be caught up in the Charlie Parker vortex.

The blues will come out if it's in you. I hear blues in Lee Konitz, without him sounding like he's sitting on a porch in Mississippi, in a rocking chair with somebody playing a guitar with two strings left, and two teeth, eating a watermelon! He's bluesy enough, for a Jewish man. There are a lot of people who can blow their teeth off on saxophone and you still don't know who they are. With Lee Konitz, within two or three notes, you know.[8] ☛

In 2000 Konitz recorded *Some New Stuff* with Greg Cohen and Joey Baron.[9] As discussed earlier, it's notable for including new Konitz compositions, many not based on standards.

The record with Greg Cohen and Joey Baron was for John Zorn's label. It was made after I went to New York in May [2000] to do a concert in honor of Tristano, with the Jazz Composer's group. They had been studying different musicians—Lennie Tristano and Herbie Nichols this time—and honoring them. We did some special arrangements and it was a very nice concert. Four days later I did the record with Joey Baron and Greg Cohen, who are really fine. I brought in a handful of pieces that I had written, and Greg and Joey were very involved, making suggestions about rhythmic things they could do. We got a good record I think.

And the next day I went in the hospital and had two heart operations, without a clue that this was imminent. I woke up about four days later and I had amnesia, I didn't remember doing the record date. Joey Baron called me from Norway, and I asked, "Did we record?" He said, "Yeah, it was great." That was very nice to hear, but very strange.

I took a few months to recuperate, but I'm back to full force now. I had been practicing slowly to get my chops back, and then I did a week in Chicago and a week in New York and three days in Boston. I just played my brains out and it felt great, no aftereffects. So I feel like I'm on my second life now.

It's very important for me to really feel what I'm playing and not depend on the mechanics to carry me through. I don't have that much more time left, and I'd like to make it as real as possible while I can.

Konitz's music has been the subject of many tributes. One of the most quirky is *Sound-Lee!* by Dutch alto saxophonist Jorrit Dijkstra in a quartet with pianist Guus Janssen.[10] This album of Konitz themes on standard progressions includes "Sound-Lee" and "Palo Alto," a Konitz composition named after Tristano's house on Palo Alto Street in Queens, NYC. "They missed the point—but made another one!" was Konitz's observation. "They didn't try to play in the tradition, but more avant-garde."

❧ Interview with Guus Janssen

Pianist, harpsichordist, and composer GUUS JANSSEN *was born in Heiloo, near Amsterdam, in 1951. His music ranges from composed improvisation ("Brake" for piano solo) to improvised composition (Violin Concerto or the opera* Noach*). He has performed with musicians from John Zorn to Gidon Kremer, and since the early 1980s has led his own ensembles. His compositions include piano music, string quartets, and orchestral works.*

In the 1990s Jorrit Dijkstra played in my groups and he gave me a bunch of lines by Lee Konitz. What interests me most is balancing on the edge of derailing. After playing free forms for years now in all kinds of different groups, I like to operate in strict forms to broaden my musical field of operation. I never really played jazz and that I am not very familiar with the Broadway songbook. At the same time I have the idea that the conceptions of strict forms confronted with the anarchy of free forms enriched my music a lot, especially that of the trio with Ernst Glerum on bass and Wim Janssen on drums.

What Lee says about "missing the point" is interesting. We in Holland have a proverb, "Somebody hears the bell ringing but can't find the clapper"—they hear the bell but don't understand how it works. So seeing the charts makes the music more accessible to me. When I see them without hearing the actual music, I see them much more through the eyes of, let's say, Frescobaldi or Bach, who in fact belong to the roots of my own tradition.[11] With a score by Frescobaldi, for example, I have no idea how he would have played it and how it would have sounded in the tuning systems of those days. The same kind of thing happens with the lines of Konitz. In this case I do know how he played them, but I must try to forget that, [in order] to hear this music with fresh ears. The same thing happened in the history of jazz the other way around, when piano players started to use chords invented by Debussy, without knowing what he meant with them or how he used them within the context of his own music.

I have a deep respect for Tristano's school, but leaving their point of view and adding the touch of free improvisation led to *Sound Lee!*. I think that the uneven phrases in the themes of Konitz are especially challenging. They invite you to play games with the tension between the regularity of the chord changes of the old standards and their own whimsicality. It was a revelation that his lines didn't suffer at all when played in a kind of over-the-edge free hard bop! On the contrary, they seem to like this kind of treatment. They become like naughty students in the strict school class of Tristano.[12] 🐾

¶ Interview with Bill Frisell

Guitarist **BILL FRISELL,** *born in Baltimore in 1951, was inspired by blues guitarists such as B. B. King and Otis Rush, but became involved in jazz and studied at Berklee from 1971. He moved to New York in 1979, where he worked with Paul Motian, Paul Bley, and Bobby Previte, and was virtually house guitarist for the ECM label in the 1980s. His activities now embrace a wide range of Americana, including country music.*

I first listened to Lee's records when I was in high school at the end of the sixties. He was up there amongst my biggest heroes, as soon as I started to immerse myself in jazz. The first time I heard him live, he was playing with Charles Mingus at the Village Vanguard, around 1972—that was a kind of odd combination, but it was great. I played with him first when I was working with Paul Motian—but we've done a lot of gigs actually. I've done a few duet concerts with him, and about a year and half ago we played a week at the Iridium with Gary Peacock and Matt Wilson. In the late nineties I had a group with trombone, violin, and trumpet—Curtis Fowlkes, Eyvind Kang, and Ron Miles—and a couple of times Lee played with us as a guest. He's so unafraid to try anything. This was mostly my music, completely unfamiliar to him. One of the first times I met him, I was playing at the Vanguard with my band, and we were playing some kind of country song. I thought, "Oh God, Lee Konitz, what's he going to think?" But he was there the whole night, and he said, "Wow, it felt like I was in a bar in Texas!"

In about just one phrase of his playing, there's so much information. It's like looking at a plant, something growing in nature. There's so much possibility for other things to happen in all these little kernels. There's possibilities for him to develop them, and it gives you something to go off from. In the moment, it gives you a lot to deal with, but also just thinking about music in general, it makes me want to rethink what I'm doing. It's goes back so deep, but it's not confining in any way.

For the last few years I've been working on "Subconscious-Lee." I've actually been playing it a lot with this string group I'm working with, with violin, viola, and cello. There's so much in that tune. If you look at it one note at a time, it's as if half the notes are wrong, but the momentum of the thing is so strong. I've been wanting to learn that tune well enough that I can just jump on it. Sometimes we'll play "What Is This Thing Called Love" [which "Subconscious-Lee" is based on] and he'll sort of refer to that line—but I've never been fast enough to jump on it with him! He'll play it for a second, and as soon as I get myself together he's on to something else. . . . It seems like a dream that I get to play with him![13] 🕭

The Audience

Lennie Tristano was a purist, commenting, "The polluted, acquisitive nature of bookers and cafe owners . . . has instilled in the musician the attitude that they must either conform, commercially, or starve, causing them to commit artistic suicide."[14] Konitz, however, has played in a wide variety of venues, while still maintaining his mentor's uncompromising artistic standards. His dislike of "showboating" means that theatricality isn't a large part of his stage performance. This was true when he played at the Coventry Jazz Festival in 2002 with Kenny Wheeler. At the start he came on stage alone, to dedicate the concert to Charlie Parker and Lester Young, then announced "The Prologue"—an unaccompanied version of "The Song Is You." When the band appeared, to kick off with "Thingin'," Konitz asked each musician to solo unaccompanied in turn—Dave Cliff, Dave Green, and Martin France on guitar, bass, and drums—and operated duos within the group, in a chamber-ish approach. Two of Wheeler's melancholy, yearning compositions were featured, plus Konitz's "Kary's Trance," dedicated to his daughter, and based on the camp gypsy hit from 1932 "Play, Fiddle, Play." If the stagecraft was low key, afterward Konitz told a very good joke. A man goes to the doctor, who tells him that he has two pieces of bad news: "The first is that you've got Alzheimer's." "Oh my God, that's terrible!" the man replies. "The second is that you've got Parkinson's Disease." "Oh that's awful," the man says—"I'm just glad I don't have Alzheimer's!"

I usually close my eyes in a concert, because I get distracted. If I open my eyes I see someone looking bored, or I just study them. It's a drag, because I don't think it's a good idea to stand there in front of an audience with your eyes closed. When I see some guys able to keep their eyes open, I know they're not looking at anything. A singer like Frank Sinatra, singing some meaningful lyrics, can spot a beautiful woman and sing to her. But it's hard to be playing something that you're not even sure of, most of the time, and look someone in the eye—especially a beautiful woman!

What do you feel about playing in concert halls compared with clubs?
I love concert halls. Usually the equipment is better, there's more room,

there's usually a better sound, there's an attentive audience, they're compelled to sit and listen and not drink and talk. It could be fun if people danced, though. You usually get paid more in a concert hall than a club. I like the idea of the music being formalized to that extent, after the gin mills. But the gin mills are intimate places, and if they have a decent piano and a decent sound and air quality, they can be great. I've had great moments in clubs that I probably couldn't have had in the concert hall.

The audience at Coventry were slow to react.

There's always a very small amount of theatricality in my stage presentation, and Kenny stands there looking like he'd rather be someplace else. Birmingham—what do they hear here, besides rock and roll?[15] I love an enthusiastic audience as well as the next guy, but I don't try to milk that response.

I was pleased that Kenny played so nicely. He's a special musician, writer, player, and person. It's kind of a jam session; give everybody the chance to play a little bit, and play a few original things so that we don't look like complete "fakers." Kenny was nice enough to learn my little études. He's a real songwriter, and I love his tunes.

You've had problems with people not listening in clubs. Have you ever played at the Pizza Express in London, which has a quiet policy?

I have, and didn't like the tables close to the stage. It's okay otherwise. I used to play Ronnie Scott's once in a while. I don't think this is the reason I haven't played there again, but some years ago—around 1994—I was there with Kenny Wheeler and a nice rhythm section, enjoying the situation. The second set frequently had the heavy-drinking tourists. One guy shouted out some dumb thing and I shouted back, "Shut up, you prick!" You should have seen Kenny's face! That was a result of years of tolerating boorish people, sitting directly in front, and talking loud.

Did Tristano's view of club owners and promoters affect you?

Well, I've been very fortunate, I think. I've had a lot of help to get places to play, and usually the people are decent enough. I got angry recently with a man at a club in Paris—he was taking advantage of the players, getting shitty hotels, and small fees, and asking for extra sets.

I think Lennie was looking for a way to get off the public hook. He could talk about the bad pianos, and stay home in his slippers and pajamas. It's more difficult out here.

I'm not a great hustler. I think that's a distinct breed. Some of the Italian guys, they're talking to somebody on their phone while they're playing! Constantly doing business. A hustler to me is a musician who's also a businessman. I don't think of myself as ever being a businessman.

You strike me as pretty organized.

I'm fairly well organized. Consent to play, travel there, play, get paid, travel back—I have that down pretty well.

And you're known as reliable—certainly compared to people like Charlie Parker and Chet Baker!

I think so. But this, incidentally, was part of their mystique. That dramatic element raised a lot of interest. Are they going to make it? When they finally arrive, everybody's going, "Oh, there they are!" Coming late was a very hip thing to do. I love to be early—does that mean I'm not hip? I felt that since I was taking a chance with the playing, I couldn't take a chance with being late. I want to make good time for the gig, and if my time is laid back in the music, that's something else!

You've made a huge number of recordings.

Well, I have. I have a shelf of them in front of me here, and whenever I start to question, "What the hell have I done all these years?" I look up there and I'm reminded. I appreciate the records. Otherwise I'd only have my recollections of inspired moments.

The truth is you're going to make most of your living from live gigs. The albums are a means to getting people to come to the gig.

I think so. They're kind of paid demos.

The "theme and variations" approach, it's not going to have a huge audience.

It depends, largely, on who is playing the theme and variations. A large audience like the Rolling Stones get is out of the question, of course. This is basically a classical music, in the sense that, at best, it is not intended to tickle an audience's fancy. It's a specific, artistic discipline, for the people who love to identify with a serious effort. Pop music, in all its various forms, can be very well achieved, but with a different goal in mind.

I think [my audiences] are people who don't need the aggressive, more macho kind of jazz. But everyone needs a good show too, sometimes. I heard Joe Lovano with his big organization—blistering trombone player, guitar player at top volume, and some very beautiful ensembles.[16] They did *Pagliacci,* for Christ's sake. Joe was playing the melody; his wife, Judi Silvano, was singing the harmony part.

Joe Lovano is a great saxophone player, full of good music and spirit. With his lovely and talented wife, they've contributed greatly to the music. I have a little trouble sometimes with his many-noted, nonstop kind of phrases, but he's certainly masterful in playing the instrument. I recorded with him, with Paul Motian, Bill Frisell, and Charlie Haden. We play some duos, which are really nice; he really simplifies, and plays very melodically.[17]

You spoke in the *Down Beat* interview with David Kastin in 1985 about "trying to be true to what I think were valid principles [of Tristano's]— and that means above all to deliver an ethical product at all times." What is an "ethical product"?

I think of something connected with my own true musicality, which I investigate every day. Acknowledging who I'm playing for, to a degree, but playing basically for myself and the people that I'm playing with—and expecting the same from them, somehow. If the music comes out clearly to people that can hear and react to it, then that sounds like an ethical attempt and result, I think.

Warne Marsh worked with that in mind. He was just primarily concerned with playing the music, which takes 100 percent of your effort. He knew that there were a few people out there who would appreciate that—and that's who it was designed for.

You're still bothered about some of the language in these transcriptions.

To write all of these idiomatic expressions down, one can sound like an idiot. It's different in the conversation.

Well, you'll just have to rely on my good taste in editing it.

Yeah, I will have to, and I do!

It's got to feel like a conversation, otherwise there's no point in having it in this form.

Do you think anyone is going to be interested in all this stuff?

Sure—it'll be a classic of the literature!

Thanks, Andy.

Musical Examples: Transcriptions and Lead-Sheets of Konitz Improvisations and Compositions

For those interested in pursuing Konitz's music further, I am happy to present transcriptions and lead-sheets of a small selection of his improvisations and compositions. The improvisations—the classic "Subconscious-Lee," and the recent "Friend-Lee" and "Joanna's Waltz"—are either on his own compositions or that of recent musical partner Frank Wunsch. I am grateful to Ohad Talmor for his work in presenting the compositions "Chromatic-Lee," "General Cluster," "Moon," "Sound-Lee," and "Springin'."

Improvisations

Eb Alto Saxophone

Lee Konitz's solo on

Friend-Lee

1999

Friend-Lee. *Lee Konitz—Sound of Surprise* (RCA Victor 74321–69309), recorded 1999. Transcription by Mike Baggetta.

242

Eb Alto Saxophone

Lee Konitz's solo on

Subconscious-Lee
1949

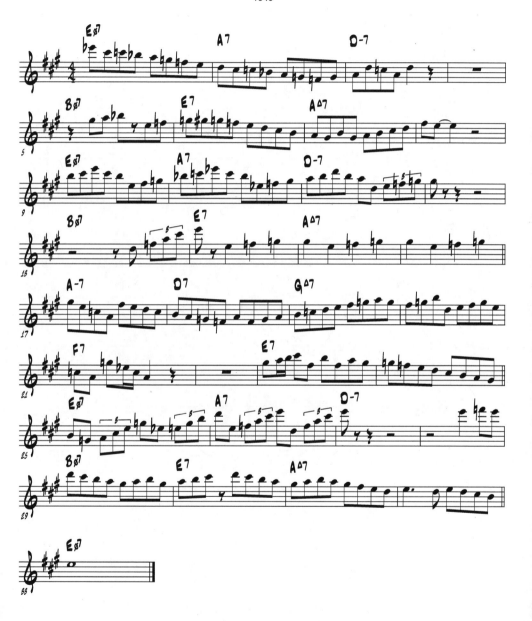

Subconscious-Lee. *Lee Konitz* (Prestige OJCCD-186–2), recorded January 11, 1949.
Transcription by Conrad Cork.

Lee Konitz's solo on

Joanna's Waltz

(2004)

THEME:

- 1 -

SOLO:

-2-

Joanna's Waltz. *Kee Konitz/Frank Wansch—Laika* (Kaika), recorded 2004. Transcriptions by Frank Wunsch.

CONCERT

CHROMATICLEE
(PART 8)

LEE KONITZ
(OHAD TALMOR)
2004/2005

MED FAST

BLOWING ON A♭ BLUES OR FREE

Chromatic-Lee

GENERAL CLUSTER

LEE KONITZ
(2002)

MED TO MED FAST

SOLOS FREE OR OVER CLUSTERS

General Cluster

Concert

MOON

Lee Konitz
(2003)

Chord Changes based on "How High the Moon" in G

Moon

Sound-Lee

Lee Konitz

CHORD CHANGES BASED ON "TOO MARVELOUS FOR WORDS"

Sound-Lee

Springin'

Notes

Full publication details of titles in these endnotes are given in References at the end of the book.

AUTHOR'S INTRODUCTION

1. The only other example I know is Meehan, *Time Will Tell,* which appeared in 2003, long after the present project was under way.

CHAPTER 1

1. Konitz pursues the question a little in the discussion of the blues in chapter 10.

2. Gavin, *Deep in a Dream.*

3. It does—in chapter 4.

4. Abraham Konitz, born Austria 1898, died 1959; Anna Getlin, born Pinsk, Ukraine, ca. 1900, died 1964.

5. The Jones family of Elvin, Thad, and Hank, and the Heath family of Jimmy, Percy, and Albert.

6. "Blacks" in Yiddish.

7. Paul Bley was joking—I think.

8. Email and telephone interview with the author, September 2005.

9. Discussed in chapter 8.

CHAPTER 2

1. As early as 1950, Michael Levin in a review described their music as "too cool, [with a] constant, omnipresent, cerebral . . . element" (*Down Beat,* August 1950).

2. As Tristano recalled it, this was in 1943: "I was playing at the Winkin' Pup in Chicago, and this kid comes up and asks to sit in. He was playing tenor saxophone then, and he was horrible, atrocious. He was playing with a mickey band at the Paradise Ballroom. I told him, 'Forget the tenor, play alto' . . . Lee studied with me until I left [Chicago] in '46, about three years. We got together in New York again in 1948" (quoted in Chamberlain, *An Unsung Cat,* 50). By "mickey band" Tristano meant one that played "[schmaltzy] two beat society music." [Lennie Tristano, "What's Wrong with Chicago Jazz," *Jazz Quarterly* 2, no. 3 (1945), quoted in Shim, *Lennie Tristano.*]

3. The Charlie Parker "Chili House" anecdote is discussed in Woideck, *Charlie Parker,* 16–17; the issue of inaccurate journalistic transcription arises again with Barry Ulanov's interview with Konitz discussed below.

4. Ted Brown's interview in chapter 3 explains in detail Tristano's teaching method of writing out improvised lines.

5. Association for the Advancement of Creative Musicians, a Chicago-based free or avant-garde jazz collective founded in 1965.

6. Other students included Bob Wilber, Bill Russo, Sheila Jordan, JoAnne Brackeen, Britt Woodman, John LaPorta, Ted Rosenthal—as well as faithful Tristano-ites such as Peter Ind, Sal Mosca, Connie Crothers, and Lenny Popkin.

7. Quoted in Gitler, *Jazz Masters of the Forties,* 226.

8. Konitz later pursues the difference between Parker's very specific phrases and Tristano's more adaptable ones.

9. Interview with Nat Hentoff, *Down Beat,* August 11, 1954.

10. Reported in Ulanov, *A History of Jazz in America,* 328.

11. The Jamey Aebersold series of play-along records, with the soloist's part removed so that horn players or pianists can practice with a rhythm section.

12. Woideck, *Charlie Parker,* 96.

13. Interview in 1996, in Jack, *Fifties Jazz Talk,* 124.

14. Quoted in Woideck, *Charlie Parker,* 127.

15. Konitz develops his account of melodic as opposed to chord-based improvisation in chapter 6.

16. Konitz discusses touring with Parker and the Kenton band in chapter 5.

17. There is further discussion of Parker in chapters 5 and 6.

18. Telephone interview with the author, July 2005.

CHAPTER 3

1. The session was issued under Konitz's name on LP and CD as *Subconscious-Lee,* along with other material for which he was always regarded as the leader. It has also been issued under Tristano's name. Bob Porter, working from Prestige files, said in his notes to the *25 Years of Prestige* double LP (P-24046), "The date was Lee Konitz's, but the records were issued under Tristano's name." The title "Subconscious-Lee" was thought up by bassist Arnold Fishkin.

2. There is some dispute about dates of these 1949 recordings, but the following seem to be correct: March 4, "Wow and Crosscurrent"; March 14, the Tristano trio's "Yesterdays"; May 16, "Marionette," "Sax of a Kind," and the two free pieces.

3. "Descent Into The Maelstrom," which features Tristano's most extraordinary free playing, was not issued until the late 1970s (East Wind EW 8040, then Inner City IC 6002). It is still not available on CD.

4. According to Connie Crothers, who got the story from Tristano, the album was originally intended to consist entirely of the live material, but Konitz was unhappy with his playing on some tracks. When Nesuhi Ertegun of Atlantic Records found Tristano's multitracked tapes in the pianist's studio, these were substituted (email to the author, 25/10/05). This was one of the Atlantic label's first attempts at stereo recording. Five live tracks were issued on the original album, and further tracks appeared later on *Lennie Tristano Quartet* (Atlantic). Konitz does not recall these events, though he believes that quite possibly he was unhappy with his playing on some tracks.

5. Nat Hentoff, "'Why Don't They Leave Me Alone?'—Tristano," *Down Beat,* December 3, 1952, 6.

6. These issues are pursued in chapter 6.

7. This episode is discussed in chapter 4.

8. Gunther Schuller comments on this in his sleeve notes to *Duets,* 1967, and in his interview in chapter 8.

9. Compare George Schuller's interview in chapter 6.

10. Telephone interview with the author, August 2005.

11. "Caught in the Act," *Down Beat,* November 5, 1964.

12. Interview in *Down Beat* with Bill Coss, quoted in sleeve notes to *Lennie Tristano: Intuition* (Proper).

13. Interview with Dan Morgenstern in *Down Beat,* November 1964.

14. Quoted in notes to the Mosaic boxed set, *The Complete Atlantic Recordings of Lennie Tristano, Lee Konitz and Warne Marsh.*

15. Gitler, *Jazz Masters of the Forties,* 233.

16. In his sleeve notes to the Mosaic boxed set.

17. Some writers argue that Tristano slowed down the recording by a minor third—a little faster than eight-tenths speed. Konitz would say that it is half speed because on standard tape-recorders of the time, the speed could be changed only by doubling or halving. But according to Lewis Porter, Tristano may have had a machine that allowed chromatic half-step changes—such machines were at some point available to the blind. Besides, it would be difficult to play along with half-speed bass and drums, because they sound atrocious at that speed. The issue remains a mystery, but see Shim, *Lennie Tristano,* for more discussion.

18. Eunmi Shim comments (email to author, April 2006): "What Lee means, I think, is that the basis of all Tristano's polyrhythms was 4/4, and he superimposed different meters and rhythms on top; he never played music in 5/4 like Brubeck did in 'Take Five.'" In her book on Tristano, she analyzes "Turkish Mambo" on *Lennie Tristano* (Atlantic) as having four different layers, each in a different meter—4/4, 5/8, 12/8, and 7/8—with the layers coming in individually and finally all happening at the same time. These meters are implied by accents over a basic pulse of 4/4, rather than 5/8, etc. in the time of 4/4 (i.e., ten quavers over eight).

19. Konitz has made a Music Minus One LP (MMO 4017) intended to help players use a trinome. Trinome markings are on the sheet music.

20. These issues are pursued in chapter 6.

21. The original recording on Atlantic was *Lennie Tristano;* the reissues were in the Mosaic boxed set.

22. This club must be the Half Note, in the late 1950s.

23. Telephone interview with the author, July 2005.

CHAPTER 4

1. Owens, *Bebop,* 66.

2. The original ten-inch LP issued by Capitol from their studio recordings was called *Classics in Jazz: Miles Davis.* The band didn't gain its title until 1957, when eleven out of the twelve studio tracks were released on LP as *The Birth of the Cool.*

3. Telephone interview with the author, June 2005.

4. Email interview with the author, January 2005.

5. Telephone interview with the author, November 2005.

6. In 1980; the results were released as *Heroes* and *Anti-Heroes.*

7. Lee's memory seems to be mistaken here. Ornette Coleman came in 1959, not 1958, according to George Schuller, who has researched the Lenox School of Jazz.

8. On *Rhapsody II* (Evidence, 1996).

9. Email interview with the author, September 2005.

10. Quoted in Chamberlain, *An Unsung Cat,* 280–81.

11. Quoted in Chamberlain, *An Unsung Cat,* 250. Here, and when Konitz uses the term, counterpoint is meant in a loose sense: "polyphonic jazz in which independent melodies are superimposed on a common chord progression." Formal, baroque counterpoint of the kind that Bach created is a subset of polyphonic music, with its own strict rules.

12. Gitler, *Jazz Masters of the Forties,* 236; Tirro, *Jazz,* 30*. Classic collaborations are found in *The Complete Atlantic Recordings of Lennie Tristano, Lee Konitz and Warne Marsh,* issued on Mosaic in 1997. It includes *Lee Konitz with Warne Marsh* from 1955, also issued on CD in 1998 on French Atlantic, and rarer items such as *Warne Marsh,* a 1958 trio recording without Konitz, which features Paul Chambers and Paul Motian.

13. This is one of several places where Konitz may not recognize that although not consciously oriented toward Parker, in tonal terms he came out of bebop. This, at least, is what Gunther Schuller argues in chapter 8.

14. A cartoonist for the *New Yorker* who favored a dark, morbid humor.

15. *Warne Marsh,* in Mosaic boxed set.

16. *Body and Soul* (Camerata, 1995).

17. A "viper" is a 1930s hipster who smoked marijuana; it is onomatopoeic from "sssssssssst," the sound made by an inhaling pot-smoker (http://www.concept420 .com/marijuana_cannabis_dictionary.htm, accessed 2005). Hence Fats Waller's composition "Viper's Drag."

18. Telephone interview with the author, August 2005.

19. The interview appears in *Jazz Review,* October 2002.

20. In his interview in chapter 3, Ted Brown gives a fuller description of this practice of Tristano's.

21. *Warne Marsh–Sal Mosca Quartet at the Vanguard—1981 Volumes 1 and 2* (Zinnia 103 and 104).

22. Telephone interview with the author, 2005. Konitz responds: "Tristano never told me that I should not imitate Bird, and do my own thing to make a name for myself. He encouraged me to study Bird's genius and use it to help my own understanding of my music. And I've played with some marvelous players over these many years."

23. *Swish* (New Artists Records, 1982).

24. Released as *Live-Lee* and *More Live-Lee* (Milestone, 2003 and 2004).

25. Konitz questions that he became more introverted during the 1950s. He began smoking marijuana, which made him less inhibited, in the 1940s and continued till the 1960s.

26. Telephone interview with the author, October 2002.

27. Owens, *Bebop,* 66.

28. The Paris performances are on *The Saxophone Collection: Lee Konitz/Hans Koller/Lars Gullin* (Vogue/BMG).

29. Hodeir, *Jazz,* 118, 121.

30. Reported in Daniels, *Lester Leaps In.*

31. Bernhardt, *I Remember,* 95. "Snakes" are long chromatic passages.

32. Interview in *Down Beat,* January 1948; quote in Blindfold Test, *Metronome,* July 1950.

33. Gillespie, *To Be or Not to Bop,* 359.

34. Schuller, *The Swing Era,* 843.

35. Gridley, *Jazz Styles,* 178.

36. Interview in *Down Beat,* January 1953; interview in *Down Beat,* December 1952.

37. Sleeve notes to *Duets* (1967).

38. Dave Brubeck and Lee Konitz, "A Conversation with Two Jazz Musicians," *Northwest Review* 1, no. 3 (1958), quoted in Woideck, *Charlie Parker,* 92.

39. "What's Wrong with the Beboppers," *Metronome,* June 1947, 16.

40. Konitz commented to Ira Gitler that he "never felt, as much as other people have led me to believe, that Paul was that influenced by me. I think he heard me, and he was affected in some way by me, and that parts knocks me out. But I don't know that he played anything that I played except a suggestion of a phrase. I thought it was a healthy influence, because it wasn't one of vocabulary, but more of sound" (Gitler, *Jazz Masters of the Forties,* 259).

41. Pepper, *Straight Life,* 374–75.

CHAPTER 5

1. Gitler, *Swing to Bop,* 15.

2. *Dedicated to Lee: Lee Konitz/Lars Sjösten Octet Plays the Music of Lars Gullin* (Dragon).

3. Telephone interview with the author, August 2005.

4. Conversation with Dr. Luther Cloud in 1958, reported in Daniels, *Lester Leaps In,* 353.

5. Blindfold Test, *Down Beat,* May 1951.

6. *Charles Mingus and Friends in Concert* (Columbia), recorded 1972.

7. Tristano described Monk as "about the dumbest pianist I've ever heard" (interview with Irv Schenkler on WKCR-FM, August 1973, quoted in Shim, *Lennie Tristano*).

8. Konitz is saying that Tristano only ever wrote new lines over existing progressions; unlike Konitz himself, he never created entirely new chord progressions.

9. I.e., "Stop asking me these questions about dates and places!"

10. Peter Ind tells the following alarming story in his book *Jazz Visions,* from the time Tristano was at a school for the blind in Chicago: "While he was waiting on the curb for assistance to cross a very busy six-lane highway, someone approached him and said 'Going across?' Then, arm in arm, they both crossed. On reaching the other side, the man turned to Lennie and said, "'Thank you.' Neither had been aware that the other was blind!" (100).

11. *The Great Jazz Concert at the Original Royal Roost* (1948, released on JungCat and on Beppo) is said to feature Benny Harris and Bud Powell, but not Miles Davis. However, Konitz believes that he never played with Benny Harris.

12. This is "No Figs," a Tristano line on "Indiana," recorded January 10, 1950—the only session of the Metronome All-Stars with Tristano, Konitz, Getz, and Chaloff. It ends with a very complicated descent.

13. On Miles Davis, *Dig* (OJC, 1951).

14. The bootleg is *Sonny Rollins in Denmark 1* (Moon MCD037–2).

15. *Sonny Meets Hawk* (RCA, 1963).

16. Konitz responds: "I'd be a dead duck!"

17. Konitz responds: "My God! What Sonny is saying here has to be tongue in cheek or something!"

18. Telephone interview with the author, September 2005.

19. Quoted in Pettinger, *Bill Evans*, 35.

20. Quoted in Pettinger, *Bill Evans*, 256.

21. Konitz says more about this problem in chapter 8.

22. Recorded in 1965, first Japanese release 1976, partial U.S. release 1982. With regard to the Half Note sessions, it may just be, as Brian Priestley commented to me, that as with other unissued Verve sessions from 1957–60, label proprietor Norman Granz had lost interest and successor Creed Taylor dropped the artist.

23. Lee Konitz/Jimmy Giuffre Octet, on *Lee Konitz Meets Jimmy Giuffre* (Verve).

24. *Chet Baker—Lee Konitz in Concert* (India Navigation).

CHAPTER 6

1. *Down Beat,* October 30, 1958.

2. Quoted in Mike Zwerin, "Lee Konitz: How to Get Away from Fixed Functions," Culturekiosque, 1999, www.musicmoz.org.

3. Barry Ulanov: "Conscious Lee: A Thoughtful Musician Demonstrates the Large Value of Thinking Musicianship. Lee Konitz Has Arrived," *Metronome,* December 1948, 35. Perhaps Ulanov's quotation is inaccurate. In the era before portable tape-recorders, writers took down musicians' words by personal shorthand.

4. ECM, 2002.

5. Quoted in Woideck, *Charlie Parker,* 164. Red Rodney was a trumpet player in Parker's group in the 1950s.

6. Email interview with the author, January 2005.

7. Konitz here seems to concede the point about needing to hear internally. This is one of our less conclusive discussions, but it was very hard to clarify the issues, and I have decided not to edit it further.

8. This and other issues are discussed in Hamilton, *Aesthetics and Music,* and in Hamilton, "The Art of Improvisation and the Aesthetics of Imperfection."

9. Konitz means: It was so complicated that you feel that it could not be improvised, yet it was.

10. This is the famous solo on *Konitz Meets Mulligan* (Pacific Jazz), 1953.

11. There are various versions of Heraclitus's ancient pronouncements, presented in Freeman, *Ancilla to the Pre-Socratic Philosophers.*

12. Telephone interview with the author, August 2005.

13. The interview with David Kastin from *Down Beat,* quoted from later in this chapter.

14. Konitz has more to say on this in chapter 8.

15. Telephone interview with the author, August 2005.

16. The group appears on *Jazz at Storyville* (Black Lion, recorded 1954).

17. *Three Guys* (Enja, 1999).

18. Telephone interview with the author, September 2005.

19. Frank Wunsch's interview is at the end of chapter 8; Lee's solo on one of his waltzes is found at the end of the book.

20. Telephone interview with the author, August 2005.

21. Konitz means that he can't identify because he's not black. He discusses the blues in chapter 10.

22. *Rhapsody II* (Evidence, 1993).

23. "You Don't Know What Love Is" on *Rhapsody II* (Evidence, 1993).

24. Telephone interview with the author, September 2005.

25. The article is also located at http://www.melmartin.com/html_pages/ Interviews/konitz.html. Numerous efforts to contact copyright holder David Kastin, both through *Down Beat* and other channels, regarding permission to use his article, have been unsuccessful.

26. Konitz's occasional comments about not being "harmonically astute" should be taken with a pinch of salt, I think! They simply reflect a basic preference in his approach to improvisation.

CHAPTER 7

1. Gitler, *Jazz Masters of the Forties,* 256.

2. The results appeared as *Continuity* (Jazz Records).

3. Owens, *Bebop,* 67. *Motion* finally appeared in a complete edition in 1998. The material unissued until that point features Nick Stabulas, the fine drummer who worked with Tristano; Sonny Dallas plays bass on all sessions.

4. Telephone interview with the author, August 2005.

5. Telephone interview with the author, September 2005. Konitz says: "I haven't given up on swing!"

6. Branford Marsalis, *Footsteps of Our Fathers* (MarCD, 2002).

7. Ornette Coleman, *Sound Museum: Three Women* (Verve/Harmolodic, 1996).

8. Konitz's solo is on a date led by Gerry Mulligan, *The Gerry Mulligan Songbook* (Pacific Jazz, 1957).

9. Extract from interview with the author at the Sage Gateshead, April 29, 2005. The complete interview appeared in *The Wire,* July 2005. There's some discrepancy between the two musicians' recollections.

10. *Cecil Taylor Feel Trio: 2 Ts for a Lovely T* (Codanza, 2002).

11. Universal, 2002.

12. Konitz pursues this question in the next chapter.

13. At the Nice Jazz Festival. In Billy Bauer's *Sideman,* Konitz comments that Shorter sang the first eight bars of "Marionette" from the 1949 date.

14. Telephone interview with the author, September 2005.

CHAPTER 8

1. One miscreant was the present writer in "Invisible Jukebox: Lee Konitz." *The Wire,* November 1999, 22–24; the entry on Konitz in the *New Grove Dictionary of Music and Musicians* is also in error here.

2. Frank Tirro, in an interesting discussion in his book *Jazz: A History,* describes it as "so devoid of overtones that it closely approximated the timbre of an electronically-generated sine wave" (338), which is unlikely!

3. Hodeir, *Jazz,* 121.

4. Telephone interview with the author, November 2005.

5. According to Jack Goodwin, this is known as Marsh's "bubblegum" period!

Later he held the mouthpiece quite steady in his mouth. The TV program was an episode of the series *The Subject Is Jazz* from 1958. In fact, classical players avoid the "double-lip" embouchure.

6. Carr et al., *Jazz*; Pettinger, *Bill Evans*, 77–78.

7. There is also timbral vibrato, and volume vibrato.

8. Konitz is picking up on Davis's comment that as a teenager he was into Harry James—but he was well over the influence before he first recorded, and Konitz never heard him play that way.

9. Konitz responds: "I don't like the word *slurring*—it sounds kind of sloppy to me. I think it's synonymous with *legato,* which is what I had in mind—not touching every note with my tongue to the reed."

10. Schuller is referring to the "triplet" feel of swing.

11. Telephone interview with the author, October 2005.

12. Pettinger, *Bill Evans*, 242.

13. Lewis Porter wrote in his editorial comments on the book manuscript: "You and Lee are both dead wrong. The research shows unequivocally that people with perfect pitch do not remember the pitch. They simply hear an 'A' sound as being different from a 'B' sound, just as everyone sees the color red as being different from blue—there is nothing to remember. That's why the old theory of trying to remember the pitch of a tuning fork never worked for anyone."

14. Telephone interview with the author, October 2005.

15. Email to the author, September 2005, translated by James Clarke. The changes in "Rhythm" are the chord progression of Gershwin's "I Got Rhythm," commonly used by bebop and later musicians.

CHAPTER 9

1. Telephone interview with the author, July 2005.

2. In chapter 11, Konitz compares the comping of Solal and Brad Mehldau.

3. Email interview in French with the author, August 2005, and translated by him.

4. *Chet Baker with Konitz and Jarrett* (Jazz Conn, 1974).

CHAPTER 10

1. A standard "fake book" with lead sheets of songs—melodies with chord symbols. The term "fake" refers to the way the book provides enough material for musicians to play any song well enough to appear as though they knew it beforehand. *Faking* is a rather derogatory term for improvising. Also, the idea is that a "fake book" contains pirated music on which copyright has not been paid.

2. According to Brian Priestley, this insight originally came from Sy Johnson, Konitz's arranger for the nonet.

3. Telephone interview with the author, August 2005.

4. Carl Woideck argues that Parker's creativity declined after 1950, for health and drug-related reasons, his huge repertoire of motifs deployed increasingly mechanically—though still with a brilliance his peers could not match (*Charlie Parker,* 175–76, 199–200). Other authorities date the decline from after 1952.

5. *Lee Konitz & The Axis String Quartet Play French Impressionist Music from the 20th Century* (Palmetto).

6. Referred to in chapter 1.

7. Tristano wrote several lines over this song in a minor key, including "Lennie's Pennies" and "Pennies In Minor."

8. Email interview with the author, July 2005.

9. "Intuition" was released late 1950 with "Yesterdays" by the Tristano trio on the reverse. "Digression" was first released by Capitol in 1954 as part of a 45 rpm disc along with three already issued titles.

10. Chamberlain, *An Unsung Cat,* 76. The reference to atonality is exaggerated. In much jazz writing, "atonal" just seems to mean "dissonant." But Frank Tirro shows how the melodic line of Konitz's composition "Tautology," recorded in 1949, approximates to serial composition in using all twelve tones in the octave (Tirro, *Jazz,* 339).

11. Quoted in Berliner, *Thinking in Jazz,* 338; interview with Chris Parker, *The Independent,* November 1989; Gitler, *Masters of Bebop,* 235.

12. In an article in *Metronome* in 1949, Roy Eldridge is quoted by Barry Ulanov as saying that he had played "free improvisation": "Clyde Hart and I made a record like that once. We decided in front that there'd be no regular chords, we'd announce no keys, stick to no progressions. Only once I fell into a minor key; the rest was free, just blowing." Dan Morgenstern comments: "Roy [Eldridge] told me about this several times. He said it was done backstage at the Apollo, on a disc recorder. He no longer owned the original disc, but said that his friend, Eldridge collector Tony Perry, had a copy. Perry died some years ago; as far as I know, his collection remains in private hands. This was a home recording made by and for the musicians involved." (Email communication with the author, 2006.)

13. Jost, *Free Jazz,* 41.

14. Litweiler, *The Freedom Principle,* 29.

15. Interview in *Coda,* December 1976.

16. Quoted in. Berendt, *The Jazz Book,* 104, who doesn't cite a source. Tristano's liner notes to the LP issue, *Crosscurrents,* say that "Miles Davis is the only noted musician who acknowledged in print the real nature of those sides."

17. *Rhapsody II* (Paddlewheel, 1994).

18. Email interview with the author, July 2005.

19. Telephone interview with the author, July 2005.

20. *The Wire,* November 1999.

21. On *Woodstock Jazz Festival* (Douglas DVD, 2 vols., 1981), Braxton can be seen singing a solo to Konitz.

22. *One in Two Two in One* (Hatology, recorded 1979).

23. Interview in *The Wire,* March 2002.

24. Telephone interview with the author, July 2005.

CHAPTER 11

1. *Three Guys* (Enja, 1999).

2. *Pride* (Steeplechase, 2001).

3. French pianist Michel Petrucciani, who died in 1999, had a bone disease that retarded his growth. Konitz was the first to present him in the United States, in 1982.

4. On *First Song* (Soul Note, 1990).

5. From an interview with the author, Rome, August 2002, which subsequently appeared in *Jazz Review,* December 2002.

6. Konitz means that he has been concentrating on paring his style down, and simplifying it.

7. Quoted in S. Futterman, "Tristano's Trust," in *Jazziz,* December 1997.

8. Telephone interview with the author, May 2005.

9. On the Japanese label DIW.

10. *Sound-Lee!* (Geestgronden, 2003).

11. Girolamo Frescobaldi (1583–1643), Italian composer and organist.

12. Email interview with the author, October 2005.

13. Telephone interview with the author, August 2005.

14. Lennie Tristano, "What's Wrong with Chicago Jazz," *Jazz Quarterly* 2, no. 3 (1945), quoted in Chamberlain, *An Unsung Cat,* 51.

15. A little unfair after the era of Simon Rattle at the City of Birmingham Symphony Orchestra!

16. At the London Jazz Festival, November 2002.

17. *Rhapsody* (Evidence, 1993).

Selected Album Listing

This list was compiled with the assistance of Conrad Cork. The label is the one currently issuing the album (or if unavailable, the original issue), followed by year of recording. A complete discography is available online at the publisher's website. Go to www.press.umich.edu and follow the links to this title.

Lee Konitz. Prestige, 1949.
Sax of a Kind. Dragon, 1951.
Konitz Meets Mulligan. Pacific Jazz, 1953.
At Storyville. Black Lion, 1954.
Konitz. Black Lion, 1954.
Timespan. Wave, 1954.
Lee Konitz with Warne Marsh. Atlantic, 1955.
Inside Hi-Fi. Atlantic, 1956.
The Real Lee Konitz. Atlantic, 1957.
Very Cool. Verve, 1957.
Lee Konitz Meets Jimmy Guiffre. Verve, 1959.
Live at the Half Note. Verve, 1959.
You and Lee. Verve, 1959.
Motion. Verve, 1961.
The Lee Konitz Duets. Milestone, 1967.
Peacemeal. Milestone, 1969.
Spirits. Milestone, 1971.
I Concentrate on You. SteepleChase, 1974.
Jazz à Juan. SteepleChase, 1974.
Lone-Lee. SteepleChase, 1974.
Oleo. Sonet, 1975.
Satori. Milestone, 1975.
Windows (with Hal Galper). SteepleChase, 1975.
London Concert. Wave, 1976.
Figure and Spirit. Progressive, 1976.
The Lee Konitz Nonet. Chiaroscuro, 1977.
Pyramid. Improvising Artists, 1977.

Tenorlee. Candid, 1977.

Yes, Yes Nonet. SteepleChase, 1979.

Lee Konitz Nonet: Live At Laren. Soul Note, 1979.

Live At the Berlin Jazz Days (with Martial Solal). MPS, 1980.

Heroes (with Gil Evans). Verve, 1980.

Anti-Heroes (with Gil Evans). Verve, 1980.

High Jingo. Atlas, 1982.

Toot Sweet (with Michel Petrucciani). Owl, 1982.

Dovetail. Sunnyside, 1983.

Glad, Koonix. Dragon, 1983.

Art of the Duo (with Albert Mangelsdorff). Enja, 1983.

Wild as Springtime (with Harold Danko). Candid, 1984.

Ideal Scene. Soul Note, 1986.

The New York Album. Soul Note, 1987.

12 Gershwin in 12 Keys. Philology, 1988.

Solitudes (with Enrico Pieranunzi). Philology, 1988.

Lee Konitz Meets the Space Jazz Trio: Blew. Philology, 1988.

Frank-Lee Speaking (with Frank Wunsch). West Wind, 1989.

Zounds. Soul Note, 1990.

Lullaby of Birdland. Candid, 1991.

Lunasea. Soul Note, 1992.

Jazz Nocturne. Evidence, 1992.

The Jobim Collection (with Peggy Stern). Philology, 1993.

Rhapsody. Evidence, 1993.

Thingin'. Hatology, 1995.

Brazilian Rhapsody. BMB/Music Masters, 1995.

Alone Together. Blue Note, 1996.

Another Shade of Blue. Blue Note, 1997.

Out of Nowhere. SteepleChase, 1997.

Three Guys. Enja, 1998.

Dig-It. SteepleChase, 1999.

Pride. SteepleChase, 1999.

Some New Stuff. DIW, 2000.

Lee Konitz with Alan Broadbent: Live-Lee. Milestone, 2000.

Parallels. Chesky, 2000.

Gong with Wind (with Matt Wilson). SteepleChase, 2002.

Big Encounter at Umbria Vols 1–4 (with Phil Woods, Enrico Rava). Philology, 2003.

Inventions. Omnitone, 2006.

Lee Konitz New Nonet. Omnitone, 2006.

Portology. Omnitone, 2007.

CHET BAKER
Chet Baker–Lee Konitz in Concert. India Navigation, 1974.

MILES DAVIS
The Complete Birth of the Cool. Capitol, 1949–50.
Miles Davis/Stan Getz/Lee Konitz: Conception. Prestige, 1951.

BILL EVANS
Crosscurrents. Fantasy, 1977.
Together Again. Moon, 1965.

ANDREW HILL
Spiral. Arista Freedom, 1974.

STAN KENTON
New Concepts of Artistry in Rhythm. Creative World, 1952.
The European Tour 1953. Artistry, 1953.

FRANZ KOGLMANN
We Thought about Duke. Hatology, 1994.

WARNE MARSH
Jazz Exchange Vols 1–3. Storyville, 1975.
Warne Marsh Meets Lee Konitz Again. Pausa, 1976.

CHARLES MINGUS
The Young Rebel. Proper, 1945–53.

CLAUDE THORNHILL
Claude Thornhill 1947. Hindsight.
The 1946–7 Performances Vols 1 and 2. Hep.

LENNIE TRISTANO, LEE KONITZ, AND WARNE MARSH
The Complete Atlantic Recordings. Mosaic, 1955–58.

LENNIE TRISTANO
Continuity. Jazz Records, 1964.
Lennie Tristano: Intuition. Proper, 1945–52.
Live in Toronto 1952. Jazz Records, 1952.

KENNY WHEELER
Angel Song. ECM, 1976.

VARIOUS ARTISTS
Charlie Parker 10th Memorial Concert. Verve, 1965.

References

Bauer, Billy. *Sideman*. New York: W. H. Bauer, 1997.

Berendt, Joachim. *The Jazz Book*. St Albans: Paladin, 1976.

Berliner, Paul. *Thinking in Jazz: The Infinite Art of Improvisation*. Chicago: University of Chicago Press, 1994.

Bernhardt, Clyde. *I Remember: Eighty Years of Black Entertainment, Big Bands, and the Blues*. Philadelphia: University of Philadelphia Press, 1986.

Bley, Paul. *Stopping Time: Paul Bley and the Transformation of Jazz*. Montréal: Véhicule Press, 1999.

Carr, Ian, et al., eds. *Jazz: The Essential Companion*. St Albans: Paladin, 1988.

Chamberlain, Safford. *An Unsung Cat: The Life and Music of Warne Marsh*. Lanham, Md.: Scarecrow Press, 2002.

Cork, Conrad. *The New Guide to Harmony with LEGO Bricks*. Leicester: Tadley Ewing Publications, 1996.

Daniels, Douglas Henry. *Lester Leaps In: The Life and Times of Lester "Pres" Young*. Boston: Beacon Press, 2002.

Freeman, K. *Ancilla to the Pre-Socratic Philosophers*. Cambridge: Harvard University Press, 1983.

Gavin, James. *Deep in a Dream: The Long Night of Chet Baker*. London: Chatto and Windus, 2002.

Gillespie, Dizzy. *To Be or Not to Bop*. New York: Da Capo, 1985.

Gitler, Ira. *Jazz Masters of the Forties*. New York: Macmillan, 1966.

———. *Masters of Bebop*. New York: Da Capo, 2001.

———. *Swing to Bop*. New York: Oxford University Press, 1985.

Gordon, Robert. *Jazz West Coast: The Los Angeles Jazz Scene of the 1950s*. London: Quartet Books, 1986.

Gridley, Mark. *Jazz Styles: History and Analysis*. New Jersey: Prentice Hall, 1988.

Hamilton, Andy. *Aesthetics and Music*. London: Continuum, 2007.

———. "The Art of Improvisation and the Aesthetics of Imperfection." *British Journal of Aesthetics* 40 (January 2000). Also in *Aesthetics in Britain,* ed. Peter Lamarque (Oxford: Oxford University Press, 2000).

Hodeir, André. *Jazz: Its Evolution and Essence*. New York: Grove Press, 1956.

Ind, Peter. *Jazz Visions: Lennie Tristano and His Legacy*. London: Equinox, 2005.

Jack, Gordon. *Fifties Jazz Talk*. Lanham, Md.: Scarecrow Press, 2004.

Jost, Ekkehard. *Free Jazz*. New York: Da Capo, 1994.

Kart, Larry. *Jazz in Search of Itself*. New Haven: Yale University Press, 2004.

Litweiler, John. *The Freedom Principle: Jazz after 1958*. New York: William Morrow, 1984.

Meehan, Norman. *Time Will Tell: Conversations with Paul Bley*. Berkeley, Calif.: Berkeley Hills, 2003.

Owens, Thomas. *Bebop: The Music and Its Players*. New York: Oxford University Press, 1995.

Pepper, Art. *Straight Life: The Story of Art Pepper.* Edinburgh: Mojo Books, 2000.

Pettinger, *Bill Evans: How My Heart Sings.* New Haven: Yale University Press, 1998.

Porter, Lewis. *John Coltrane: His Life and Music.* Ann Arbor: University of Michigan Press, 1998.

Schuller, Gunther. *The Swing Era.* Oxford: Oxford University Press, 1989.

Shim, Eunmi. *Lennie Tristano: His Life in Music.* Ann Arbor: University of Michigan Press, 2007.

Tirro, Frank. *Jazz: A History.* 2nd ed. New York: Norton, 1993.

Ulanov, Barry. *A History of Jazz in America.* New York: Viking, 1952.

Washut, Bob. *Lee Konitz' Transcribed Solos.* Lebanon, Ind.: Houston Publishing, 1994.

Woideck, Carl. *Charlie Parker: His Music and Life.* Ann Arbor: University of Michigan Press, 1996.

Bibliography: Major Articles on Lee Konitz

Barry Ulanov. "Conscious Lee: A Thoughtful Musician Demonstrates the Large Value of Thinking Musicianship. Lee Konitz Has Arrived." *Metronome,* December 1948, 17, 34–35.

Robert Aubert and Jean-François Quievreux. "Lee Konitz." *Jazz Hot,* July–August 1950, 7.

Bill Russo. "Jazz off the Record: Lee Konitz' Solo on 'Move.'" *Down Beat,* February 1952, 12.

E. Jackson. "Lee Konitz—I'll Remember April." *Melody Maker,* 1954, 8.

Jack Maher. "Lee Konitz a Winner." *Metronome,* June 1958, 10.

J. McKinney. "The Shadow or Substance of Lee Konitz." *Metronome,* November 1958, 18.

Max Harrison and Michael James. "Controversialee." *Jazz Review,* 1960, 10–12.

Don DeMichael. "Lee Konitz/Teddy Charles—'Ezzthetic' (New Jazz)." *Down Beat,* October 22, 1964, 31–32.

Ira Gitler. "Lennie Tristano and Lee Konitz." In *Jazz Masters of the Forties.* 1966; reprint, New York: Collier, 1974. 226–61. Updated in Ira Gitler, *The Masters of Bebop: A Listener's Guide* (New York: Da Capo, 2001), 226–61.

Martin Williams. "Lee Konitz. A Career Renewed." *Jazz Journal,* September 1966, 22–23. Reprinted in Martin Williams, *Jazz in Its Time* (New York: Oxford University Press, 1989), 65–70.

Gunther Schuller. "Lee Konitz." In *Musings: The Musical Worlds of Gunther Schuller.* (New York: Oxford University Press, 1986), 98–101.

Alan Surpin. "Inside Lee Konitz." *Down Beat,* July 11, 1968, 15–16.

Jim Szantor. "Lee Konitz Sax Duets (Music Minus One Saxophone)." *Down Beat,* April 16, 1970, 21–22.

Thomas Tolnay. "Lee Konitz. Creative Communicator." *Down Beat,* February 18, 1971, 12–13.

Gordon Kopulos. "Lee Konitz." *Jazz Journal,* June 1974, 8–10.

Mark Gridley. "Transitional Figures of the 40s: Lennie Tristano and Lee Konitz." In *Jazz Styles.* Englewood Cliffs, N.J.: Prentice-Hall, 1978. 147–50.

Tom Everett. "Lee Konitz Interview." *Cadence,* January 1978, 12–14, 16.

Neil Tesser. "Lee Konitz Searches for the Perfect Solo." *Down Beat,* January 1980, 16–18, 69.

Lee Jeske. "Gil Evans–Lee Konitz Duo, Greene Street, New York City." *Down Beat,* May 1980, 59–60.

Whitney Balliett. "Ten Levels." In *Jelly Roll, Jabbo & Fats: Nineteen Portraits in Jazz.* New York: Oxford University Press, 1983. 177–86. Reprinted in Whitney Balliett, *American Musicians: Fifty-six Portraits in Jazz* (New York: Oxford University Press, 1986), 374–80. Reprinted in Whitney Balliett, *American Musicians II: Seventy-One Portraits in Jazz* (New York: Oxford University Press, 1997), 480–86.

Herbert Hellhund. "Lee Konitz—Ezz-thetic!" In *Cool Jazz: Grundzüge seiner Entste-hung und Entwicklung.* Mainz: Schott, 1985. 205–10.

David Kastin. "Lee Konitz: Back to the Basics." *Down Beat,* December 1985, 12–14.

Mike Baillie. "Lee Konitz: While His Fellow Altoists Were Following the Example of Charlie Parker, Lee Konitz Was Developing a Distinctive Style of His Own." *Jazz Journal,* May 1987, 6–9.

Thierry Quénum. "L'Europe des 12 de Lee Konitz." *Jazz Magazine,* December 1991, 24–29.

Alberto Bazzurro, Maurizio Franco, and Claudio Fasoli. "Lee Konitz." *Musica Jazz,* March 1992, 35–50.

Frank Tirro. "Lee Konitz/Warne Marsh—Marshmellow." In *Jazz: A History.* 2nd ed. New York: Norton, 1993. 29–32.

Lewis Porter and Michael Ullman. "The Tristano School." In *Jazz: From Its Origins to the Present.* Englewood Cliffs, N.J.: Prentice-Hall, 1993. 246–50.

Peter Niklas Wilson. "Instant Composing als Lebensaufgabe: Lee Konitz im Gespräch." *Jazzthetik,* July–August 1993, 42–45.

Paul F. Berliner. *Thinking in Jazz: The Infinite Art of Improvisation.* Chicago University of Chicago Press, 1994.

Thomas Owens. "Alto Saxophonists: Lee Konitz." In *Bebop: The Music and Its Players.* New York: Oxford University Press, 1995. 65–68.

Gordon Jack. "Lee Konitz." *Jazz Journal,* December 1996, 6–8.

Greg Robinson. "Lee Konitz: On His Own Terms." *Jazz Times,* June 1997, 72–74, 76.

Art Lange. "Changing the Shape of Music: Another View of Lennie Tristano, Lee Konitz, and Warne Marsh." *Coda,* January–February 1999, 12–17.

Andy Hamilton. "Invisible Jukebox: Lee Konitz." *The Wire,* November 1999, 22–24.

Andy Hamilton. "Intuition and Digression: In This Major Interview, Andy Hamilton Talks to Master Saxophonist Lee Konitz about a Lifetime in Jazz Improvisation." *Jazz Review,* December 2000, 10–14, 16–20.

Francis Davis. "Some Recordings." In *Like Young: Jazz, Pop, Youth, and Middle Age.* New York: Da Capo, 2001. 191–94.

Ted Panken. "Lee Konitz: Alto Saxophonist of the Year." *Down Beat,* August 2002, 32–35.

Matthias Wegner. "Lee Konitz. Mister Cool." *Jazz Podium,* February 2003, 14–16.

Andy Hamilton. "Another Word With Lee." *Jazz Review,* December 2003, 22–28.

Michael Jackson. "Alone Together: Two Great Chicago Players Come Together in an Interview for the First Time, and Talk to Michael Jackson." *Jazzwise,* February 2004, 30–34.

Gordon Jack. *Fifties Jazz Talk: An Oral Retrospective.* Lanham, Md.: Scarecrow, 2004. Chapter on Konitz, 122–28.

Larry Kart. *Jazz in Search of Itself.* New Haven: Yale University Press, 2004. Three arti-cles on Konitz and the Tristano school, 219–37.

Index

A set of short biographies of the main musicians mentioned in the text, compiled by Mike Baggetta but not included due to lack of space, is available online. To find them, and also the online discography, go to http://www.press.umich.edu/ and follow the links to this title.

JAZZ PERSPECTIVES
Lewis Porter, Series General Editor

Open the Door: The Life and Music of Betty Carter
By William R. Bauer

Jazz Journeys to Japan: The Heart Within   By William Minor

Four Jazz Lives   By A. B. Spellman

Head Hunters: *The Making of Jazz's First Platinum Album*
By Steven F. Pond

Lester Young   By Lewis Porter

The Last Miles: The Music of Miles Davis, 1980–1991
By George Cole

The André Hodeir Jazz Reader
By André Hodeir   Edited by Jean-Louis Pautrot

Someone to Watch Over Me: The Life and Music of Ben Webster
By Frank Büchmann-Møller

Rhythm Is Our Business: Jimmie Lunceford and the Harlem Express
By Eddy Determeyer

Lennie Tristano: His Life in Music   By Eunmi Shim

Lee Konitz: Conversations on the Improviser's Art
By Andy Hamilton

OTHER BOOKS OF INTEREST

Before Motown: A History of Jazz in Detroit, 1920–60
By Lars Bjorn with Jim Gallert

John Coltrane: His Life and Music   By Lewis Porter

Charlie Parker: His Music and Life   By Carl Woideck

The Song of the Hawk: The Life and Recordings of Coleman Hawkins
By John Chilton

Let the Good Times Roll: The Story of Louis Jordan and His Music
By John Chilton